CATALONIA: A NEW HISTORY

Catalonia: A New History revises many traditional and romantic conceptions in the historiography of a small nation. This book engages with the scholarship of the past decade and separates nationalist myth-history from real historical processes. It is thus able to provide the reader with an analytical account, situating each historical period within its temporal context. Catalonia emerges as a territory where complex social forces interact, where revolts and rebellions are frequent. This is a contested terrain where political ideologies have sought to impose their interpretation of Catalan reality.

This book situates Catalonia within the wider currents of European and Spanish history, from pre-history to the contemporary independence movement, and makes an important contribution to our understanding of nation-making.

Andrew Dowling is Reader in Spanish History at Cardiff University and researches the history and politics of Catalonia. He has previously published *The Rise of Catalan Independence: Spain's Territorial Crisis* with Routledge in 2018 and *Catalonia since the Spanish Civil War: Reconstructing the Nation* (Sussex Academic Press, 2012).

Routledge Studies in Modern European History

For more information about this series, please visit:
www.routledge.com/Routledge-Studies-in-Modern-European-History/
book-series/SE0246

CATALONIA: A NEW HISTORY

Andrew Dowling

Routledge
Taylor & Francis Group

LONDON AND NEW YORK

Cover image: Blasón de Aragón: el escudo y la bandera

First published 2023
by Routledge
4 Park Square, Milton Park, Abingdon, Oxon OX14 4RN

and by Routledge
605 Third Avenue, New York, NY 10158

Routledge is an imprint of the Taylor & Francis Group, an informa business

© 2023 Andrew Dowling

British Library Cataloguing-in-Publication Data
A catalogue record for this book is available from the British Library

Library of Congress Cataloging-in-Publication Data
Names: Dowling, Andrew, 1965 July 18– author.
Title: Catalonia: a new history/Andrew Dowling.
Other titles: Catalonia, a new history
Description: Abingdon, Oxon; New York: Routledge, 2022. |
  Series: Routledge studies in modern European history | Includes
  bibliographical references and index.
Identifiers: LCCN 2022010367 (print) | LCCN 2022010368 (ebook) |
  ISBN 9781032111919 (hardback) | ISBN 9781032111926 (paperback) |
  ISBN 9781003218791 (ebook)
Subjects: LCSH: Catalonia (Spain)—History.
Classification: LCC DP302.C62 D69 2022 (print) | LCC DP302.C62
  (ebook) | DDC 946.7—dc23/eng/20220304
LC record available at https://lccn.loc.gov/2022010367
LC ebook record available at https://lccn.loc.gov/2022010368

ISBN: 978-1-032-11191-9 (hbk)
ISBN: 978-1-032-11192-6 (pbk)
ISBN: 978-1-003-21879-1 (ebk)

DOI: 10.4324/9781003218791

Typeset in Bembo
by Apex CoVantage, LLC

CONTENTS

INTRODUCTION

On 1 October 2017, consciousness of Catalonia and the Catalan question exploded into global awareness. The holding of a referendum on the independence of Catalonia, deemed illegal by the Spanish authorities, saw over two million Catalans participate, some 43 per cent of eligible voters. In a number of polling stations, harsh and brutal police action provided the media with a compelling news story. It seemed particularly dramatic as these scenes played out in a member state of the European Union. Spanish police and civil guards used reckless violence to stop a vote which even its organisers largely recognised as being mostly symbolic. The following weeks demonstrated the inability of Catalonia to achieve independence. However, the events of October 2017 and beyond meant that the story of Catalonia, its people and culture was centre stage in a way it had not been before. Prior to this dramatic episode, knowledge of Catalonia centred on the city of Barcelona, including its hosting of the Olympics in 1992, the global brand associated with the city's football team, FC Barcelona and mass tourism. Catalonia receives almost 20 million tourists a year with 12 million visiting the city of Barcelona. Few visitors could name a Catalan writer, artist or historical figure with perhaps only Salvador Dalí or Antoni Gaudí having what we might term widespread name recognition. However, since 2017, with the question of independence both resonating and unresolved, and the harsh prison sentences handed out to the leadership in October 2019 provoking another wave of protest that again attracted extensive media attention, it is now common to see Catalonia or Catalans referred to in the media, rather than 'the Spanish artist', etc. The association between Catalonia and its struggle for independence from Spain has attracted extensive commentary. With this new awareness of a Catalan distinctiveness, it seems an appropriate time to publish a New History of Catalonia.

The little that is available in English on the general history of Catalonia too often falls victim to traditional narratives of kings and queens. New readers are

DOI: 10.4324/9781003218791-1

often lost in the plethora of names and dynasties, not helped when one medieval ruler Ramon Berenguer called his son and heir, Berenguer Ramon. Whilst royal rule is a useful device for periodisation, the focus on royalty and high culture alone leaves the vast majority of the population as passive actors. As we will see, Catalonia has a rich history of popular rebellion, which has continued right into the very present. Catalonia has seen repeated patterns of internal conflict. From the early modern period, there has been pressure to be absorbed within a wider state entity that became simply known as Spain. In the modern period, particularly the past 150 years, we see attempts to preserve and develop a distinct Catalan identity. Though in itself a new form of political expression, the goal of independence should be situated within this context. Catalonia's position as a gateway between France and Spain, as well as its coastal position, has ensured constant renewal of its population. Even in the past 20 years, a further million or so arrivals have been added. These population movements into Iberia over thousands of years played a major role in shaping both its pre-history and its history. Fewer than 20 per cent of contemporary Catalonia can claim four grandparents as having originated within the territory. The focus of this work will be on the political, social and economic development of Catalonia and the Catalans. It will not be a cultural history or one centred on the territory's art or architecture as these have been well covered in the English-speaking world. Rather its purpose will seek to situate the story of one European people, the Catalans, in all its complexity and in their encounter with greater phenomenon and processes such as conquest, feudalism, capitalism and the contemporary world. This will be a national history but never a nationalist history.

The Danish philosopher Søren Kierkegaard once noted that whilst life is lived forwards, it can only be understood backwards. A collective consciousness of being Catalan is improbable before the early middle ages and what national awareness we find in this period would be largely confined to ruling elites. Identity was local, not national. Yet even medieval figures who spoke Catalan at court were part of a wider world of Latin Christendom. Amongst the European aristocracy as a totality, cultural and class identity was shared but it was not framed in a national sense. Territory was sought but dynastic interests predominated. Marriages were contracted on the basis of power relations across the continent and should not be seen as exercises in nation building. We should note that there were no real institutions in Catalan territory before at least the twelfth century and be careful about the use of terms such as a Catalan state before this era. We must always be guarded against using the present-day map of Europe as providing any meaningful reading of the past, particularly prior to 1700. With these caveats, this New History of Catalonia is a national history but is one that notes that neither Catalonia nor the Catalans existed in any meaningful sense before the middle ages. Of course, nor did the 'French', 'English', 'Germans' or any other European people as we might understand them today. Yet landscape, territory and cultural mixing do flow into the formation of a people, so I will follow the established convention in the writing of national histories by seeking national origins and distinctiveness from the beginnings. I will also refer at times to Catalonia or Catalan territory as a simple shorthand for the area under consideration in the earlier sections of the book.

If to be Catalan, as many argue today, is to speak and use the Catalan language, all observations made before the language emerged fully formed from Latin perhaps in the eleventh century, refer to the inhabitants of the territory we know today as Catalonia. However, they were not 'Catalans'. The Iberian language, unrelated to Latin, and which is still not deciphered, was spoken for longer in the territory of Catalonia than that of Catalan, which has existed for perhaps nine centuries. The Iberian language is now mostly lost, except for inscriptions on stone and lettering on coins. It was Roman conquest which ended the speaking of Iberian and its substitution by Latin, which in time became medieval Catalan. This process took hundreds of years and some mountain communities were speaking forms of Iberian until at least the eighth century. We have no prior evidence of the existence of either the term 'Catalans' or 'Catalonia' before the twelfth century. The political emergence of the Catalan-speaking territories is to be found in the medieval Kingdom of Aragon, which participated in the formation of the modern Spanish state. In this period, Catalan was the language of the court. Catalan culture held high status not only in Spanish territory but also across Europe. This is the golden age of Catalonia when it was a European power with extensive overseas possessions. Internal divisions including a civil war gradually ended this period. The processes of Spanish unity further contributed to the decadence and decline of this culture. The first phase came about through the unification of the Kingdoms of Aragon and Castile in the late fifteenth century and in a second phase following the Wars of the Spanish Succession in the early eighteenth century. The consequences, in particular of the latter period, led to the abolition of the cultural and political autonomy of the territory and a century or more of cultural and political decline. A further pivotal element of Catalan belonging is attachment to its institutions, in particular to the revived Generalitat, seat of the regional government of Catalonia. This institution, medieval in origin, was abolished in 1714 and finally restored in the 1930s. Francoist victory in the Spanish Civil War led to its abolition in 1939. With the end of the dictatorship of Franco, it returned again in 1978 and has remained the present-day symbol of Catalan political nationhood.

Before we begin our narrative, we must also note that the stories we tell ourselves about our past seep into our notion of the present. All national movements manipulate the past for contemporary political purposes. From Braveheart to the American Founding Fathers, from the battle of Kosovo to Masada, usable pasts are chosen to help construct a current world view. In 1988, the Catalan nationalist government celebrated 1,000 years of the formation of Catalonia as an independent realm, terming the events of 988 as the beginning point of Catalan history. In this year, the count of Barcelona ceased to be a vassal of the Franks but as we have noted neither Catalonia nor the Catalans can be said to exist at this point. This form of rendering of the past occurs everywhere and I do not intend to mean that these observations undermine the present-day claim to nationhood of the Catalans. In my view that fact that Catalonia is a nation is unanswerable. Rather we need to note how widespread is the case that how the past is presented is often fundamental for explaining the present. Catalan schoolchildren are told that Catalonia became independent in 988 and that Catalonia was an independent state until the later middle ages. The claim to independence today is usually framed as one of restoring national sovereignty, which was deemed lost in 1714. It is also appropriate to note in this context that notions of an eternal Spanish unity dating back to the Romans is also a historical myth and is one further indication of how the past becomes the battleground of the present. As we will see later in this book, definitions and terminology of Catalonia, the Catalans, Spain and Spanishness continue to be highly charged and politicised. For some there is only one nation, and that is Spain. For many, Catalonia has no right to independence: Spanish unity is eternal. Given that the Catalan question continues to be Spain's greatest political challenge, the search for historical legitimacy and justification is unresolved and more pertinently, unresolvable. In the writing of history, the answers you obtain are mostly determined by the questions that you ask.

1

ORIGINS, FROM PRE-HISTORY TO THE ROMANS

National formation is a lengthy process, subject to dramatic rupture, which can include conquest, civil war, famine or plague. Human history is incomplete unless we also consider the physical features of the landscape. The mountain of Montserrat is at least 35 million years old, yet it and other features of the landscape have become part of a nationalist reading of the past. It is a holy place and one of many symbols of Catalan nationhood. Place can be a useful enhancement for a collective sense of identity. In the nineteenth century, as Catalan identity was being reframed, poets and others wrote of the eternal elements of the land and mountains. One striking poetical epic, Canigó, written by the religious mystic Jacint Verdaguer in 1886, is set in the early medieval period on a mountain within the Pyrenees. The poem is focussed on the story of Catalan national formation in the eleventh century. There are features of the landscape of Catalonia that have determined its history: the sea and the mountains. The Catalan coast forms part of the Mediterranean Sea, stretching from the Pyrenees to Valencia. This geography has had lasting impact with the coastline today substantially more inhabited than the interior. Some 80 per cent of the present-day Catalan population of over seven million inhabitants are concentrated along this coast or in towns that serve these urban areas. This Mediterranean location has determined that sea faring was an early component to the local culture as the coastline contains extensive natural places to land. This required familiarity with currents and the winds. It was in the Mediterranean that important advances in the field of navigation took place. Sea going facilitated trade and communication. Sailors returned home with news of the wider world. The ports of Catalonia developed an urban trading tradition. For example, as the Roman Empire expanded, it was certain that the ports along the Iberian coast were to become of key strategic importance. Until the arrival of the railways, transport by sea remained the most rapid means of moving goods. Though for much of his period, the urban trading zones were lowly populated

DOI: 10.4324/9781003218791-2

whilst the interior farming area contained the dominant core of the population. The sea-bound aspect to Catalonia enabled two further elements. Firstly, a mutual relationship between Catalonia and the sea was formed. Secondly, as territorial expansion beckoned in the early middle ages, the option of overseas conquest in the Mediterranean seemed a natural choice.

As the territory that became Catalonia developed and consolidated, it found it had four main expansion options. To the west was the rest of the Iberian peninsula but this was rapidly blocked by the expansion of Castile. This was a path not taken. To the north over the Pyrenees; this did occur for a period in the early middle ages but in time French expansion blocked this route. To the east was the Mediterranean Sea and to the south were the Valencian territories, and these became the two outlets for Catalan expansion. As we will see in Chapter 4, for a time, Catalonia itself was a pivotal and conquering Mediterranean power. The next important physical feature that has contributed to the making of Catalonia are mountains. After Switzerland, the Iberian peninsula is the most mountainous area of Europe and historians have long noted how these physical features contributed to intense local identities. The Pyrenees have acted as a physical frontier between the two major states of Spain and France, yet they have not always functioned as such. Mountain peoples have a long tradition of independence and self-sufficiency and are usually the last areas to be incorporated within a state. They have provided refuge for Catalan rebels from the middle ages to the early Franco period in the 1940s. There is a deeply rooted Catalan tradition of banditry with these mountain-scapes providing perfect hideouts. The Pyrenees were also a route for smuggling well into the modern era. Mountains are vast and impenetrable to the uninitiated yet also provide opportunity for transport and communication for those with deep knowledge of their morphology.

Linked to both the sea and the mountains is the River Ebro. This river, which is Spain's longest, was navigable which meant coastal goods could be supplied, transported and distributed inland. Other rivers too were key to these patterns such as the Ter and Llobregat.[1] Rivers also contribute to the fertility of nearby land and are places where humans from the earliest periods settled. For example, settlement situated on the Ebro dates back at least 2,500 years, testament to its pivotal location between the Mediterranean and the interior of the peninsula. The Ebro has often functioned as a natural frontier and was used by the Romans to divide the peninsula between its sphere of interest and that of its geo-political rival, Carthage. Other important Catalan settlements such as Lleida and Girona are also on rivers. It has been the geographical location of Catalonia, and the wealth that became possible because of it that has attracted the attention of conquerors. The territory has no coal and little in terms of gems or precious metals. It is thus poor in terms of natural resources though the land is abundant in parts. This has ensured that trading has been not only a natural outcome but also essential.

For most of the period until the present, the Catalan climate has been marked by winters that are mostly mild with summer periods of heat. Spring and autumn are also mild facilitating farming and growing. Rain is usually sufficient in these two seasons to ensure successful harvests. A further factor to note is the temperatures between higher, coastal and lowlands as this can determine internal micro-climates. This climate has not been unchanging and general periods of apparent stability also contained long periods of extensive cold or heat. The end of the last ice age approximately 10,000 years ago enabled greater sharing of knowledge and population movement. Over many generations, the slow build-up of knowledge combined with a mostly benign climate enabled the move towards farming. Settlement also enabled the introduction of new technology including the smelting and working of metals. It also contributed to new forms of building such as earthworks to provide greater security. Continuous occupation is a further indicator of the relationship between people and their landscape. Colder periods were experienced during parts of the Roman era and the middle ages, the latter known as the Little Ice Age. In the case of the latter, poorer conditions for farming contributed to social conflict and unrest. The changing climate and disease have directly impinged on and disrupted societal stability in Catalonia whilst a benevolent environment contributes towards societal stability. The land, sea, rivers and mountains inscribe the human experience and play fundamental roles for the knowledge that must be developed to shape their usage.

Pre-history

Neanderthals were amongst the earliest inhabitants in Catalonia and only in three other places in Europe, wooden tools are found which were used by Neanderthal population groups. One of these four locations is Abric Romaní, located inland at around 60 miles from Barcelona.[2] The preservation of wooden tools dating back more than 40,000 years is rare because wooden tools rarely survive, unlike metal objects. Neanderthals were skilled hunters of large mammals and they co-existed with other populations including the ancestors of modern humans (Homo sapiens sapiens). As with elsewhere in Europe, modern humans gradually displaced the Neanderthal population groups. Catalan territory formed part of larger regional networks and patterns. Catalonia in pre-history can be situated within an arc from Gibraltar along the Mediterranean almost to northern Italy in terms of the shared experience of transformation. This included forms of settlement, hunting and farming patterns, religious beliefs and societal structure. Farming arrived in the period 5800 to 5300 BCE. The gradual arrival of a pottery form known as Cardium spread through Italy, southern France and the Mediterranean coast.[3] In broad terms, this geographical spread was repeated in terms of advances in copper, bronze and iron, usually arriving from the near east.

The co-existence and admixture of different population groups determine much of pre-history.[4] Genetic analysis has shown that early inhabitants can find shared lineage with farmers from Anatolia, North Africa as well as eastern Europe.[5] This was all before new arrivals such as Romans or Goths. At the site of Ullastret, some 20 miles inland, is the largest Iberian settlement discovered so far in Catalonia. Permanent structures began to be built there around 550 BCE. Analysis has confirmed the existence of population groups with diverse genetic origins. A macabre feature of this site is the severed heads of Ullastret. Skulls of both men and women have been found with evidence of nails inserted and other injuries likely produced by stabbing. Scholars continue to debate the cause with one view being the public display of defeated enemies as assertions of power and victory.[6] However, the later finds of female heads with similar injuries have caused some doubt as to the veracity of this theory. Yet we should note that these specific finds are not typical of the record elsewhere. Evidence of conflict and violence is mostly lacking in general terms. Cooperation was also an essential element to social life. Whilst this was not some harmonious rural idyll either, intense violence is mostly associated with resistance to outsider rule, for example in the case of the Roman conquest. Ullastret was the urban centre of a tribal grouping known as the Indigetes, whose territory included much of north eastern Catalonia. These Iberian societies were developing new forms of iron working and extensive domestication of a range of animals.

The rock art along the Mediterranean is the largest group of rock-art sites in Europe and in Ulldecona, near Tarragona, a series has been found containing around 400 examples of this art. They are at least 8,000 years old. Significantly, the art that survives depicts few scenes of violence, except against animals being hunted.[7] This art is subject to a wide range of interpretations but their public location should be seen as instances of prehistoric inscribing on the landscape. They thus served a different social function from that found within caves. The scenes mostly affirm the priority of hunting to the society so mostly male figures are represented. Prehistoric belief systems were firmly rooted in the land, which was expressed in the building of burial mounds and other monuments. Some 650 grave sites have been located in Catalan territory from pre-history. As settlement stabilised and became normalised, from around 4000 BCE, we see increasing evidence of cults of fertility. In Gavà, in the province of Barcelona, a figurine of a pregnant Neolithic woman has been found, dated to around 3500 BCE. This is one of only three early figures that have human form found in this zone. Ever greater importance was shown in the burial of the dead as can be seen for example in the site at Solsona region, deep in the Catalan interior, some dating back to 3000 BCE.

As the transition to stable settlement occurred, familiarity with the land had been obtained over hundreds of generations through hunting and consuming. Animals were often a guide to the most fertile terrain. In the entire Catalan region, settlement choices were favoured towards sites with potential for the development of agriculture. The gradual transition from a hunter-gatherer economy to one based mostly upon farming brought about a range of social changes. Initial groupings were usually in the range of 70–100 or so individuals. This settlement pattern remained basically unchanged until around 1000 BCE. As society developed, settlement size gradually grew. From this period, we find increasing evidence of extensive permanent settlement, some displaying increasing complexity. For example, the settlement of Els Vilars, near the city of Lleida, which was built by the second half of the eighth-century BCE, housed up to 200 people. This was protected by a wall, a series of towers and an extensive moat. The settlement was also supported by a network of roads.[8] Settlement in Els Vilars lasted some 500 years. Choice of settlement location was key to ensuring stable social organisation. There is now evidence for over 1,000 settlements of varying sizes located across Catalonia and these are, of course, only those so far unearthed by archaeologists. Whilst some hierarchy gradually emerged within these societies, chiefdom was substantially less powerful than something approaching kingship. A clan or tribal chief amongst the Iberian groups was not a figurehead like a monarch but one who worked the land and was given some decision-making powers. Authority was dependent on consent. Status was defined by the ability to distribute gifts rather than conspicuous displays of personal wealth.

For hundreds of years, these population groupings and settlements were mostly self-sufficient though internal and external trading emerged. Trading between different tribes began in the eighth-century BCE. The evidence indicates that it was the growth of trading activity that led to greater disparities of wealth both within and between communities.[9] With the emergence of early social classes, there is increased evidence of conflict. This is particularly clear in the lower Ebro River area, where settlements such as Sant Jaume Mas d'en Serra, south-east Catalonia, was destroyed by fire and permanently abandoned around 550 BCE.[10] A newly expansive trading society from modern day Lebanon, who have become known to us as the Phoenicians, is believed to have contributed to this change. These traders, from city-states on the Lebanese coast, developed relations with some tribal heads. In Sant Jaume Mas d'en Serra, for example, around 30 per cent of pottery finds are of Phoenician origin, leading to the belief that the site belonged to a local chieftain. Thus, this seems to demonstrate that elites were beginning to distinguish themselves from the majority.[11] Trading posts were established on the Catalan coast. These early settlements were solely for the purpose of trade and did not represent an attempted colonial form of domination. Together with that of the Greeks, the impact was also socio-cultural through the arrival of new products, such as olives and grapes. These products marked a new phase in agriculture as crops such as these take many years to establish before harvesting is possible. Wine making in Catalonia dates back over 2,500 years. However, consumption was not initially widespread as it functioned more in religious rituals and for ceremonial usage.[12] Wine drinking outside of this context was confined to tribal elites. Again, we see how outside influence impacted on local societal structure. New fruits and other plants were also introduced by the Romans.

Greeks

The ancient Greeks also founded new outposts at coastal sites across the Mediterranean. This was a form of imperial expansion without the trappings of imperial control. Empúries (the word for market or trading place), located to the north of Barcelona, functioned as a site of trade between Greeks and a local tribe, the Indiketes.[13] The location of Empúries, on the coast and between two rivers, was key to its founding and success. This was a relationship that was mutually beneficial, where goods were exchanged between trading partners. This trading post also encouraged the parallel development of native urban centres in the vicinity. Empúries was a multi-ethnic settlement, one that included both locals and Greeks. There has been a tendency to exaggerate the significance of Empúries. Part of this exaggeration has come from later authors who wished to claim an early Catalan heritage of classical culture. As noted, the impact of Greeks and Lebanese-Phoenicians was most evident in the case of the local elites. Analysis of pottery found in the vicinity has confirmed that at least 95 per cent was not of Greek origin but was of local manufacture.[14] This indicates that consumption of Greek goods did not impinge on the majority of the population. Given that Empúries continued to develop through Greek and Phoenician patronage, it was inevitable that as Rome expanded, it would play a role in Roman rule. As part of the complex inter-relations and alliances that emerged during Roman ascendancy, inhabitants of Empúries welcomed Roman forces, even as the Iberian tribes revolted. Before Rome embarked in Empúries, however, it had gained the attention of its Mediterranean rival Carthage.

Romans

Urbanisation was well underway before the impact of Rome with the town of Ullastret reaching a size of up to 6,000 inhabitants. From around 550 BCE, local tribal cultures continued to develop, peaking in the third-century BCE, before Roman arrival disrupted and ultimately destroyed pre-existing patterns. By the time of Roman intervention in the peninsula, around 190 BCE, we find up to ten main tribal groupings in the Catalan territory. It would partly be this internal fragmentation which contributed towards ultimate Roman victory. Iberia became one of the central areas of dispute between two imperial powers: Rome and Carthage. The Carthaginians, originally from Lebanon, developed in North Africa and gradually came to be Rome's rival for domination of the Mediterranean. The north-east, mostly Catalonia, held an important role in this conflict due to urban settlements and its strategic situation. Whilst Iberian tribal groupings had initially supported Rome against the Carthaginians, once it became clear that one power was simply to be replaced by another, local discontent rapidly escalated. Roman rule rapidly became unpopular, with mass rebellion one outcome. At least 40,000 took up arms and the full force of Roman power was necessary to defeat them. The Ebro valley was the scene of fierce fighting between the Iberian populations and Rome. This climate of instability culminated in a large-scale uprising by the Iberian tribes both in the interior and on the coast in 197 BCE. The siege of Empúries was a notable event of the campaign. Some 20,000 Roman soldiers and allies defeated a larger besieging army. Subsequent repression was ruthless with many built settlements razed to the ground and survivors sold into slavery.

Whilst further rebellions occurred in subsequent years, Roman rule was not shaken in the same way again. Local revolts were normally no match for the Roman army when it intervened. It was the revolt of 197 BCE that pushed Rome towards the full incorporation of Hispania into the empire. The consequences of defeat in Catalan territory were extensive. Tribal groupings such as the Lacetans or Bergistans were harshly repressed and were subject to the imposition of Roman forms of landholding.[15] The long process of the loss of a local tribal identity began, with assimilation into the Roman world its ultimate end result. The main tribal urban settlements were abandoned. Defensive walls were destroyed as part of a generalised policy of violent destruction to not only subdue a defeated enemy but also crush collective morale. The population growth that had been occurring in Catalonia prior to Roman intervention now stabilised or reversed. This was due to intermittent war with Rome and the consequences of defeat, where substantial local populations were enslaved. Others were given the option to fight for Rome in the army but this meant departure from the country. Some fled to the mountains to avoid Roman domination. Whilst intermittent rebellions continued to occur, most of the territory was subdued by 180 BCE. Catalonia was fully conquered before many other regions of Spain and it frequently became the launch base for Roman forces in their attempts to force submission of the rest of the peninsula. The priority of initial Roman domination was coastal, including the Catalan site of Empúries. In this early phase, there was no attempt at cultural Romanisation but simply the determination to prevent further rebellion and ensure that taxation was paid. There was substantial disruption with population movement usually towards mountainous terrain to avoid the Romans.

Romanisation

It was the Roman military presence which was initially most effective at disrupt-ing the then existing society. For at least a hundred years, the traditional order, whilst militarily defeated, remained mostly intact.[16] However, the tribal elites lost much of their prestige, which may explain why it was the higher echelons of this society that moved most quickly to submit to the new conquerors and embrace Romanisation.[17] Traditional belief systems were disrupted as some attributed native defeat and Roman victory to their abandonment by their gods. Due to internal developments within Rome itself, from around 100 BCE (if not a little earlier), a full strategy of colonisation was adopted. The first period of control was marked by militarisation and repression.[18] This was followed by establishing relations with local elites who had agreed to submit. The shift to full colonisation represented a major policy change. This would find expression in terms of infrastructure: cities, roads and bridges. This physical change was an expression of the permanence of Rome, perhaps not imagining that some of this would still be visible 2,000 years later. In cultural terms, we find the ascendancy of Latin and Roman philosophy, literature and learning, particularly applied to the elites. Finally, Romanisation rep-resented economic change and a shift towards a new model of trade and agricul-ture. The Romans imposed their law, and members of the local elite who wished to deal with the Roman authorities and to function in the new system had to learn Roman cultural practices and the Latin language. The adoption and acceptance of the Roman legal code was directly related to the obtention of citizenship. The spoken language did not have the same association with identity as we might find today, and in the early phase of Roman rule, the adoption of Latin was simply a pragmatic one to enable communication with the new rulers. Settlers from Italy were also introduced to the area and they did not learn the local languages. Therefore, Latin was central. The old world of Catalan society was to begin a process of overhaul and transformation, leaving little in terms of legacy or cultural memory of an extensive past. Catalonia, like other territories, now belonged to Rome.

Urban change

Whilst urbanisation had been increasing in the period prior to the arrival of the Romans, its scale now accelerated. Hilltop settlements which had been growing before Roman arrival in 200 BCE and smaller rural villages were now displaced by larger Roman urban centres.[19] The new Roman cities had a number of goals. As well as asserting dominance, they were designed to marshal agricultural production and improve trade. Roman conquest resulted in enormous changes in settlement patterns, in architecture and in the lifestyles lived in the major settlements. An extensive building programme was undertaken and included the creation of large urban settlements such as Tarragona together with smaller cities such as Baetulo (Badalona), Gerunda (Girona) and Iluro (Mataró).[20] Stone became the principal material for a permanent expression of Roman rule. This new urban form was the model adopted throughout Catalan territory. These settlements were usually built close to previous Iberian sites that had been abandoned or destroyed and previous inhabitants now often relocated to these new cities. Yet as we have noted, not all previous Iberian population groups chose to accept this new reality as some fled to the mountains in an attempt to preserve a previous way of life. In the early decades after conquest, the actual overall urban population fell. The new cities symbolised Romanisation. As with other features of Catalan physical infrastructure, Catalonia's contemporary cities have their origins in the Roman era.

Here we must note the primary importance given to the city of Tarragona. It became one of the two most important military and political centres in all of Roman Hispania in 25 BCE. Tarraco, as the Romans called Tarragona, was the administrative capital when Barcelona was little more than a small urban settlement. At its height the city had over 30,000 inhabitants. Tarragona retained primacy over the future Catalan capital until the third century and was the last Catalan city to fall to Gothic invasion in the fifth century. Strategic needs were key to the locations chosen for Roman cities. Tarragona had held some importance in the Iberian period when it was the most important urban settlement of people called the Cessetani.[21] Rome split the Iberian peninsula in two and later into three zones for imperial purposes. Tarragona was responsible for the administration of a vast zone of northern Spain from the Mediterranean to the Atlantic. The first group of inhabitants of the new city were mostly Roman military and governing officials.[22] As in all phases of Roman domination and control, the initial phase centred around military functions. Tarragona was an entry point into the peninsula. It was a city built on a hill, close to a river and a port. It thus combined in one place many of the features desired by the conquerors: security, ease of communication and transport. Rome could be reached by sea in just five days. Tarragona was given vast fortifications, with walls 20 metres high. To this was added an aqueduct and a bridge of almost 30 metres. Tarragona was the centrepiece of Romanised Catalonia, and its inhabitants embraced features of its new rulers. Within its secure walls were found a large Roman temple, arena and theatre. The full range of Roman festivities, religious rites and games, including chariot races was adopted. Seating in the arena demonstrated the status of the new ruling elite.[23] Tarragona grew in importance over the following century becoming a site of attraction for traders and other settlers with its port in near constant activity. As a truly Roman city, its destiny was affected by the development of the wider empire. In 260 CE, during a period of imperial instability, Tarragona was seized by the Franks. However, the city walls remained standing though much outside of the walls was destroyed. The city retained its importance by later becoming a seat of Christendom.

The founding of cities conveyed to the conquered their complete domination. In all cases, social division was evident in the cities' structure and ordering.[24] Those elites who had embraced Romanisation as well as the newcomers from the Empire expressed their social prestige by supporting the building of works of varying kinds in the city, from temples to theatres to public monuments. We find clear evidence in these cities of powerful Roman or Romanised families engaged in public display and patronage as expressions of their social dominance.[25] Within their walls, the free and the slaves served their new rulers. Stones found in the city of Tarragona contain inscriptions referring to slaves owned. The cityscape of Roman Catalonia formed a series of major and minor urban settlements to ensure collection of tax and the assertion of Roman order. They also functioned as poles of attraction for those wishing to embrace the new ruling order. Architecture functioned as a form of colonial expression. Barcino (Barcelona) was founded in the late first-century BCE with extensive walls. The new city exactly modelled Italian building style and no concessions were made to the previously existing cultures.[26] This was a form of empire where pre-existing culture, identity, religion and society was expected to fully submit. Imperial ideology can be seen, for example, in the capital Tarragona through decoration paying homage to the achievements of the emperor. Local notables petitioned the emperor to erect a temple in his honour.[27] Temples are also found in locations small and large throughout the territory in a sign that the old religious idols of the Iberian populations were being replaced by cults of the Roman Gods. The Roman bath affirmed a combination of the sacred and a new form of sociability. In the mid-first century, baths such as those in the city of Ilerda (Lleida) were testimony to the rising affluence of the main city residents.[28]

A new city such as Barcino asserted the power of Rome through its vast structure to both opponents and to those who had chosen to accept Roman rule and its benefits. The walls of Barcelona were later strengthened and added to as the later Roman period was marked by raids and assault by Goths and others. The Roman city sought to offer security. Prominent homes in Barcino adopted the full range of Roman interior decoration including mosaic and tiling. The Roman mosaic was a further expression of the newly dominant culture as it communicated religious and historical expressions of Rome. Those found in Baetulo (Badalona), for example, follow the latest Roman styles of the period.[29] It was in the urban settlements that cultural Romanisation occurred most rapidly and city-based dominance of the rest of Catalonia was affirmed. The wider territory had been pacified and the conflict that remained was usually to do with factional struggles within Rome itself that impacted on elites throughout the empire. These range from the overthrow of an emperor to a Roman civil war that spread to other areas of the empire. The transformation brought by Rome occurred not only in the urban arena. There were also major upheavals in the countryside.

Agriculture

Whilst the focus of Roman impact is often mostly concerned with urban settlements usually found on the Catalan coast, partly because these are the most prominent remains existing in the present, this urban population remained a clear minority of the population. The Catalan land, as in other parts of Roman Hispania, held great potential due to its climate and productive land. Once the territory was conquered, Roman interest was above all economic. From the trafficking of slaves to quarrying and mining, agriculture and trading, this region was to prove its economic worth. Whilst initially slow to take off under the new Roman system, the economy boomed in the second century. The countryside experienced new forms of land ownership and peasants were subject to new taxes. The turn towards a new agricultural order was facilitated by changes in the climate. The climatic situation from 100 BCE to 200 CE, known as the Roman Warm Period, favoured an increase in agrarian production. This 300-year period combined warmth and sufficient rainfall.[30] The intensification of agriculture and the type of crops grown such as cereals, grapes and olives led to a transformation of the surrounding landscape. Roman intensive agriculture increased the clearing of forests. In an area close to the city of Lleida, a vast clearing was created to introduce and grow new fruit varieties.[31] Imperial change thus had a range of consequences including new culinary traditions. The introduction of the Roman economic form of landholding had a negative impact on the majority. Repeated tax demands produced a near subsistence existence for many as the conquered population resettled. At the height of the empire, the average income level was at the lower end of the empire average overall as surplus from Catalonia was sold for trade or consumed by Romanised elites.

Land was used as a tool to ensure social control through its distribution to locally favoured elites as well as former veterans from the army. Evidence in the city of Baetulo (Badalona) points to increased pork production to satisfy the dietary demands of soldiers from Rome.[32] There is also clear evidence of other Italian settlers in the territory. The Roman villa was transplanted and developed as a system of agricultural exploitation. An example of this form is found at Vilauba Villa, near

Banyoles in the north of the region, where olive oil and wine was produced.[33] A villa of this kind was where the central activity took place in a rural area, including important trades such as pottery production. In this sense, the villa can be seen as a small outpost of Roman rule but one scattered throughout the land. In the Maresme region, over 70 Roman villas and 50 other Roman buildings have been located in a zone of around 15 square miles.[34] The villa, where the new elite lived, organised the rural workforce and was also a privileged zone for social life in a rural area. Whilst the urban world predominated over the countryside in the early centuries of Roman rule, growing imperial instability shifted the focus of stability to the Catalan countryside. The new economic conditions produced a growing surplus which led to a vast trade of goods from Catalonia leaving for Rome or other outposts of the empire. The rural population grew, yet the total number of villas declined and wealth became more concentrated in fewer individuals.

Romanisation occurred at a slower pace in the countryside, particularly in terms of the slow shift to a Latinised language.[35] Other changes were more visible. Dietary changes are evident including the increasing use of salt even deep into the interior of the country.[36] Only in the Pyrenees was Romanisation slow and halting with little physical evidence to indicate much Roman presence. Here were the last and longest lasting outposts of the speaking of the Iberian language. It would be several generations before a new mode of existence became assimilated and accepted in the countryside. Following the conquest, a period of consolidation and transition occurred to a new Roman order. It was during the first and second centuries that major changes took place. Greater agricultural activity is visible in much of the central area of the country. The greatest impact felt by the population at large was the introduction of the Roman form of property. Roman property law was a now a firmly embedded part of social life. The small peasant plot which provided sufficient produce for a family and a small surplus went into decline as slavery expanded the ability of the richer farmer to produce at scale.[37] The new agricultural elite consolidated their dominance. Slave labour and that of the newly impoverished peasantry enabled the growth of production and the creation of surplus that could be sold abroad. The Roman economy was an agrarian regime that produced mainly cereal, wine and olive oil combined with livestock farming. Rome also introduced a form of consumer model to economic activity through pottery, earthenware, mosaic and other forms of decoration. The wine industry was one symbol of this transformed landscape and economic model. Whilst vines had been known previously, it was the intensification of their use that marked the Roman era. Wine production for both internal consumption and export contributed to the growth of coastal cities such as Baetulo (Badalona) and Iluro (Mataró). Wine from the Catalan region became a major export.

The physical infrastructure transformed

With the full incorporation of the region into the empire and the growing potential of the territory for agricultural riches, a process of vast infrastructural building was undertaken. The former model of settlement in the countryside was no more than a memory and the new cities, inspired by Rome and many situated around the most important land and sea routes, had become the main element around which the territory and its inhabitants were organised and integrated. The next step involved connecting the interior through a network of roads, most of which were completed by 120 to 110 BCE. Improved communication and the facilitating of rapid troop movements as well as trade was a further tool of Romanisation. As previously noted, given that it was conquered early, Catalonia was used as a base to attack other parts of the peninsula that had not submitted to Rome. Roman roads played a key role in this development. The main route built was the Via Augusta which reached as far south as Cadiz. The location of the road also meant the consolidation of urban settlement along its path. The Romans undertook an extensive project of planning and mapping of the territory for military and trading purposes. Roman cities were distributed around 50 miles apart to ensure rapid internal communication should revolt or raids occur. The Via Augusta was the main route but feeder routes were also an important component to communication within Catalonia. This is visible in an area such as the plain of Vic, found in the interior, where minor roads linked the new city to the Via Augusta.[38]

It was only deep in the countryside where, in the absence of a river, areas remained isolated. However, even here some Roman settlements existed in the lower Pyrenees. In spite of the vast road-building project, transport by land continued to be slow and expensive. Ports retained their importance as sea transport was usually safer and more reliable. Rivers continued in their role as for example in the case of Empúries which made use of three forms of transport in the Roman period: sea, land and river. The Ebro retained its pre-eminence since it passed through so much of the interior. Tarragona, given its status as capital remained the main port of the Roman period. The Pont del Diable, the Devil's Bridge, is the largest construction of its kind in Catalonia and was built as a key strategic element as it connected the local capital Tarragona to the Via Augusta.

Romanisation of culture and lifestyle

Rome treated its conquered territories as provinces, meaning they had been annexed. They were ruled by Roman appointed officials, backed by the military power of the army.

Romanisation occurred at different paces, being most rapid in these urban, coastal settlements. Mixed population groups of Romans and natives were more common in the coastal urban settlement, whilst a regime of colonial domination was found in the countryside. As noted, Romanisation was most visible amongst the elites who saw this avenue as an opportunity to maintain or obtain privilege. This social sector embraced Roman culture in all aspects and within a century they had been culturally Romanised. They retained power but in a new guise.[39] This process lasted hundreds of years amongst the majority of the population in a slower moving transition from a dying old order to the new world. We should see this process as existing on an arc from complete Romanisation to little impact, particularly in isolated zones. The erosion of the native population's traditional identity intensified over the hundred years between 50 BCE and 50 CE. By around 70 BCE, only one Roman legion was stationed in Spain. It was literacy and access to the Classics that accelerated elite Romanisation. After conquest, Rome was able to provide a stable social order. For around the next 250 years, imperial ideology was increasingly assimilated. Enlistment in the Roman army was the fastest route to citizenship to those without means and with it the future promise of land. The army was also the most popular mechanism for the transmission of Latin to those without literacy.

Imperial domination was achieved through a range of measures. The shift to Romanisation was enabled because Roman culture held high prestige. This was a confident culture. Local elites were the quickest to find a mechanism of accommodation with Roman rule. Citizenship was granted to loyal local elites. The assertion of newly Romanised status amongst elites was evident in clothing, language shift to Latin and building. The adoption of the worship of Roman Gods was required. Those with the wealth directly copied the Roman villa. The transition from the Iberian languages to Latin was a lengthy process. Whilst written Latin remained static, language evolution occurred with the spoken variety, though this occurred slowly. Thus, the initial phase of vulgar Latin in Catalonia, which lasted hundreds of years, was the gradual appearance of some dialectal differences with written Latin. Until we find the final emergence of the Catalan language, not earlier than the eleventh century, it is easier to speak of the language spoken as the Catalan form of Latin. This is a difficult process to trace as it occurred for most people over many generations. Dialectical change occurs slowly with shifts in pronunciation and the arrival of new words. At a certain point, a new mother tongue will emerge. The shift from the Iberian languages to Latin was a process that occurred most intensely in the major Roman urban centres.[40]

Roman imperialism adopted two main methods to achieve control: repressive violence and diplomacy. The latter entailed building alliances with local elites, ensuring that they never faced a truly unified opponent. This was the articulation of the classic Roman method of divide and rule. Rome affirmed its domination and once it was accepted, it offered order and peace. Generation by generation, the old ways fell from use and the population increasingly accepted their sense of being Roman. The new ruling system clearly offered benefits, in particular that of acquiring Roman citizenship. Rewards to the elites were most evident. Iberian identity was gradually diluted, and a form of Roman identity emerged. Whilst Rome brought with it a colonial relationship, its willingness to bestow what Rome termed its benefits made it highly attractive for those willing to accept the abandonment of old practices and cultural habits. As we will see in the next chapter, the Pyrenees did not act as a cultural frontier in this latter period, as social structure was broadly similar in Catalonia to that of southern Gaul. Language differences in these two zones were small, ultimately producing the languages of Catalan and Occitan.

Roman legacy

The golden age of Roman rule was the first and second centuries. From the third century and until the arrival of a Germanic people known as the Visigoths in 409 CE, Catalonia experienced periods of disruption as well as the stability that the later Roman Empire was able to achieve. We have previously mentioned the assault on Tarragona in 260 CE. Crisis periodically hit Catalonia and some cities, such as Empúries, entered a period of decline. The decline of the Roman warm period and a general cooling of the climate is believed to have contributed to this disruption.[41] It was during the latter phase of the empire that Tarragona began to lose its dominance to the city of Barcelona. Other Roman cities such as Girona also declined in importance as the profile of Barcelona rose. Notably, the Germanic invaders who came in the fifth century chose Barcelona not Tarragona as their base. Romanisation in social and cultural terms was however so deeply embedded that only a relatively small military force was kept in the territory. Romanisation is perhaps the most deeply felt of all foreign influence in the making of Catalonia. We have noted how little legacy of the lengthy Iberian period was remembered or evoked. Romanisation was so extensive that it ended collective memory of the Iberian period. Roman religion had swept the native cults aside though traditional religious practices survived longest in isolated rural areas. Christianity emerged in some small communities in the third century but it remained a religion of dissent until the Roman Empire decreed it as its official religion. Roman law also prevailed, and survived the presence of the Visigoths, to the point of becoming the basis of medieval Catalan law. The Roman system of landholding had a lasting legacy with the villa economy remaining the dominant form. The smallholder or peasant would not retain significant rights of tenure or access to land until rebellions over landlord abuses in the later feudal period.

The commonly held view of Rome as bringing order, hierarchy, roads and culture means that key aspects of Roman civilisation such as slavery and brutal violence are quickly passed over. Yet together with Christianity, the Roman legacy is the most apparent and long lasting in the making of Catalonia. This legacy as we have seen is physical and can be seen across the landscape. The urban and rural geography of contemporary Catalonia follows the pattern articulated in the Roman period. A legal code, as in much of Romanised Europe, led to the model of a Catalan legal form heavily influenced by Roman law. As in other areas of Catalan life, little legacy of the Iberian systems of justice survived. Conquered earlier than other parts of the Iberian peninsula, Catalonia was one of the most fully Romanised areas of the empire. This Romanisation was largely preserved by the next conquering people, the Visigoths. Whilst some societies evoke the pre-Roman period, in the case of Catalonia, because Romanisation brought the language which is central to contemporary identity, there is no attempt to celebrate the period before Rome. The Iberian era is not seen as making any useful contribution to the formation of the Catalans. The subsequent period, as we will see in the next chapter, entails three new influences in the making of Catalonia. Christianity, the Visigoths and the arrival and occupation of the Arabs.

Notes

1 Bolòs i Masclans, J. (2004) *Els orígens medievals del paisatge català. l'arqueologia del paisatge com a font per a conèixer la història de Catalunya*, Barcelona: Institut d'Estudis Catalans, p. 48.

2 Vallverdú Poch, J., Gómez de Soler, B., Vaquero Rodríguez, M. and Bischoff, J. (2012) 'The abric romaní site and the Capellades region, High Resolution Archaeology and Neanderthal Behavior: Time and Space in Level J of Abric Romaní (Capellades, Spain)', in Carbonell i Roura, E. (ed.) *High Resolution Archaeology and Neanderthal Behavior*, Dordrecht: Springer, pp. 19–46.

3 Whittle, A. W. R. (1996) *Europe in the Neolithic. The Creation of New Worlds*, Cambridge: Cambridge University Press, p. 309.

4 Cabanilles, J. (et al.) (2017) 'New Approaches to the Neolithic Transition: The Last Hunters and First Farmers of the Western Mediterranean', in García Puchol, O. and Salazar García, C. (eds.) *Times of Neolithic Transition Along the Western Mediterranean*, Dordrecht: Springer International Publishing, 2017, pp. 33–65.

5 Pinhasi, R., Fort, J. and Ammerman, A. J. (2005) 'Tracing the Origin and Spread of Agriculture in Europe'. *PLoS Biology*, vol. 3, no. 12, p. e410.

6 Pujol Puigvehí, A. (1979) 'Los cráneos de Ullastret y su posible significado', *Pyrenae: revista de prehistòria i antiguitat de la Mediterrània Occidental*, no. 15–16, pp. 267–276.

7 Lillios, K. (2019) *The Archaeology of the Iberian Peninsula. From the Paleolithic to the Bronze Age*, Cambridge: Cambridge University Press, pp. 150–152.

8 Junyent Sánchez, E., Garcés i Estallo, I., López Melción, J. and Lafuente Revuelto, A. (1993) 'Els Vilars (Arbeca, Les Garrigues): primera edat del ferro i època ibèrica a la plana occidental catalana', *Laietania: Estudis d'historia i d'arqueología de Mataró i del Maresme*, no. 8, pp. 41–60.

9 Aranegui Gascó, C. and Vives-Ferrándiz Sánchez, J. (2007) 'Encuentros coloniales, respuestas plurales. Los ibéricos antiguos de la fachada mediterránea central', in *De les comunitats locals als estats arcaics. La formació de les societats complexes a la costa del Mediterrani occidental*, Barcelona: Universitat de Barcelona, pp. 89–107.

10 Munilla Cabrillana, G., Garcia i Rubert, D. and Gracia Alonso, F. (1998) 'San Jaume-Mas d'en Serra (Alcanar, Tarragona) Un asentamiento de transición entre los S. VII y VI a. C en el área de la desembocadura del Ebro: primeros resultados', *Revista de estudios ibéricos*, no. 3, pp. 23–44.

11 Arteaga, O., Padró, J. and Sanmartí, E. (1986) 'La expansión fenicia por las costas de Cataluña y el Languedoc', in Del Olmo, G. and Aubet, M. E. (eds.) *Los fenicios en la Península Ibérica*, Sabadell: Ausa, pp. 303–314.

12 Ramon, J. (2008) 'El comercio púnico en occidente en época tardorepublicana (siglos II-I aC). Una perspectiva actual según el tráfico envasado en ánforas. Los Fenicios y el Atlántico', in González, R., López, F. and Peña, V. (eds.) *Iberia e Italia: modelos romanos de integración territorial*, Madrid: Universidad Complutense, pp. 67–100.

13 Sanmartí Grego, J., Asensio i Vilaró, D., Belarte Franco, M. C. and Noguera Guillén, J. (2009) 'Comerc colonial, comensalitat i canvi social a la protohistòria de Catalunya', *Citerior: arqueologia i ciències de l'Antiguitat*, no. 5, pp. 219–238.

14 Barberá i Farras, J. (2001) 'La ceràmica griega arcaica a la laietània', in Cabrera Bonet, P. and Santos Retolaza, M. (eds.) *Ceràmiques jònies d'època arcaica: centres de producció i comercialització al Mediterrani occidental*, Barcelona: Museu d'Arqueologia de Catalunya, pp. 277–284.

15 Pérez Conill, J. (2010) 'La Segarra entre els lacetans i els ilergetes. Una aproximació a la cultura ibèrica en aquesta comarca', *Miscel·lania Cerverina*, no. 20, pp. 11–22.

16 Sanmartí, J. (2014) 'L'Estat del coneixement sobre la cultura ibèrica a Catalunya', *Butlletí de la Societat Catalana d'Estudis Històrics*, no. 25, pp. 227–260.

17 Burch, J., Castanyer i Masoliver, P., Nolla Brufau, J. M. and Tremoleda i Trilla, J. (2010) 'Temps de canvis. La romanització del nord-est de Catalunya', in *Època de canvis: als inicis de la romanització = Time of Changes: in the Beginning of the Romanization*, Girona: Laboratori d'Arqueologia, Universitat de Girona, pp. 89–108.

18 Noguera Guillén, J., Asensio Vilaró, D., Ble, E. and Jornet, R. (2014) 'The Beginnings of Rome's Conquest of Hispania. Archaeological Evidence for the Assault on and Destruction of the Iberian Town Castellet de Banyoles', *Journal of Roman Archaeology*, no. 26, pp. 60–81.

19 Sanz Martínez, M. (1979) 'Población ibérica del valle del Ebro (III). Aportación al estudio del oppidum ibérico de San Miguel, Vinebre', *Butlletí arqueològic de la Reial Societat Arqueològica Tarraconense*, no. 1, pp. 11–42.

20 Pérez Centeno, M. (1998) 'Análisis evolutivo de "Gerunda, Baetulo e Iluro" en el siglo III DC', *Annals de l'Institut d'Estudis Gironins*, no. 39, pp. 31–38.

21 Canela Gràcia, J. (2012) 'De la cabana a la ciutat. El poblament a la cessetània occidental entre el bronze final i l'ibèric final (XII-VIII ane–II/I ane)', *Cypsela*, no. 19, pp. 141–157.

22 Nolla i Brufau, J. M. (2019) 'El món romà i la Hispània Tarraconense precatalana', *Butlletí de la Societat Catalana d'Estudis Històrics*, no. 30, pp. 21–78.

23 Capra, R. (2015) 'Chariot Racing in Hispania Tarraconensis: Urban Romanization and Provincial Identity', in Kemezis, A. (ed.) *Urban Dreams and Realities in Antiquity: Remains and Representations of the Ancient City*, Leiden: Brill, pp. 370–392.

24 Cabrelles, I. (2013) 'Elits urbanes i propietat rural durant l'Alt Imperi. El cas dels Clodii de Tarraco', *Pyrenae: revista de prehistòria i antiguitat de la Mediterrània Occidental*, vol. 44, no. 2, pp. 7–32.

25 Prevosti i Monclús, M. (2010) 'Els grans canvis del poblament a Catalunya: de la protohistòria a l'antiguitat', *Butlletí de la Societat Catalana d'Estudis Històrics*, no. 21, pp. 45–76.

26 Rodà de Llanza, I. (2016) 'Tarraco y Barcino en el Alto Imperio', *Revista de historiografía*, no. 25, pp. 245–272.

27 Mierse, W. (1999) *Temples and Towns in Roman Iberia. The Social and Architectural Dynamics of Sanctuary Designs, from the Third Century B.C. to the Third Century A.D.*, Berkeley: University of California Press, p. 132.

28 Xavier Payà i Mercè (2003) 'Les termes públiques de la ciutat romana d' Ilerda (Lleida, Segrià)', *Tribuna d' arqueologia*, no. 1999–2000, pp. 147–164.

29 Dunbabin, K. (1999) *Mosaics of the Greek and Roman World*, Cambridge: Cambridge University Press, p. 145.

30 Scheidel, W. (2019) *The Science of Roman History Biology, Climate, and the Future of the Past*, Princeton: Princeton University Press, pp. 33–34.

31 Alonso Martinez, N. (2005) 'Agriculture and Food from the Roman to the Islamic Period in the North-East of the Iberian Peninsula: Archaeobotanical Studies in the City of Lleida (Catalonia, Spain)', *Vegetation History and Archaeobotany*, vol. 14, no. 4, pp. 341–361.

32 Colominas, L., Fernandez Rodriguez, C. and Iborra Eres, M. (2017) 'Animal Husbandry and Hunting Practices in Hispania Tarraconensis: An Overview', *European Journal of Archaeology*, vol. 20, no. 3, pp. 510–534.

33 Castanyer i Masoliver, P., Tremoleda i Trilla, J., Colominas Barberà, L. and Antolín i Tutusaus, F. (2015) 'Després de les villæ. La transformació del camp al nord-est català en els segles VI i VII a partir de l'exemple de Vilauba / Villa Alba (Pla de l'Estany)', *Estudis d'història agrària*, no. 27, pp. 43–65.

34 Marta Prevosti i Monclús, M. (1995) 'Prospecciones sistemáticas en el Maresme y los orígenes de la romanización del territorio', *Studia historica. Historia antigua*, nos. 13–14, pp. 125–141.

35 Nolla i Brufau, J. M. (2001) 'Aspectes de la romanització. De la llengua dels indigets al llatí. Algunes dades', *Estudi General*, no. 21, pp. 415–428.

36 Buxó, R. (2005) 'L'agricultura d'època romana: estudis arqueobotànics i evolució dels cultius a Catalunya', *Cota Zero*, no. 20, pp. 108–120.

37 Lara Peinado, F. (1978) 'Materiales para el estudio de la esclavitud romana en las tierras de Lérida', *Ilerda*, no. 39, pp. 79–84.

38 Panosa, M. A. (2012) *Els ibers del Vallès Oriental*, Barcelona: Publicacions de l'Abadia de Montserrat, pp. 176–177.
39 Morley, N. (2010) *The Roman Empire: Roots of Imperialism*, London: Pluto Press, pp. 52–54.
40 Pérez i Conill, J. (2010) 'La Segarra entre els lacetans i els ilergetes. Una aproximació a la cultura ibèrica en aquesta comarca', *Miscel·lània cerverina*, no. 20, pp. 11–22.
41 Westin, A., Crumley C. and Lennartsson, T. (2018) *Issues and Concepts in Historical Ecology. The Past and Future of Landscapes and Regions*, Cambridge: Cambridge University Press, p. 47.

2

NEW INFLUENCES. VISIGOTHS, CHRISTIANITY AND THE ARABS, 400–800

Examination of the map of Europe in 500 or 700 CE shows us kingdoms ruled by Franks, Saxons, Slavs, Ostrogoths, etc. To the modern eye, it is an unfamiliar map in almost any area we look. So just as Catalonia as we understand it did not yet exist, nor did the vast majority of today's European nation states. A battle lost here, a better ruler there would have led to some important differences to the map that is so familiar to us today. By the end of our period in this chapter, the Latin spoken in the territory we know as Catalonia will have sufficiently evolved to be closer to a different language, a process that has taken hundreds of years.[1] Though even here it is a very close linguistic cousin of a parallel development in southern France: the language that will become known as Occitan. We can call these languages at the end of our period proto-Catalan and proto-Occitan.[2] The population of Catalonia is now mostly formed by a grouping who are usually called Hispano-Romans. This refers to the majority of the population of the Iberian peninsula as other languages such as Castilian or Portuguese have not yet evolved from Latin either. Only in the case of the Basques and the slowly diminishing speakers of Iberian is there a differentiated linguistic community.[3] Some of these speakers were still found in Catalan territory, particularly in the zone close to the Pyrenees. As we noted in the previous chapter, the majority population group had largely abandoned the speaking of Iberian languages and Latin, or the Catalan version of it, was now the spoken tongue for most.[4] It is notable that in spite of the arrival of two new conquering groups in the following centuries, Catalanised Latin remained the vernacular for most. The Germanic influence from the Goths on Catalan was very small, as it was in other Latin languages of the peninsula. Unlike in the case of the Romans, who achieved full and complete cultural conquest, the Germanic Visigoths were themselves conquered by the civilisation of their subjects.[5] Equally for the main part of Catalonia, Arab occupation was short lived and its linguistic legacy on the Catalan language is minor.

DOI: 10.4324/9781003218791-3

The fall of the western Roman Empire continues to have great symbolic appeal in the west, as perhaps offering lessons for the present. One historian has even traced the 50 or so main theses as to why the empire fell. However, work in recent decades shows a more nuanced binary picture than the destruction of Roman civilisation by 'barbarians'.[6] There was not a simple collapse as might be signified by defeat in war and occupation. The term 'barbarian' is of course heavily loaded and generally unhelpful and will not be a term I will use. Whilst originally it simply meant 'foreigner', its overwhelmingly negative association today means it is highly unsatisfactory as a term of description. Equally unhelpful is the use of the Dark Ages to describe our period. This coinage emerged in the Renaissance and was part of a movement that evoked the civilisation of the ancients and saw the intermediate period as one largely without culture or value. This reading of the period from around 400 to at least 1000 as lacking much merit became the standard narrative in European history and has only begun to be questioned in recent decades.

From the middle of the third century, Rome began to lose influence in parts of its borderlands. The subsequent period is one marked by periodic disruption as well as long periods of relative stability. As Roman power tended to weaken in Spain in the latter phase of the empire, a Germanic people, the Visigoths acted for a time as Rome's proxies, including suppressing rebellions on Rome's behalf in the Tarraconense region in the mid-fifth century.[7] The Visigoths first arrived in Catalonia as an ally of Rome to fight against other people: Swedes, Vandals and Alans. A Visigothic court was briefly established in Barcelona between 415 and 418. The murder in quick succession of two kings in the city saw the third newly crowned king leave with his forces and head for the south of Spain. Seemingly, Barcelona was too just too dangerous a city to remain.[8] In general terms, however, Roman taxation had become so burdensome that most inhabitants actually welcomed invading Visigoths and there is little evidence of the repeated revolts as occurred in the early years of Roman occupation. For example, the main route known as the Via Augusta, which crossed Catalan territory, continued its traffic and there is little to indicate that this vital road was marked by violent conflict for control. Overall, roads from the Roman period continued to be used across Catalonia.[9] The principal change represented by Visigothic control was a change at the elite level. Simply put, the Romanised ruling elite was displaced or replaced by new Germanic rulers.

Yet much of the legacy of Rome continued. We find that the Germanic conquerors of Spain were highly Romanised.[10] Furthermore, as with late Rome, they had Christianised, though in the variant known as Arianism. This religious difference between a majority Catholic population may have been the most important division at a popular level. Arianism and Catholicism maintained minor theological differences around the nature of God but these were intensely felt.[11] It was only the much later adoption by the Visigoths of the dominant Catholic form of Christianity that ensured their integration with the native population. Whilst it is often common to refer to the intense divisions and dynastic conflicts during the

Visigothic period, we should recall the large number of Roman civil wars and emperors who were removed and usually killed. The new Visigothic conquerors adapted to a written Latin language. Those most opposed to the new rulers were the fully Romanised elites, the large landowners as well as the Catholic church which saw Arianism as heresy. In general terms, the broad mass of the population were not hostile to the Visigoths nor did their economic condition worsen or change. In 470 AD, the Visigoths broke with Rome and conquered the peninsula for themselves. The domination of the Tarraconense region, which included Catalonia, was not easy as the Hispano-Romans put up resistance led by the aristocracy. However, with little popular support, the former rulers were subdued and all Catalan territory fell to Gothic rule, likely to have been not later than 476. A further indicator of lack of broad resistance to Visigothic rule was the complete failure of an invading Frankish force to control the territory, attempted in 541.[12] The Franks were forced to return over the Pyrenees as native populations chose not to assist them.

The Visigothic presence did not mean any significant change in the socioeconomic structures characteristic of the period of the later Roman Empire as the Visigoths were a substantial minority of the peninsular population. In all of the Iberian peninsula, they are unlikely to have ever comprised more than 5 per cent of the total population. Even in urban settlements, it was rare for the Visigoths to comprise half of a town's inhabitants. With the absence of resistance to their rule and their relatively minor population compared to the native population, the general pattern in time was one of Visigothic adaptation to the local culture rather than its transformation. Some elements remained a constant in the Visigothic period. Visigothic laws did not represent a rupture with Roman rule though Visigoths and Hispano-Romans were governed by different legal codes. With the religious divide around Catholic or Arian development of Christianity, the Visigothic period was initially marked by the parallel development of two mostly separate communities. This only changed with a new legal code adopted in the mid-seventh century. This new legal regime also allowed for security of land tenure if continuous possession could be demonstrated over a period of 30 years.[13] Perhaps the most important difference other than the religious was the militarisation of the aristocracy. This entailed changes in dress codes and the development of warrior ethos. This change marked a major shift from the character of the Roman elite who not only did not fight but also attached importance to their own personal cultivation. This militarised warrior class and its culture continued its central role until the high middle ages and is the origin of what will become known as the knightly class. Army size was another consequence as the emergence of a horse-bound militarised cast meant a much smaller military force than that mustered by Rome. The fortified building at Puig Rom, near to Girona, is one of the important examples of this change. It was built in a location that had little strategic value. Yet its militarised form can be seen as an example of a transformed culture and one that is markedly different from a Roman villa.[14] It bears more relationship to a medieval castle than a Roman building.

Urban change

Unlike the Roman conquest, Visigothic domination did not entail the destruction of the pre-existing culture. Rather, much of the Roman legacy was adapted for new uses. Building in towns and villages tended to be much less ordered and structured than under Roman rule. With the Visigoths a series of changes became evident. The Visigoths preferred heavily fortified urban centres. They adopted and adapted the major cities of Barcelona and Tarragona for their own purposes. The cities continued to maintain their prestige, and the city continued to be the preferred residence of the local Visigothic elite. There was some abandonment of cities by Hispano-Romans who were displaced by a new ruling class.[15] It was these former elites who were most likely to relocate to their rural estates. This dynamic caused the cities to lose gradually their predominant role in the economy, which shifted to the countryside. With this change of elites, the period of donations to cities as expression of social status came to an end. Without patronage, for a period little renovation or new building took places. The patronage that was a feature of the Roman period did not return until the building of churches emerged as an expression of status from the sixth century. However, not all was economic decline. Barcelona grew in importance. Its key strategic location and its strong fortifications from the late Roman period accentuated its role in the later Visigothic period. By the end of the fifth century, it had become an important economic centre in its own right and taxes from all of the main Catalan cities were collected there.[16] Barcelona's trade with North Africa grew in importance and it became a centre for the distribution of ceramics from other areas of the Mediterranean.

Changes in the economy

It was both during the later Roman period and Visigothic rule that we see a general pattern marked by population decline or little population growth. However, this was not simply because of political instability or change due to new Gothic rulers. The climate was generally less favourable to increased agricultural production and plagues also decimated populations. In the mid-540s, a plague similar in character to the Black Death though much less virulent and known as the Justinian pandemic spread through North Africa and into Europe.[17] It reached Catalonia 541–542, though little record remains of its impact and likely devastation. Trade became more of a subsistence activity, meaning production was mostly concerned with satisfying local need rather than creating a surplus for trade. This change, however, had already commenced in the later Roman period as the period from around 400 is marked by the decline of overseas trade. Production was focussed on maximising the available resources for local distribution and consumption. We also find a change from the Roman period in the reappearance of moving of flocks for grazing purposes. In the latter part of our period, this trade was usually controlled by the emergent religious centres as the Church grew in wealth. Imports from the Mediterranean seem to be limited only to coastal towns, particularly following

Byzantine control of North Africa in the mid-fifth century. However, whilst there was an overall decline in economic activity, this did not mean the period was static. Many of the key features that we interpret as medieval begin in this period. For example, we find cultivated land increasingly sub-divided according to different crops. The principal means of income in the Roman period had come through rent but the new period marked a shift to profit making through owning land.[18] The transformation in many villas in Catalonia indicate a series of changes in the fourth and fifth centuries. The cities ceased to be the centre of agricultural trade in the area, which began to be done directly in the large agricultural villas.

Rural world in the Visigothic

As with Rome, agriculture remained central to the Visigothic economy. The Visigothic period represents substantial change in the countryside. In the post-Roman period, we now see the growth of villages, rather than scattered settlements associated with the Roman villa. These villages will consolidate in time and provide a further manifestation of a new rural form of existence, as the city did under Roman rule. This will represent a transformation of the landscape from one where the villa was dominant to the village-type structure which will continue until the middle ages.[19] Village names will be established in this era that in most cases will continue in some form until the present. Identity formed around local place will become a permanent feature. There is some revival of simpler construction for occupation such as those made of wood and mud. An example of this type of settlement has been examined in Castellar del Vallès, some 20 miles inland from Barcelona, where the dwellings were made of perishable materials.[20] A range of agricultural activity took place, including wine making. Thus, much of the knowledge developed from the Roman period was retained and transmitted. As an indicator of how localised trade had become, there was very little pottery from outside of the surrounding area found in Castellar del Vallès.[21]

With the emergence of the village, burial tended to be concentrated rather than isolated and formed part of the greater village. From the later sixth century, burial became firmly associated with a church. Whilst in the early Visigothic period as in Rome, burial had been largely associated with the highest strata of society, this gradually changed to permit burial of the ordinary peasant in consecrated ground. The emergence of the graveyard makes a change in popular relations with the village as it provides a source of familial lineage and memory. Large areas of these villas seem to have been converted from residential space to new, productive uses. Mosaic floors were removed or built over, dwelling spaces and baths ceased to serve their original functions and in their place olive presses or ovens were installed. Part of the difficulty in assessing this period is the decline of stone as primary material for building, which was used by Rome and again in the later middle ages. For example, there is evidence of castle building under the Visigoths but the form of materials used prevented it lasting such as a medieval castle. New building did occur but it usually combined clay and stone and hence did not have the longevity of medieval stone constructions. It was not simply a pattern of changing the usage of Roman buildings. In the north of Catalonia, for example, we find at l'Hort d'en Bach a substantial building from the late Roman period which continued its role, with some extensions, until well into the sixth century.[22] An innovation of the new elites was the seated banquet around a table as a display of wealth and generosity. Prior to this, the Roman custom had been to eat and dine reclined. The banquet of this new kind is another feature more suggestive of the middle ages. Another example is that of Vilauba, near Banyoles in the northern Catalan coast, where post-Rome, the house was divided internally for a range of uses, including a range of agricultural tasks.[23] The Roman order had been able to maintain control over all social sectors. Under the Visigoths, some peasant communities attain much greater autonomy and were able to work and manage their own farms. This varied across Catalan territory, where areas closer to the Mediterranean coast saw elites, the aristocracy and the Church, maintain a lot of power over the population.[24] In these areas, poorer peasants had what was closer to a feudal relationship where land was exchanged in protection by the local lord.

Under the new rulers, we see the appearance of a new type of settlement.[25] This was usually surrounded by a wall, often with milling facilities, with a number of inland examples excavated such as Castellfollit del Boix, some 40 miles inland from Barcelona or Collet dels Clapers, in central Catalonia.[26] These constructions can be situated as transitional between the Roman and medieval worlds. By the seventh century, many of the future patterns of the medieval world are well established. These changes in the structure of the villas and in the population in general are linked to a change in the model of livestock exploitation. Animal and crop practices during the transition from antiquity to the middle ages in Catalonia show the emergence of a different land use linked to goat herding after the arrival of the Visigoths. The areas around Empúries, Tarragona and Barcelona saw the continuing clearance of forest and other changes due to intensive animal farming. An increase in crop cultivation for animal feed for sheep and goats has also been documented.[27] Settlement tend to be organised around small family units devoted mainly to cereal and olives, as well as animals for personal consumption. Whilst pork consumption rose substantially under Roman rule, we now see pork displaced by lamb and goat.

Early Church

By the middle of the third century, practising Christians had already emerged, though they were small scale and often isolated communities. However, in the same period, Rome began a series of anti-Christian persecutions. All citizens of Rome were required to sacrifice to the Roman gods and produce an officially verified certificate that they had complied. This persecution wave led in January 259 CE to the imprisonment of the bishop of Tarragona, Fructuós, who was tried and burned alive in the city, together with his two deacons. In 303 and 304, the emperor Diocletian further hardened the persecution, and new martyrs were produced: Feliu in Girona and Eulàlia in Barcelona. Eulàlia was only 13 when she was reputed to have died from torture and became a powerful and lasting symbol of the new religion. Saints would provide names for future towns and cities, such as that of Cugat who gave his name to Sant Cugat del Vallès or became patron saints, such as Eulàlia in Barcelona.[28] Once Christianity became the official religion of the empire from the mid-fourth century, a new phase began and one was the cult dedicated to martyrs. Catalan martyrology has five martyrs from the early Christian period. In Girona for example, a basilica was built to commemorate Saint Feliu and it became a place of pilgrimage cementing the areas role in the expansion of Christianity. At the beginning of the fifth century, Tarragona built a basilica in honour of its martyrs as a way of establishing a collective memory for believers.

The conversion of Emperor Constantine and merging of Roman power with Christianity marked a major change in the fourth century and the establishment of a new type of religious organisation. Christianity first expanded amongst the Romanised elites. In this final period of Roman rule, it became the duty of the cities to ensure that the peasant population practised the new religion and abandoned the old pagan rituals. From Roman paganism persecuting Christians, the reverse came about. Pope Siricius expressed concern at the continuance of pagan practice in the Tarragona area in the early 400s. The turn to Christianity was a slow process and there are many indications that pagan and Christian practices existed side by side in mixed and confused form over many generations. Religious elites regularly demanded the adherence to official Christianity and the ending of pagan celebrations. Bishops and other religious figures became ever more important in late Roman and Visigothic society. They were overwhelmingly recruited from aristocratic families. The power vacuum left by the Roman Empire from the fifth century was filled by the Church, which gradually became an autonomous and powerful entity within the late Roman state. The Church, which was exempt from taxes, began to accumulate a huge amount of property and land, as early as the fourth century. With its growing prestige and wealth, the Church led a building wave, again a pattern that is intensified in the middle ages.

Christianity formed a fundamental component of early medieval Catalan identity. Most villages and rural settlements did not have their own church building however. There are still very few in Catalonia until well into the sixth century. Older Roman buildings were sometimes used and converted into churches. From the seventh century, we see the expansion of church building and the first monasteries appear. It is from this period that we begin to see the first baptism of children taking place. As it expanded and consolidated, Christianity changed the local relationship to the land and to a sense of time. Saints' days and other religious holidays marked the pattern of the year. However, where they could, the Visigoths established an Arian religious order, as for example in the city of Barcelona. The Arian and Catholic division lasted in Spain till 586 until Catholic victory at the third council of Toledo. After Arianism was condemned as heretical, King Reccared ordered the seizure and destruction of all Arian texts. The conversion of the Visigothic monarchs to Catholicism contributed to the ever-growing church influence in society as elites were now united. The later Visigtholic rulers combined military, aristocratic and religious values. Church councils become one of the most important events in Visigothic society and at the same time became political assemblies within the kingdom. The church Council of 546 held in Lleida established new rules on when churches and monasteries could be established and a number of these councils were also held in Barcelona and Girona.

The Jews in Catalonia

Before the fifth century, some Jewish merchants are evident in trading in cities such as Tarragona and Tortosa though the overall Jewish population remained very small in Catalonia. Tarragona, as regional capital, contained the largest and oldest Jewish community in this period.[29] Visigothic treatment of the Jewish population became more intolerant after conversion to the Catholic variant of Christianity, with some theologians terming Judaism as seditious.[30] The Jews were frequently portrayed as being anti-Christian and hostile to the Gothic kingdom. Jewish communities were increasingly subject to an explicit anti-Jewish policy, with forced conversions, persecution and prohibitions.[31] Jews were forbidden from undertaking legal action against Christians and from giving evidence against them in court. The Muslim conquest (711–718) was welcomed by the Jewish communities. During the Arab conquest of Catalonia, Jews preferred to remain in Moslem rather than Christian territory and this entailed the movement of some Jewish groups. The harassment that the Jews had suffered from the Visigoths meant many Jews welcomed Arab rulers as a source of liberation from Christian persecution. However, this would add to Christian suspicion and a Christian chronicle of 852 accused the Jews of having opened the gates of the city of Barcelona to the Moslems. In the later medieval period, relations would vary between being relatively stable and conflictual until new Christian repression and pogroms permanently changed relations.

Cross-Pyrenees relations

The Visigoths divided their territory into six regions and followed the model established by Rome. This included Catalan territory within the area still known as the Tarraconense. For the first hundred years of Visigothic rule, control was exercised over extensive territory in southern France. This cross-Pyrenees relation is important to the future development of Catalonia. Initial Visigothic territory in France was substantial but after military defeat by the Franks in 507, this was reduced to a much smaller strip. This conflict was not just territorial as the Frankish leader Clovis was hostile to the Visigoths for following what was deemed by his court as the heresy of Arianism. The Frankish rulers saw this cross-Pyrenean zone as a natural zone for annexation as their own kingdom consolidated. However, the Franks were unable to push the Visigoths over the Pyrenees. Although the Visigothic kingdom was likely to have been the strongest state in Western Europe in the period, this did not mean that control was exercised as in a modern state.

Some areas were so geographically distant from the capital in Toledo that local elites had a reasonable degree of autonomy. This was the case in much of the north of Catalonia and extended to the area of southern France controlled by the Visigoths. In the final period of Visigothic rule, this zone was increasingly prone to rebellion, at times including Girona and Barcelona. This area became of further significance following the Islamic conquest of Spain. Visigothic elites, who were now of course Catholic, found refuge in these cross-Pyrenees borderlands and they would seek alliances to restore their land and status. The Arab kingdom established in Spain was not without its own internal revolts and in time, Al-Andalus would become a kingdom that was completely separate from other Arab-ruled dominions of the Caliphate. Al-Andalus was also not one that exercised control as in a modern state. It too was dependent on a system of localised alliances, though in theory it was centrally ruled from Cordoba.

End of the Visigoths

Few rulers have maintained strong central control of the Iberian peninsula and Visigothic Spain was prone to instability and turbulence. Its final decades were marked by aristocratic factionalism evocative of the feudal period and this weakened overall military coordination. This once again marks this period as sharing parallels with the high middle ages. Unrest, and at times civil war, followed the death of kings, as rival factions of nobles sought to back their claimant to the throne. This occurred in areas including Catalonia where in 673, Barcelona and Girona supported a revolt against the king by a noble based across the Pyrenees. This became known as the rebellion of Paulus.[32] The Visigothic king was forced to move his forces to the Catalan and southern French zone to repress the rebellion. The Visigoths dominated the territory until the beginning of the eighth century but the monarchy had been gradually losing its capacity to impose its rule across its regions. In the middle of a Visigothic civil war for the succession of the kingdom in 710–711, one of the claimants sought aid from the Umayyad Empire. The Umayyad dynasty, from 661 to 750, ruled from Damascus. This Arab dynasty had expanded from its heartland across much of the Mediterranean. Once intervention in the Iberian peninsula began, Visigothic weakness became evident and led to full Arab conquest. The Visigothic kingdom, which had lasted 250 years, rapidly collapsed. The Arab and Berber forces led by Tariq ibn Ziyad, taking advantage of the internal factionalism of Visigothic power, occupied the Peninsula in a short period of time. An Islamic empire from Spain to Afghanistan emerged, which now contained within it substantial numbers of non-Arabs. For later Christian chroniclers, the conquest was mostly attributed to internal division, rather than the prowess of the invaders. Though some also attributed to a Christian legacy of sin and the decadence of the Visigothic court. End times narratives were also evident in some Christian accounts. The coalition of Arab and Berbers established a series of agreements with the leading figures they encountered locally. As with Rome and the Visigoths, once again a new ruling order came into being.

Arab conquest and pushback

Muslim conquest of the peninsula in 711 was relatively unopposed. The conquering Arab force was not large. We can note that Rome needed extensive forces to subdue Catalonia and the rest of Spain, whilst the Visigoths marshalled much smaller forces. The Arab army was the smallest of the three conquering powers at a maximum of 15,000.[33] The areas of southern Catalonia such as the city of Lleida and the surrounding area fell into Arab hands at an early stage of conquest. Resistance in an area stretching from Girona, including Tarragona and Barcelona, was stronger. The former province of the Tarraconense, that included all of Catalonia and the Ebro Valley, was however under Muslim control by 720. The river Ebro again functioned as a frontier zone. Due to its strategic value, for both trade and communication, the northern stretch of the Ebro was disputed by Muslims and various Christian kingdoms. The Ebro and the river Segre were key rivers for internal supply with cities such as Lleida and Saragossa. We noted earlier how Barcelona had increasingly displaced Tarragona in regional importance. Tarragona, however, had remained an important city in religious terms. Arab conquest saw its abandonment by leading figures. Following conquest, new population groups came from North Africa and other parts of the Islamic world. Thus again, the population in the future Catalan zone, like much of the peninsula, experienced a new social and cultural infusion, following that of Rome and the Visigoths.

The new conquerors did little in terms of eroding religious practices or customs of the Christians. In that sense, the initial conquest should not be seen as a traumatic rupture with what came before. Following consolidation and a stable frontier, we do see the appearance of a new form of existence in Al-Andalus. A society emerged that fused pre-existing elements with those brought by the new rulers. However, this new society offered advantages for some. Peasants and small holders could improve their socioeconomic status by converting to Islam. However, conversion to Islam was not yet encouraged as it would mean a reduced tax base for the new rulers. Marrying into local families by Arabs and Berbers was adopted as a strategy for ensuring good relations with local aristocracies. Catalan territory formed part of a Muslim kingdom that lasted until the mid–twelfth century and was centred on the city of Cordoba, Europe's largest city with over 100,000 inhabitants. The Arab presence, lasting less than a 100 years in the northern zone and, lasting some 400 years in southern Catalan territory, led to separate development in these two zones.

It would be mistaken to interpret this early phase of conquest as marking a religious struggle amongst either Christians or Moslems. Islam was sufficiently new for most Christians not to be aware of it as a religion whilst areas of the countryside had still not fully Christianised. Islamic religious culture itself did not appear fully formed until the mid-eighth century. The principal concern of the new Arab rulers was not religious conversion but tribute and stability. Except for the frontier zones, this was not a military occupation beyond a number of strategic fortresses found further north. The poorly defended churches and monasteries of Christendom often held important booty made of gold and silver. Christians who remained preserved their property and were allowed to practise their religion. Those who resisted were normally enslaved. However, as had happened with the Iberians becoming Romans, they were certainly substantial numbers who chose to adapt to the new rulers and converted to Islam. In doing so, they were not required to pay taxes or if they did, the tax burden was minor compared to Christians.

We can divide popular responses to the new rulers into three broad categories. The first was broadly well disposed to their new rulers and substantial numbers would convert to Islam as a sign of adaptation to a new reality. Hispano-Goths elites chose conversion to Islam to maintain their social position. The second category remained under Moslem rule but continued as Christian or Jewish. This category was influenced culturally and socially by the new rulers. In most cases, there was little or no resistance to the new rulers. Islam did not necessarily mean a dramatic rupturing to pre-established identity. Arab social structure had also been heavily influenced by Rome prior to its expansion. Islam was not imposed from above but was adopted by personal choice. The third category of the populace fled to the north, usually into Frankish-dominated terrain. This included leading aristocrats and bishops as well as a large number of farmers and peasants. There was substantial abandonment of the land in the central Catalan zone. In this category, we can speak of a collapse of the traditional social order. The failure of armed resistance and the fact that those defeated were often enslaved ensured that those most committed to the resistance fled. From this first wave of migration, Archbishop Pròsper of Tarragona, with his senior clergy fled to Italy after the taking of the See in 720.[34] They brought with them holy relics such as those of martyr Saint Fructuos and as well a number of manuscripts. In the zone that will become Christian, there is little evidence of a Moslem population remaining after territories were regained. In the Islamic zone, however, the experience was very different.

Early Arab Catalonia

By the time of the Islamic conquest of Iberia, the new religion had barely existed for a hundred years and it was, as with early Christianity, still developing doctrinally. Islamic law and Arabic custom began to impact across society in a range of areas, from dress codes, acceptable public behaviour, diet and entertainment. Whilst some bishops fled from the conquest, sizeable Christian communities remained. Church authorities worked closely with the new Islamic rulers. Church building did not cease over the course of the eighth century. The new rulers brought with them important techniques in irrigation. They introduced crops of cereals, fruit trees and vegetables previously unknown and had a long-lasting impact on dietary habits. After the hiatus of the Visigothic period, cities became revitalised and a new urban civilisation emerged. Lleida and Tortosa became the most important Muslim cities in Catalonia.[35] Tortosa was conquered and remained under Muslim control until 1139. Its location on the river Ebro gave it an important role as a transport hub and strategic asset. It was fortified and became a key city in the area.[36] In the early

Islamic period, a major military force was stationed there to respond to Frankish incursions. It also became a key city for ship building and repair of the Arab fleets. During the four centuries of Muslim rule, Lleida became a cultural, economic and political centre. The invasion and conquest by the Arabs had ruptured much of Spain's natural economic development towards feudalism, which continued uninterrupted in the rest of Western Europe. Whilst in the south of Catalonia Islamic rule brought with it a new prosperity through increased agricultural production in the hortes (market gardens), in the north, that will be become known as Old Catalonia, was a feudal, unsophisticated warrior society. It was overwhelmingly rural, and compared to the Byzantine and Islamic worlds, it was technologically and culturally backward.

Frontier

After conquering most of Spain, the Muslim governors in Al-Andalus made repeated advances into southern France. We should remind ourselves that this zone had remained part of the Visigothic kingdom until its end. The Frankish leader Charles Martel met and defeated the invaders in 732, which marked the high point of Islamic advance in Western Europe. This defeat would begin a series of developments leading to the overthrow of the Umayyad dynasty and ultimately the separate development of Islamic Spain from the Caliphate. The defeat of 732 would begin the gradual pushback against Arab forces, forced back beyond the Pyrenees, which became for a period a geographical frontier between the two powers. In the mid-eighth century, the Emir of Córdoba ordered the strengthening of fortifications on this northern frontier of Al-Andalus, as the new kingdom was termed. This zone became a highly militarised region where neither clear Christian nor Islamic zones of domination were firmly established for some decades.[37] Three border zones, given special status within the emirate, were created across the peninsula and that including Catalonia was termed by Arabs as the upper zone (Marca Superior) of their territory.[38]

From an early point, the incipient Muslim occupation also introduced innovations in the field of fortifications and territorial defence, as happened with the creation of an extensive network of circular and raised watchtowers, known as husun, constructed across the eastern half of Catalonia.[39] In this frontier zone, a number of fortresses were built or those already in existence were repaired. An example is that found at l'Esquerda, previously a Visigothic site, some 50 miles north of Barcelona, where watch towers were built and walling extended.[40] Given its key strategic role, its defenders were given high status as defenders of Al-Andalus. This zone embarked on an Arab-led military-building programme. Girona, the principal Catalan city near to the Pyrenees, had been strengthened as a key city for the Arabs in 760. It retained its military importance after falling to the Franks in 785. The acquisition of Girona was partly enabled by the support of Muslims to the Umayyads in Cordoba and opened the city gates to the besiegers. The city defences prevented it falling again to the Moslems in a renewed intent in 793, though the surrounding areas were devastated in the Arab retreat.[41] Until 801, Girona was the key base for the Frankish forces as they sought to push back the Arab forces. As in other cities that fell to the Franks, the new rulers owed their position to Charlemagne.

As the Visigoths had followed many of the patterns of Rome, so Al-Andalus maintained much of the regionalised system of rule of Visigothic Spain. This semi-regional arrangement had begun from an early stage of the conquest. This had its own pitfalls as Al-Andalus too was confronted with internal attempts at rebellion by its own local officials. The new conquerors had their own divisions between Arabs and Berbers and other factional differences, which resulted in conspiracies, rebellions and military conflict. In the late 770s, an Arab governor Sulaiman, installed near Barcelona, sought to break from control from Cordoba. He formed alliances with both Arab and Hispano-Goths south of the Pyrenees, and his revolt included the taking of the Aragonese capital, Zaragoza. As an indication that conflict at this time was not framed in a purely Christian-Moslem binary, Sulaiman sought the assistance of the Frankish king Charlemagne. He proposed becoming a vassal lord and offered control of the Ebro and the Catalan coast in exchange for military aid against the Umayyad government. This was not sufficient to prevent suppression of the revolt by the Umayyad ruler of Córdoba. These changing alliances were common and crossed religious boundaries. For example, in the 710s, the Muslim advance to the Pyrenees was partly enabled by local support.[42] Land, territory and strategic alliances were far more important in motivating alliances, and Christian hostility to Islam in religious terms was not yet the primary focus of military mobilisation.

Christian Catalonia

Frankish territory beyond the Pyreness became the centre of an exiled Hispano-Goth community who were determined to reclaim their lands. Catalan territory was at the epicentre of the conflict for control of these borderlands. From around 720 until 800, northern Catalan territory experienced intermittent conflict as Arab and Frankish forces sought domination. The territory remained under overall Islamic control but it was subject to a range of challenges until it was finally lost by the early ninth century. In the period from 788 and 796, the Umayyad rules faced intense political instability with rival claimants for power seeking control. Partly facilitated by this, Girona was the first major city to fall to the Franks in 785. The fall of Girona was an example of a city ruled by Moslems, yet its rulers opened its gates to the Franks. An attempt to regain the territories for Cordoba was pursued in 793 but failed. A band of territory from the Pyrenees to the coast was gradually incorporated within the Frankish or Carolingian Empire. Now ruled by Charlemagne, this narrow band of territory was gradually extended. Following a lengthy siege, Barcelona was taken by the Franks in 801. After the fall of Barcelona, the frontier was extended towards the River Llobregat. To prevent Muslim penetration, the Carolingians built a series of wooden watchtowers in higher locations to allow surveillance of the river. A Frankish attempt at the taking of Tortosa was resisted in 808, whilst a new Arab intent at the reconquest of Barcelona was halted in 815.[43] In this case, a local lord allied with the Arabs against the Franks. Peace was restored for a period but both Barcelona and Girona were besieged by Saracen forces in 817 and again in 850. This would not be the last time. The general instability of the zone meant that farming activity remained basic and little trade beyond local consumption developed.

Marca

Arab holding of Barcelona and the northern zone of Catalonia ended with less than 100 years of control. The comparative brevity of Islamic rule in northern Catalonia meant that Hispano-Gothic sentiment was little disrupted and continued to be the basis for identity in the subsequent decades. Again, in the historical development of Catalonia, we can note how a relatively small area was found in a position of dependence with its two largest neighbours, in this case Al-Andalus and the Franks. The population in the latter zone of influence continued to follow the Visigothic legal code. This survival will also be important in a process of differentiation with the new Frankish rulers. Frankish sources use the term 'Spanish March' over 20 times between 821 and 850 in a clear expression that this zone at this time was not fully part of the overall Frankish territory. The Marca Hispanica described a geographical, political and military zone in the border area below the Pyrenees.[44] It came under Frankish rule. The inhabitants of the lands on both sides of the Pyrenees were known by the Franks as Hispani. However, the Spanish March zone remained of central importance in the maintaining of cross-Pyrenean social and cultural linkages. Lands taken from the Moslems, sometimes declared to be abandoned, were granted out in return for military service. These estates were then used by these new landowners to reward their own followers. Administration of these conquered zones was delegated to various counts. In this phase, the Frankish nobles were more likely to be trusted than the Hispano-Goths who saw the territory as their own. This allocation of land and vassalage to the Frankish king were rewards for loyalty and to enable the building of a warrior class in this zone. As a borderland, with its attendant instability, taking on this role within the kingdom might allow for personal advancement. As the Christian zone stabilised, Christian population groups also began to move to it from Al-Andalus. This was partly because of internal changes from the late eighth century within Al-Andalus marking a greater Islamisation.

The transition to the Catalan language

The language spoken in the early eighth century, when the Arab invasion took place, had continued its evolution from standard Latin. By this time, spoken speech was much closer to medieval Catalan than it would have been to Latin of the later Roman Empire. Evolution would occur in a range of everyday vocabulary which was passed on within families and villages. Classical Latin had remained relatively static and thus could only be learnt. Yet written Latin retained its prestige in Christian Catalonia, which it will maintain throughout the following centuries though literacy was heavily dominated by the Church. The small bastions of literacy that existed in this society knew only Latin or, in the south, Arabic. The conquerors formed a small proportion of the overall population of this new province of the Islamic empire. The adoption of Arabic was a slow process which entailed the gradual intrusion of Arabic vocabulary into Catalanised Latin. This transmission was more rapid in towns than the countryside. During the period of Arab rule, initial co-existence of late Latin with Arabic was apparent, though need for Arabic was greater higher up the social ladder as it became the language of government and administration. Arabic was also central to scientific and cultural advance. Until at least the 850s, Latin was used within Al-Andalus by those who remained Christian for internal communications, particularly within the Church. The newly Arabised, who became known as the Muladites, used classical Arabic for cultural purposes and this became more common.

In the Pyrenean areas and the zone that will become known as the Spanish March, the influence of Arabic was slight as a result of the short duration of Arab control.[45] Refugees from the conquest took refuge in the mountains and also across the frontier, where Visigoth leaders were integrated into Frankish society, yet maintained their wider political and cultural identity as goths. With a narrow band of territory in northern Spain embarking on separate development, the languages that will emerge in the peninsula such as Castilian, Portuguese and Aragonese, increasingly diverge from their common Latin source.[46] The ninth century is key for the last phase of transition from vulgar or Catalanised Latin to the emergence of the Catalan language in its own right. Documentary evidence increasingly appears such as legal texts, contracts, etc. which contain words or phrases that can be identified as close to Catalan. As an indication of recognition of the divergence of Latin from everyday speech, the Third Church Council held in Tours in 813 decreed that sermons in the Catholic Mass should be given in the common tongue of the populace. It will not be until the year 917, however, that the word 'Catalan' first appears, yet a new language is clearly about to emerge.

Notes

1 Morán i Ocerinjauregui, J. (1984) 'Notes sobre la formació de la llengua catalana', *Anuario de filología*, no. 10, pp. 335–346.
2 Posner, R. (1966) *The Romance Languages*, Cambridge: Cambridge University Press, pp. 122 and 197.
3 Moncunill Martí, N. (2011) 'La llengua dels ibers: preguntes i respostes', *Quaderns de Vilaniu*, no. 59, pp. 5–20.
4 Bastardas, J. (1992) 'El llatí de la Catalunya romana i l'origen i formació de la llengua catalana', *Fonaments: prehistòria i món antic als Països Catalans*, no. 8, pp. 99–116.
5 Esmonde Cleary, S. (2013) *The Roman West, AD 200–500. An Archaeological Study*, Cambridge: Cambridge University Press, p. 364.
6 Halsall, G. (2007) *Barbarian Migrations and the Roman West, 376–568*, Cambridge: Cambridge University Press, pp. 45–47.

7 Isla Frez, A. (2011) 'Del món tardoantic a la Tarragona visigoda, Història de Tarragona', in Bonet Donato, M. and Isla Frez, A. (eds.) *Tarragona medieval, capital eclesiàstica i del camp*, Tarragona: Universitat Rovira i Virgili, pp. 21–56.

8 Beltrán de Heredia Bercero, J. (2013) 'Barcino, de colònia romana a sede regia visigoda, medina Islàmica i ciutat comtal: una urbs en transformació', *Quarhis: Quaderns d'Arqueologia i Història de la Ciutat de Barcelona*, no. 9, pp. 16–118.

9 Collins, R. (2008) *Visigothic Spain 409–711*, Oxford: Blackwell, pp. 211–212.

10 Green, D. H. (2000) *Language and History in the Early Germanic World*, Cambridge: Cambridge University Press, 2000, p. 323.

11 Bainton, R. H. (2000) *Christianity*, Boston: Houghton Mifflin, pp. 141–143.

12 Kulikowski, M. (2011) *Late Roman Spain and Its Cities*, Baltimore: Johns Hopkins University Press, p. 272.

13 Sam, S. and Wood, J. (2009) 'Unity from Disunity: Law, Rhetoric and Power in the Visigothic Kingdom', *European Review of History=Revue européene d'histoire*, vol. 16, no. 6, pp. 793–808.

14 Subías Pascual, E., Puig Griessenberger, E., Codina i Reina, D. and Fiz Fernández, J. (2016) 'El castrum visigòtic de Puig Rom revisitat', *Annals de l'Institut d'Estudis Empordanesos*, no. 47, pp. 75–96.

15 Claude, D. (1998) *Remarks About Relations Between Visigoths and Hispano-Romans in the Seventh Century*, Leiden: Brill, pp. 118–120.

16 Tarradell, M. (1979) 'La ciutat antiga: Dels orígens urbans als visigots', *Cuadernos de historia económica de Cataluña*, no. 20, pp. 17–22.

17 Bran García, F. (2021) 'Sobre la epidemia en la Antigüedad: la peste antonina y la plaga de Justiniano', in Pageaux, D. (ed.) *Pandemia y cultura*, Madrid: Instituto Juan Andrés de Comparatística y Globalización, pp. 37–46.

18 King, P. D. (1972) *Law and Society in the Visigothic Kingdom*, Cambridge: Cambridge University Press, pp. 60 and 64.

19 Salrach Marés, J. M. (2014) 'La Història de Catalunya, avui: La llarga edat mitjana', *Butlletí de la Societat Catalana d'Estudis Històrics*, no. 25, pp. 261–297.

20 Buxó, J. and Coll Riera, J. (2010) 'El jaciment de la Plaça Major de Castellar del Vallès: de l'Assentament del Neolitic al viatge de l'antiguitat tardana. 5000 anys d'evolució històrica', *Recerca: Revista d'història i ciències socials i humanes de Castellar del Vallés*, no. 7, pp. 77–108.

21 Riutort, J. (2018) 'Estudio macroscópico de las cerámicas de cocina tardoantiguas de Plaça Major de Castellar del Valles (Barcelona)', in Martín Viso, I., Fuentes Melgar, P., Sastre Blanco, J. and Catalán Ramos, R. (eds.) *Cerámicas altomedievales en Hispania y su entorno: (siglos V- VIII d. C.)*, Valladolidad: Arbotante Patrimonio e Innovación, pp. 563–572.

22 Montalbán Martínez, C., Llinàs i Pol, J. and Ramírez, A. (1996–1997) 'L'hort d'en Bach (Maçanet): una vil·la romana a la selva interior', *Annals de l'Institut d'Estudis Gironins*, no. 37, pp. 841–852.

23 Castanyer i Masoliver, P., Tremoleda i Trilla, J., Dehesa, R. and De Vilauba a Villa, A. (2010) 'L'hàbitat dels segles VI-VII dC de la vil·la romana de Vilauba (Camós, Pla de l'Estany)', *Tribuna d' arqueologia*, no. 2010–2011, pp. 9–21.

24 Carr, K. (2002) *Vandals to Visigoths. Rural Settlement Patterns in Early Medieval Spain*, Ann Arbor: University of Michigan Press, pp. 189–190.

25 Jimenez Garnica, A. M. (2003) 'Settlement of the Visigoths in the Fifth Century', in Heather, P. (ed.) *The Visigoths from the Migration Period to the Seventh Century. An Ethnographic Perspective*, Rochester: Boydell Press, 2003, pp. 93–128.

26 Enrich, J. and Pedraza, L. (1995) 'Vilaclara de Castellfollit de Boix (Bages): un assentament rural de l'antiguitat tardana', *Tribuna d' arqueologia*, no. 1993–1994, pp. 95–106.

27 Alonso Martinez, N. (2005) 'Agriculture and Food from the Roman to the Islamic Period in the North-East of the Iberian Peninsula: Archaeobotanical Studies in the City of Lleida (Catalonia, Spain)', *Vegetation History and Archaeobotany*, vol. 14, no. 4, pp. 341–361.

28 Bellavista i Ramon, J. (1998) 'El culte al màrtir sant Cugat a través dels textos de les misses de manuscrits litúrgics de Catalunya', *Analecta sacra tarraconensia: Revista de ciències historicoeclesiàstiques*, no. 71, pp. 115–130.

29 Roth, N. and Roth, A. M. (1999) *Jews, Visigoths, and Muslims in Medieval Spain. Cooperation and Conflict*, Leiden: E. J. Brill, pp. 11 and 141.

30 O'Callaghan, J. (2018) *A History of Medieval Spain*, Ithaca, NY: Cornell University Press, pp. 71–72.

31 Stocking, R. (2008) 'Early Medieval Christian Identity and Anti-Judaism: The Case of the Visigothic Kingdom', *Religion Compass*, vol. 2, no. 4, pp. 642–658.

32 Orlandis, J. (2003) *Historia del Reino Visigodo español*, Madrid: Ediciones Rialp, pp. 119–121.

33 Collins, R. (1989) *The Arab Conquest of Spain 710–797*, Oxford: Blackwell, pp. 96–97.

34 Recasens i Comes, J. M. (1972) *A propòsit de l'ocupació àrab de Tarragona i l'emigració de Sant Pròsper a Itàlia*, Tarragona: Real Sociedad Arqueológica Tarraconense, pp. 209–213.

35 Brufal Sucarrat, J. (2018) 'La arquitectura del poder en los distritos islámicos de Lleida, Tortosa y Huesca', in Sabaté i Curull, F. (ed.) *El poder entre la ciutat i la regió*, Lleida: Pagès editors, pp. 17–42.

36 Kirchner, H., Virgili Colet, A. and Antolín i Tutusaus, F. (2014) 'Un espacio de cultivo urbano en al-Andalus: Madîna Turtûsa (Tortosa) antes de 1148', *Historia agraria: Revista de agricultura e historia rural*, no. 62, pp. 11–45.

37 Adell Gisbert, J. A. and Menchón i Bes, J. (2004–2005) 'Les fortificacions de la frontera meridional dels comtats catalans, o les fortificacions de la Marca Superior d'al-Àndalus', *Lambard: Estudis d'art medieval*, no. 17, pp. 65–84.

38 Chandler, C. (2019) *Carolingian Cataloni. Politics, Culture, and Identity in an Imperial Province, 778–987*, Cambridge: Cambridge University Press, pp. 52–54.

39 Martí Castelló, R. and Viladrich, M. (2018) 'Les torres de planta circular de la frontera extrema d'al-Andalus a Catalunya (segles VIII-X)', *Treballs d'Arqueologia*, no. 22, pp. 51–81.

40 Ollich, I. (1999) 'Roda: l'Esquerda. La ciudad carolingia', in Camps, J. (ed.) *Cataluña en la época carolingia: arte y cultura antes del románic (siglos IX y X)*, Barcelona: Museu nacional d'art de Catalunya, pp. 84–88.

41 Canal i Roquet Jalmar, J. (1985) 'De la "Marca Hispànica" a la constitució de l'estat: Especial significació de la petició d'ajuda de Girona als francs', *Quadern de treball*, no. 6, pp. 45–49.

42 Folch Iglesias, C. (2003) 'Estratègies de conquesta i ocupació islàmica del nord-est de Catalunya', *Quaderns de la Selva*, no. 15, pp. 139–154.

43 Kennedy, H. (1996) *Muslim Spain and Portugal: A Political History of al-Andalus*, London: Routledge, pp. 54–55.

44 Chandler, C. (2013) 'Carolingian Catalonia: The Spanish March and the Franks, c. 750—c. 1050', *History Compass*, vol. 11, no. 9, pp. 739–750.

45 Rubiera Mata, M. (1993) 'Els arabismes del català. Història d'un rebuig', in Ferrando Francés, A., Lluís Meseguer, L. and Alemany Ferrer, R. (eds.) *Actes del novè Col·loqui Internacional de Llengua i Literatura Catalanes*, Barcelona: Abadia de Montserrat, vol. 2, pp. 301–317.

46 Muñoz Peña, P., Díez de Revenga Torres, P. and Puche Lorenzo, M. (2010) *Discurso sobre el origen y progreso de la lengua castellana*, Murcia: Universidad de Murcia Editum, pp. 42–43.

3

CONSOLIDATION AND EXPANSION 800–1150

The following period is pivotal in the emergence of Catalonia, socially, politically and culturally. By 1150, a defined territory will exist that shares substantial territorial extent to that of today as will a language, Catalan. The emergence of the term 'Catalan' will have appeared though not yet usage of the term Catalonia to describe it. These territories were more influenced by a Frankish legacy than the northern kingdoms of Spain that pushed southwards. We find here the origins of some cultural distinctiveness. Whilst full historical and national consciousness is still some way off, the contours of Catalan differentiation are being laid down. This period is important for some of the modern interpretations given to it, as was mentioned in the introduction. For those who interpret history through a nationalist prism alone, a claim is made that in already in this era we find a Catalan state and identity. It matters little, for those that make these claims, that notions such as a thousand years of Catalan independence do not stand up to scrutiny. Rather what is important here is how the past is framed. A heroic impetus is ascribed to its kings and nobles apparently acting on behalf of a ready-made Catalonia that somehow has a continuity from the ninth century to the present, with one count, Guifre, deemed the founder of Catalonia. As we have also previously noted, what happens in the case of the Catalans is also evident in most of the history narratives told within modern European nation states and their education systems. These narratives are imparted to most citizens in claims by politicians as well as television documentaries on the national history. Most history writing today is framed and written within the mental maps created by the frontiers of the present. A thousand years ago those frontiers had little real meaning beyond aristocratic or royal control. Just as there was no medieval kingdom of Spain, medieval France was formed by a series of territories, bearing only a partial resemblance to the state of today. We must also note that for most people, identity was constructed locally, with only members of the Church and aristocracy sharing broader cultural

DOI: 10.4324/9781003218791-4

attachments. Yet even amongst these elites, identity or belonging was not framed in national terms. The most important shared component within this cohort was a sense of belonging to Christendom. This was the only thing we might call a broadly encompassing ideology.

Consolidating the Spanish March

The Frankish kingdom, which extended across today's France, parts of Germany, Italy and Spain, was the largest monarchical entity in Europe after the collapse of Roman rule in the west. At its greatest extent, it comprised some 600 counties and 180 dioceses. As we saw, a small number of these counties were established just south of the Pyrenees, which in time attained a degree of autonomy from central French rule. These counties, together with much of northern Spain, are a small Christian bastion in a territory that is dominated by the Islamic Caliphate. These were militarised and frontier societies where warrior elites ruled over a largely civilian and rural population.[1] Small urban centres appeared but they remain comparatively tiny. Apart from the coastal counties around Girona and south to Barcelona, most of the area comprising the March is mountainous and communication was extremely difficult in the ninth and tenth centuries. These zones were prone to greater levels of violence than many other areas of Europe, and territorial expansion will be forged by military means. Borderlands experienced raids and regular disruption to the normal rhythm of life. Given its frontier status with Al-Andalus, these Catalan counties held vital strategic importance as in no other dominion of the vast Frankish territory was the threat posed Islamic in nature. However, Islam was not seen as a rival religion to Christendom, rather it was framed as another form of paganism.

Between 810 and 820, a line from Barcelona moving westwards defined a fairly stable frontier between Frankish and Al-Andalus forces, though even this decade was not without armed conflict. For a period after 820, a modus vivendi between both powers emerged. The first counts, marcher lords, appointed by the Carolingian Frankish rulers, emerge here. Loyalty to the Franks was exhibited by leading nobles though they were known as and described as Goths or Hispani. Their principal concern was the recovery of their land and position. As the Carolingian monarchy stabilised, it no longer had land to parcel out to followers. This caused tension particularly on the borderlands such as the March. Lords sought to expand locally. The emergence of inheritance amongst local counts was a factor that in time would contribute to their distancing from Carolingian control.[2] This process also happened in other territories on the fringes of Frankish lands, such as northern Italy and Bavaria. The main counties in territory that will become Catalonia were Barcelona, Berga, Besalú, Cerdanya, Conflent, Empúries, Girona, Osona, Rosselló, Urgell and Vallespir. Of these counties, the most important will in time be the County of Barcelona, which gradually expanded from the 820s.

Rebellion 825

Until the 880s, little further southwards expansion into the lands of Al-Andalus occurred. For most of this early period, Arab military superiority held a clear advantage over northern Christian forces. In both frontier zones, whether Christian and Islamic borderlands, similar patterns of centre–local tensions emerged. These counties were particularly prone to instability and rebellion. In 825, an uprising against Frankish domination on the plain of Vic broke out. Internal division amongst elites was the principal cause with one side advocating war and conquest against Arab neighbours with other lords advocating a policy of accommodation. Those closer to or on the frontier tended to be the war party. This revolt led to the removal of the local ruler. This conflict was in reality an elite-dominated civil war and its consequences were profound. The countryside of the Spanish March was ravaged and some territory was lost to Muslims. Much of the area would take several decades to recover the pre-conflict demographic and economic levels. This was not the first or last revolt of this kind. Catalonia, like Bavaria, another territory on the fringe of the empire, slipped from Frankish control during a Carolingian civil war in 841–842. Three counts were executed for rebellion between 844 and 880. The second half of the ninth century saw the Spanish March not as a marginal frontier zone but as a territory where factional disputes were played out. As well as internal conflict, violence came from without. In 850, the emir of Cordoba sent a large army to the territory of Barcelona, where it devastated its surroundings and also besieged the city of Girona. Girona had previously suffered two serious incursions in 793 and 827.

Towards greater local control

In time, a local elite became increasingly dominant, a process we can call regionalisation. Guifre (Wilfred) became successively count of Urgell, Cerdanya, Osona and Barcelona in the 870s. Guifre was awarded control of his territory by the Frankish king. Significantly, he was the first count to apply the principle of hereditary, ceding his titles to his sons. This principle had begun to emerge in northern Europe and facilitated the emergence of powerful ruling families and dynasties. The later distancing of Guifre and his successors from central control formed part of a trend in many zones of the Carolingian territory where local lords sought to affirm permanent control of their territory. Achieving hereditary control enabled the growth of local consciousness and identity. This began a stop–start process over the next hundred years of distancing and re-establishing relations with the Frankish court, which ebbed and flowed depending on the capacity of the ruler to ensure control across his kingdom. One assertion of local control was through the patronage of religious centres such as the monasteries of Ripoll and Sant Joan de les Abadesses. In the case of the latter abbey, it was initially created as a monastery for nuns. Although a female religious centre, it too engaged in similar practices of acquisition of land and the subjection of local villages. Christianity was increasingly utilised by local rulers for the purposes of establishing legitimate rule. In spite of the un-Christian behaviour of Charlemagne, including an often ruthless form of conquest and subsequent repression, his court defined the alliance between court and Church that will be common throughout the middle ages.[3] Whilst the local lords and counts broke with Charlemagne, Frankish influence was evident in morals, theology and political form.[4] The local Church supported these efforts as it sought to break away from control of Narbonne, located across the Pyrenees. It was the recapture of Tarragona in the late eleventh century that embedded a turn to a locally inflected Catholicism. The Papacy remained a weak institution so local bishops held great influence.

Catalonia developed a hybrid of a Visigothic legal system with the form of rule adopted by the counts also heavily influenced by the Carolingian tradition. The gradual decay and disintegration of the Carolingian empire created a power vacuum, which allowed the progressive independence of the Catalan counties. This was an intermediate period with intermittent deference to Carolingian power combined with greater local assertation of power and law until the feudalisation of medieval society ended the existing order. The counts of Barcelona continued the consolidation of their authority over other counts, barons and magnates. Between the years 950 and 1050, we also see the gradual emergence of what we will come to term the feudal form. Catalan society became fully feudalised in a period of less than a hundred years. The heirs of Guifre were now in a position to act as local barons and distribute land like a monarch. Associated with this distribution was the establishment of bonds of fealty. Wealth and the capacity to wield influence was increasingly based on land. As the local county forms developed, some locations such as the city of Girona regained their prominence. However, in spite of the process of distancing from Frankish power, these local counties faced a formidable foe in terms of Al-Andalus. This would be made apparent in the events of 985.

Islamic Catalonia 800–1000

The majority of territory that will one day form Catalonia was found within Al-Andalus in 800. The frontier of 801 remained largely unchanged for the next 300 years, with small bands of territory lost and regained. The Islamic southern zone that will be incorporated into Catalonia in the twelfth century also displayed similar patterns of tension between local rulers and central control, in this case that based in Cordoba. Islamic society was dominated by urban centres and influence extended out to rural areas. Urban sophistication permitted the emergence of an advanced artisanal system. The areas on the Muslim side of the frontier were similarly divided into Marches with the Upper March with its capital at Zaragoza including future Catalan territory. The lords of the Marches had considerable local autonomy and the power to lead defensive and offensive campaigns on their own initiative.

Islam and its practice was the principal cultural characteristic in this zone. Culture and daily life followed the rituals of Islamic practice. However, as this culture consolidated, it distanced itself from Islamic culture in the Middle East. In the ninth and tenth centuries, Arabic fully penetrated this society and literacy was widespread and encouraged. The contrast with a mostly illiterate northern Europe was notable. Under Abd ar Rahman III (912–929), Arabisation and Islamisation intensified. Arabic was extensively adopted as the language as those of higher status, education and by urban dwellers. Romance/late Latin was the language of the poor, rural, uneducated and Christians. Thus, the route for the latter into social advancement came through the adoption of their rulers' religion and language.[5] Even so, there was unlikely to be a Muslim majority before 900. The internal differences within the population meant cultural and other relations occurred between Al-Andalus and the Christian zone south of the Pyrenees. In particular, Arabic-speaking Christians and the Jewish population were key figures in this encounter.

Al-Andalus developed a more advanced economic system with harvests obtainable two or three times a year due to the sophisticated irrigation systems established in the Lleida area from the 930s. The market garden system, organised on both banks of the river Segre, was extensively farmed and highly productive.[6] A distinctive characteristic of the Arab-Islamic system is that office holding is more important in Al Andalus than land. In the Islamic system, landowners were not in control as they were in Europe. In contrast to the Christian zone which had little in terms of an efficient administration, the Umayyads managed a sophisticated bureaucracy. The dynasty itself owned vast landholdings, which were often leased out in exchange for rent, whether to small holders or large landowners required to contribute a portion of their harvest. Landholding in these zones mirrored the broad structure of Al-Andalus. Military control and tax raising were urban characteristics. This urban form gave prominence to places such as Lleida and Tortosa as locations that dominated their hinterland. In the case of the latter, its role as port gave it strategic importance given its closeness to the frontier.[7]

As with the Christian lands to the north, this zone is a frontier zone. Intermittent southwards pressure of Christians required a network of fortifications built north of Lleida which dominated the border zone. From the perspective of Al-Andalus, the coastal lands until the Pyrenees held great value as the entry point into Frankish lands and potentially other parts of Europe. A further parallel with the northern Christian counties then is that this society was built for warfare. Both sides probed the defences and for a long period, the Islamic held zone had much greater capacity at disruption and raiding. Southern pressure on Barcelona was intermittent and at times intense and in 940 AD, an Islamic fleet was visible from Barcelona. On this occasion, a new truce was the outcome. In 985, under different leadership, a greatly different outcome took place. However, alliances also took place across the religious divide, demonstrating that disputes over control and land were not yet framed as they would later be. For example, in the late eleventh century, Barcelona allied with Moslem Lleida against Castile and Zaragoza.[8]

985

In the ninth and tenth centuries, Islamic Spain was still in the ascendancy. After largely breaking from the Carolingians, the counts of Barcelona established bonds of submission to the caliph in Cordoba, a clear indication that a few counties were no match to a militarily superior power. However, the events of 985–988 demonstrated their vulnerability. A new figure, Al-Mansur (the Victorious), emerged as the real power in Córdoba after the succession of al-Hisham II in 981, and from the beginning, he began a long series of campaigns against the Christians of the north. In 985, Barcelona was sacked by Al-Mansur, an event that reverberated long afterwards and survived in the popular imagination as 'the day that Barcelona died'. When Al-Mansur captured Barcelona, its leaders were executed, slaughter was widespread and those survived were sold into slavery. A number of monasteries were burned to the ground in the area close to Barcelona. At a key moment in the conflict, count Borrell of Barcelona sought assistance from the Frankish king but once this aid was declined, the final separation of the Catalan counties was complete, though symbolic deference continued for a time.

Impact of 985

The devastation wrought by Al-Mansur revealed the defensive weakness of the counties. Yet 985 can also be now seen as a high point in the military superiority of the Arabs over the Catalan region. Tensions within Islamic society saw internal conflict, revolts and rebellions which would culminate in the rupture of Al-Andalus into smaller kingdoms, known as taifas. In 1010, a Christian force sacked the city of Cordoba, though at a high cost in terms of troops lost. Muslim rule began a slow decline and an increasing position of advantage to the northern zone. However, this took time as the county of Barcelona was severely disrupted by the destruction and loss of population. It is unlikely that the population within the city walls numbered more than 1,500 in the year 1000. The first priority was the rebuilding of a defence system and the city walls of Barcelona. This began the process of expansion of the city into the surrounding areas. As this process developed, Barcelona came to be the dominant city in the territory in both political and economic terms. Financial pressures saw the leading aristocrats pressure the peasantry and we can discern the shift towards feudal relations.[9] This incipient feudalism was already appearing in many areas of Christian Europe. The adoption of the feudal approach to the organisation of the land also lead to the other counties of the zone recognising the authority of Barcelona. The counts of Barcelona emerged as the most powerful rulers in the region and expanded their territory by acquiring control of neighbouring counties, often through strategic marriages.

The Wars of the Counts

However, as occurred in many European territories in the mid-eleventh century, including the German lands, Hungary and Poland, many nobles were not yet ready to submit to a greater lord or king. As the Catalan lands sought to rebuild following 985, financial pressure led to a series of local rebellions, at times at the level of civil war in terms of intensity. Local elites rebelled against the Count and made use of their castles to assert local control. New obligations were imposed on the peasantry, cementing the feudal process. These pressures were caused by the opportunity provided by self-enrichment for the aristocracy as central control was resisted.[10] Yet what occurred in the Catalan lands was in keeping with the patterns elsewhere, as feudal relations were closely aligned with a militarised culture.[11] All attempts to stop the spiral of violence failed. At times the Church sought mediation, at others it aligned itself with the count or rebellious lords. These conflicts intensified in the second half of the eleventh century and have become known to history as the Wars of the Counts. These were centred in three zones: Pallars, Cerdanya and Barcelona. Yet few were able to remain outside of the conflict as noble power increased. Many of the noble houses that, in the future, would be the most influential in Catalonia, rose to the forefront of politics.[12] These revolts and conflicts delayed a push south, in spite of the fact that the taifas were particularly vulnerable to being defeated due to their fragmentation. A substantial area of unoccupied land existed on the frontier between the taifas and the Christian zone, a territory that became greatly desired.[13] By 1080, the count of Barcelona had re-asserted control and subsequently feudal relations between count and the local aristocracy were re-established. The capture of the city of Tarragona in 1099 symbolised a new unity. Whilst a shadow of its former self, being somewhat abandoned and unrepaired, it still held resonance as a historic city in the collective imagination.

One consequence of the end of the Wars of the Counts was the normalisation of violence to resolve disputes. Again, this was part of a common pattern in other European territories. This also saw the emergence of a warrior ethic based on bravery and loyalty.[14] We have previously noted how future Catalan territory, whether in Christian or Islamic hands, was disproportionately prone to the experience of war and conflict. Violence was assimilated as a natural state of society and filtered down from the counts of Barcelona who used it to assert their dominance. At the same time, local counts and lords used violent means to resist central control or assert their local dominance. By these means, the basic norms of early medieval society such as bonds of loyalty and fealty were imposed. For a period, the priority of unity over the Islamic enemy prevailed, as did the distribution of vast spoils, but we will later see the devastating impact of violent civil war in Catalan society in the later middle ages. Feudalism as a social system was also built on a concept of honour. The Church-led system of moral values required the adoption of the vow of marriage, bringing with it norms of subordination and obedience. As a further indication of territorial assertion, the surnames of nobles became territorial and were often used, once a castle in the family name had been built.[15] By the tenth century, castles had become a normalised feature of the landscape, and their expansion in the century that followed was closely connected to the Wars of the Counts. Power and domination were exercised through force and intimidation.[16] The construction of castles after 1100 entailed a new permanence through the use of stone as primary material, ending the practice of partly wooden construction.[17] Castles then played a role in demarcating the boundaries of controlled territory.

Feudal relations

Between the fall of Rome in the west and the full establishment of feudal relations, for a period, the peasantry had developed a degree of autonomy and self-sufficiency. This was gradually eroded by a process of taking over land of free peasants, usually achieved by the categorisation of newly acquired land as private or public. The move towards feudal relations had begun from around 900, through what has been termed the increasing caging of the peasantry.[18] Peasant plot sizes fell and they came under increased pressure from church and the aristocracy. This value system also had implications for the position of women as the notion of the male heir, l'hereu, became normalised.[19] The loss of freedoms for women, including many who worked the land, saw their relative autonomy eroded by the Church and a new social order.[20] The dowry as a form of payment for marriage became increasingly normalised. The occasional instance of a prominent female noble reaches us, such as countess Ermessenda who co-governed Barcelona, Girona and Osona in the first half of the eleventh century. As the new economic order stabilised, instances of this kind are ever less frequent.

In the case of Catalan territory, it was proximity to the kingdom of Charlemagne and the Franks that permitted the adoption of feudalism, in contrast to hybrid and diverse models in other regions of Spain.[21] The final years of the tenth century and the first half of the eleventh was the period during which a radical transformations took place. The domination of the local lord and the privileges ascribed to their families were more intense in Catalan lands than any other part of the peninsula.[22] Local lords and the religious increasingly established monopolies around the usage of mills, ovens and presses, as well as any modest manufacturing.[23] By mid-century, a new legal code emerged, which became known as the Usatges. This code was first compiled from 1068 and became in time a rudimentary civil law. It would not be, however, until the fourteenth century that the Usatges became an established form.[24] Trade between the Christian zone and the taifas was penalised and fines introduced for those sold foodstuffs or weaponry.[25] Whilst we term this period the beginnings of feudalism, we should note that the term feudalism is a much later coinage and did not emerge until the eighteenth century.[26] A series of obligations was gradually imposed on sectors of the peasantry, known as (mals usos) misuses, which laid out the form of servitude required to the lord. Social stratification intensified with the rising wealth of the local nobility requiring a regime of defence of their interests, usually in the form of castles, which facilitated the assertion of local control.[27] The programme of castle building extended as far south as Tarragona.

A parallel and linked process in the emergence of the feudal order was the development of the Church as a key component within the society. In the Marches, the owning of land became central to status. In parallel to this, the rising influence of the Church meant status affirmation could occur through donating land to the Church. From 970, we begin to find donations and bequests where the allotments and rents were given specifically to the clergy of the see. The counts and nobles increasingly built, together with higher ranking church figures, a new social order, through the control of ecclesiastical institutions and the hereditary transmission of the offices and incomes assigned to them. Thus, a bishopric and abbacy would nearly always be led by a member of a leading noble family.

Urban life and the market

Before the eleventh century, in medieval European cities, the notion of the market as a site of sale and exchange was little developed.[28] Early markets mostly provided goods for luxury consumption. Local craft workers and merchants carried out their activity in the service of a privileged urban clientele: the count and his entourage, the bishop and his family. The local market was also a mechanism for local elites to extract profits.[29] The fair was another development, with some evidence pointing to their emergence before 900. From the eleventh century, we see the emergence of both new fairs and markets. Fairs, which occurred several times a year also contributed to the rise of status of a location.[30] Hospitals were also established. In that sense, these places stood out compared to villages that lacked these services. The emergence of the weekly market, usually held on Sundays, contributed to the growth of a settlement or town as it became a local pole of attraction. Road links were also key to determining the growth potential of a locality. Local officials were more likely to be established in these locales, as was a greater range of artisans, further contributing to the centrality of the locale. A virtuous pattern was thus created which ensured the upkeep and expansion of roads serving that community. In time, locations such as these would be construed as local capitals.

Taifa

Whilst conquest of these terrains was not yet possible, the situation of the tenth century was increasingly reversed with Christian forces now having the capacity to mount raids and excursions. Although Christianity and Islam defined the two sides of the cultural frontier, religious differences were secondary motivations in their conflicts during the eleventh century. Moreover, during peaceful intervals, a variety of cultural, commercial, social and political exchanges occurred across the religious frontiers. Al-Andalus had, however, reached its zenith and was engulfed in civil war. Central authority collapsed in the 1010s, leading to division into 30 or so locally based territorial Islamic kingdoms, the taifas. Christian territory gradually expanded southward into Muslim-controlled areas, with the raiders sacking towns, destroying crops and seizing animals, collecting loot and captives for ransom or enslavement and encouraging Mozarabs to return with the raiders and take up residence in Christian areas. Yet the Christian zone to the north was still unable to capitalise on this crisis and in spite of growing Christian pressure, these societies were not conquered.

Lleida became an independent taifa or emirate that included under its jurisdiction a large part of the current counties of Segrià, the south of La Noguera, Pla d'Urgell and La Segarra. Whilst no individual taifa could defeat Christian kingdoms of the north, Christian Spain was not yet strong enough to reconquer and repopulate extensive territories. Instead, Christian leaders intervened in the squabbles amongst the taifas, forming alliances with some taifas against others, or launching independent attacks to sack cities and capture territories. The economic damage was obviously considerable, not just in terms of the tribute paid but also of ravaged lands and deserted villages. Instead of attacking, they might threaten a vulnerable taifa into paying protection money in the form of tribute. In 1051, Yusuf b. Hud, ruler of Lleida, paid northern Christian counts to protect him against his family in Zaragoza. The count of Barcelona Ramon Berenguer received taxes from the Saracens of Tortosa and Lleida and thus was able to increase his wealth. This enabled him to cement his status as the leading count in the Christian zone. The northern Christian counties increasingly held the initiative which increased on these frontier zones as the century proceeds. Al-Andalus was gravely weakened by the later eleventh century. However, the situation was transformed for a while with the arrival of the Almoravids. This grouping, embodying an intransigent form of Islam, crossed into Spain in 1086 and began a series of reverses for the Christian powers.

Expansion of villages

Around 800, the zone under Carolingian control was populated with semi-scattered settlements made up mainly of hamlets. Some of these hamlets later became villages, others became farmsteads and others simply disappeared. The usual settlement type was one of scattered population, separated into isolated houses. This form became widespread after the eleventh century. From the 850s, the land that was more distant from the frontier experienced a new process of human intervention. Settlements stabilised and new land was cleared of woodland. The appearance of these farmsteads had an effect on the cultivated landscape. Each agricultural unit was often surrounded by its fields, orchards, and sometimes a vineyard, and even had rights over woodland or pastureland. In mountainous land, many farmsteads were made up of a large field and a group of terraces. The grazing of herds was normally the principal source of wealth with iron smelting an additional resource controlled by local lords.[31] Although it remains common to speak of a medieval climate anomaly lasting perhaps from 800 to 1300 at its maximum extent, it now seems that the increase was more modest than assumed and within the broader pattern there was substantial variation. Yet even a more modest increase in temperatures did permit increased agricultural production, which enabled population and urban growth. Village names became established as permanent features.[32]

As in many Western European locations, the eleventh and twelfth centuries saw the building of villages around churches, some were built around castles, and villages (vilanoves) were established where previously there had been none.[33] New villages were often organised along one or two streets. Both the Church and the nobility sought to influence the village-building process, with a battle for souls and tenants relevant to both. A feature that has lasted until the present, the Mas type farmhouses are the type of tenure best identified of the time, especially since the middle of the eleventh century. These peasant homes were modestly scattered, not usually more than 150 metres apart.[34] Whilst still tied to their local lord, these farmsteads usually provided sufficient surplus to permit a modest degree of security to the peasantry.[35] As society became feudalised, large sections of the population remained subject to a few lords, to whom they had to serve and swear allegiance. Some were tied to the land and could not leave it. They were the so-called remença peasants, because they had to pay a certain amount to free themselves from these obligations.[36] The Church was also a beneficiary in this social ordering.

Church development

The institutionalisation of the Church was a central component to the establishment of feudal relations.[37] The count appointed the bishops, or intervened in their appointment, because the bishop was the linkage between the count and the local population. The formation process of the parish network of the Catalan lands has traditionally been situated in the middle ages.[38] The parish, as a boundary, represented the basic foundation of religious life. Their increase is significant between the tenth and eleventh centuries, which indicates both population growth as southwards movements became safer. The proliferation of new parishes is also an indicator that Christianisation was closely connected to this population movement. The establishment of the parish was also how the Church benefited through the tithe tribute, often around 10 per cent of the harvest. Monasteries were one further element in the assertion of local control. Once consolidated, monasteries became important sources of local legitimation. New roads were built or repaired to permit the emergence of religious networks. This does not mean that churches built then were still there 500 years later. Rather, what was important was that the parish was established and a new Church would normally be built later to replace the old. Monasteries were established in areas that were dynamic economically and with stable populations, whilst religious buildings from the Visigothic period were repaired.

The establishment of doctrinal uniformity was part of the process of Christianisation. The first doctrinal divergence deemed a heresy for four centuries was associated with two bishops, one from Toledo and the other, Felix of Urgell, and appeared in the late eighth century. The doctrine was known as adoptionism and claimed that Jesus was the adopted son of God. It was condemned as polytheism. The doctrine and its supporters were repressed by the Franks and a re-Christianisation process of conventional theology was pursued in the areas that had followed adoptionism.[39] Subsequently, Catalan territory became increasingly integrated into the normal patterns of western Christendom. New monasteries were established such as Cuixà (878), Ripoll (879) and Sant Joan de les Abadesses (887), which became centres of ritualistic activity. By the year 1000, the Benedictines alone had founded over 100 monasteries in Catalan lands. Ripoll became the spiritual capital, shrine and place of burial for the Barcelona dynasty.[40] It was Ripoll, through the affluence derived from landholding, that was able to excel in manuscript copying and became a point of transmission of Islamic science to other European centres. Ripoll became strongly associated with a figure seen as central in the history of Catalan Christianity: abbot Òliba. From a noble family, Òliba was abbot of Ripoll and Cuixa, and later bishop of Vic. He was influential in the cultural terrain and also sought to promote the Truce of God, where warfare did not occur on Sundays or religious holidays. This movement existed in other parts of Europe and had emerged due to concern at the destruction wrought on religious buildings during dynastic conflicts.[41] Whilst it was of minor significance at the time, Abbot Òliba also founded the monastery of Montserrat. Many abbeys played key roles in the processes of repopulating territory that had been mostly sparsely populated due to political instability and constant war, including Ripoll, Sant Joan de les Abadesses, Sant Cugat and Montserrat. The Church and the nobility continued to have interests that spanned the Pyrenees, and exchange, whether religious, cultural or economic, was common between these zones. Whether it was genuinely practised or not, Christianity remained consolidated as the principal religious expression in the territory.

The Jews

With the main focus of the Church in the development of a crusading culture in the south, the small Jewish population in the northern zone was able to consolidate. Jews were often the principal transmitters of innovation between Christian and Islamic zones as traders were permitted to move freely between both zones. In 1105, count Ramon Berenguer III of Barcelona permitted some trading privileges for these merchants with Al-Andalus. The counts of Barcelona both owned and protected the Jewish population.[42] Barcelona and Girona became the two cities most associated with a Jewish population. As early as the late tenth century, there is evidence of a synagogue in Girona. By the eleventh century, a concentrated Jewish community is found within the city of Barcelona, which in time will become known as the Call. We can speak of a broad tolerance of the Jewish community in this period and opportunity would arise for leading figures to take roles in the court. The Barcelona-based Jewish philosopher Abraham bar Hiyya facilitated the cross-translation of works written in Arabic or Hebrew into Latin.[43] With the Almoravids and later the Almohads from North Africa expressing a more intolerant and crusading form of Islam, a northwards movement of Jews occurred into the Christian zone. With their knowledge of Arabic, some were employed as translators.

Almoravids and Almohads

Any assumption that Islamic Spain was finished was checked by the emergence of two fervent nomadic conquerors from North Africa, the Almohads and Almoravids. Their crusading form of Islam seemed to revive the collective moral of the territories of Al-Andalus and not only checked Christian advance but also were able to reverse it, which included the taking of Zaragoza. More significant for the counts of Barcelona, this brought to an end the system of tribute they had benefitted from with the taifa kingdoms. Raids were launched and in 1108 and 1109, territory as far north as Penedès was plundered, with the attendant burning of churches. As a consequence, the counts of Barcelona sought external assistance, including from England and France. European society is increasingly mobilised around the defence of Christendom and the First Crusade had launched 20 years earlier with the Second launched in 1147. It is in this context that the Christians increasingly frame their conflict in the Iberian peninsula in religious terms, mirroring that of their opponents. In response to the Almoravid threat, an internationalisation of the conflict occurred. The Papacy supported warfare against the pagans (Moslems) in Spain. Those knights who had missed the First Crusade saw Spain as an opportunity to redeem themselves amongst their social class as well as personal enrichment. This was an elite culture that valued both honour and a natural hierarchy, conveniently ordained by God. Aristocrats, knights and other leading figures thus shared a common heritage in the defence of Christendom. The leading cleric of the time, Oleguer Archbishop of Tarragona, called on foreign knights to aid in the defeat of the infidel. Oleguer, originally a Bishop of Barcelona had been rewarded by Ramon Berenguer III as Archbishop of Tarragona, restoring this historic location as the primary centre of the Catalan church. Oleguer was a leading proponent of the doctrine of the Truce of God. However, it was only to be applied amongst Christians and did not apply to pagans (as Moslems were seen). With an emergent culture of Christian unity, as well as international assistance, the Almoravid threat was gradually reduced. By around 1145, the Almoravid Empire fell apart. However, a new dynastic grouping of the Almohads entered Spain from North Africa and, by 1172, ruled all of Al-Andalus.

Creation of the kingdom of Aragon

As an indication of the rising status of the count-kings of Barcelona, they became allied in the Mediterranean with Pisa and Genoa. As with any successful medieval house, transactional and strategic marriages were made, including with Sicily. The Counts of Barcelona maintained cultural, economic and political ties with Rome as well as with the counties on the other side of the Pyrenees as well as Muslim Spain. Close cultural and dynastic connections meant that these mountains were not seen as a frontier, and a cross-cultural relation between Catalonia and Occitan territory later intensified. Attachment to a territory in this zone as well as one that could expand southwards remained strong; however, at some point, the growing ambitions of the kingdom of France ensured a conflict over this zone. The dominance of the house of Barcelona within the Christian zone had been clearly established and its leadership was accepted by the other houses.[44] It is in this period that we see the first references to the terms Catalan and Catalans used by external observers. We should note that 'Spaniard' was not used until the thirteenth century, rather regional expressions such as Castilian or Leonese, etc. were applied. However, the term to describe the land as Catalonia had not yet been adopted but would begin to be used from around the 1150s.

The Christian kingdoms throughout the peninsula were now sufficiently strong to pursue a serious project of conquest and expand the area under their control. In 1114, the house of Barcelona sacked the Balearic islands of Ibiza and Mallorca. Yet full conquest was not possible due to the Almoravid threat and retreat to Barcelona was required. The neighbouring kingdom of Aragon, extending from the Pyrenees to the Ebro valley, developed along lines similar to Castile, where the Visigothic heritage was most important. A number of Christian kingdoms had now emerged across the north and were soon to embark on a major thrust southwards. With both Aragon and Catalonia still relatively small compared to Navarre and Leon, an alliance between them seemed to make strategic sense, providing benefits to both. Aragonese elites were weakened and feared assimilation within a rising Castile. For the Catalan counties, alliance with Aragon ensured the emergence of a territory of greater size, which was deemed useful against anticipated southwards pressure from France. The union of Aragon and Catalonia took place in 1137 with the betrothal of the count of Barcelona, Ramón Berenguer, to Petronilla, then still a child. For a period, this ruler and kingdom was the most powerful in the peninsula.

From 1137, Ramón Berenguer ruled a unified Aragon and Catalonia. The union was dynastic, that is, two dynasties were merged, but the institutions of each country continued to function separately. We find here a parallel with the future union between Aragon and Castile which maintained a confederal rather than unitary relation. The new king met with the Aragonese courts in Zaragoza and with the Catalan courts in Barcelona. In these Catalan was spoken, and in the others Aragonese. Local legislative texts such as the Usatges de Barcelona continued to be in full force separately. The currency was also different. The Crown of Aragon, which existed between 1137 and 1715, was a monarchy made up of various political entities that shared the same sovereign: King of Aragon and Count of Barcelona; and later also king of Valencia, Mallorca, Sardinia, etc. However, as Catalan influence was greater than that of Aragon for most of the existence, we can also call the counts of Barcelona 'count-kings'.[45] One of the principal outcomes of the new union was an agreed division of the territory to be conquered in the south: the Crown of Aragon would move on the Mediterranean strip as far as Murcia whilst Castile would focus on the western Islamic zone of the Peninsula. The new unified Kingdom of Aragon embarked on a southern conquest that was now framed as a religious crusade.[46] Pope Urban II granted indulgences, meaning remission of sin, to those who fought in the Iberian campaigns against the Muslims as had been offered to the participants of the First Crusade.[47] The granting of property, special rights and freedoms was intended to attract settlers from the older and more secure Christian territories to the newly conquered cities and lands on the frontiers of Christendom. Warriors from elsewhere including Normandy helped make the Iberian frontier a new battleground in the development of crusading theology.[48] The king led a reconquest of frontier lands and offered generous terms to the Muslims, allowing them to live under Christian authority and to retain their religion. With the submission of Tortosa and Lleida, a vast expansion of the territory was achieved. The next century would see even greater conquests southwards into Valencia. None of these cities was retaken, and a Catalan zone that had been under Islamic rule for over 400 years came to an end.

Consequences of the conquest

As we have seen, frontier zones had experienced decades of military pressure, raids and excursions. Whilst the city of Tarragona had been taken by the count of Barcelona in 1091, the re-settlement of the region was not very successful due to it becoming a new frontier. Tarragona had become almost a no-man's-land, where settlers were afraid to live for fear of Andalusi raids.[49] Count Ramon Berenguer IV began the conquest of Tortosa in July 1148, at the head of a force that can be deemed an international alliance, with the papacy again encouraging participation. The city resisted for five months, until in December, Tortosa capitulated. With surrender, the city of Tortosa and its Muslim inhabitants were promised measures to respect their religion, the protection of mosques and preserve their property.[50] However, these promises were subsequently broken with mosques being converted into churches, Muslims enslaved and assigned to work the land. This breech in the agreement was partly because of pressure by contingents, both local and foreign, who demanded rewards for their part in the conquest. Christian colonisation of the city proceeded, with Norman, French, Catalan or Aragonese settlers, amongst the new settlers. The conquest of Lleida, together with that of Tortosa, meant the full incorporation of the lands that would define Catalonia into the present.

The Christian conquest of Tortosa and Lleida, in the mid-twelfth century, represented the acquisition of great wealth in land due to the established system of irrigation and market gardens (hortes). Military successes were combined with economic and demographic ones.[51] In general terms, there was continuity of occupation and for most of the population, the conquest represented a change in ruling elites. For now, the religious practice of Islam was tolerated. The new regime required the recognition on the part of the Moslem population of its new vassalage in exchange for permission to continue to practise its religion.[52] In most parts of the territory, there was a repopulation process with the arrival of new settlers from the northern zone. This process of populating changed the internal dynamic of Catalan territory. Dominated for hundreds of years by terrain close to mountains, a new spatial geography unfolded.

By the mid-twelfth century, the Christian zone of the Iberian peninsula was much greater than that remaining under Islamic control. One hundred and fifty years later, only the small kingdom of Granada survived. All the differing Christian kingdoms that had emerged were now strong enough to embark on further southwards conquest. However, first a period of internal consolidation was required to assimilate the recently gained territory including a large non-Christian population. Each Christian kingdom brought with it a new economic and political tradition into the newly conquered lands. New land to distribute was in abundance. Knights received fiefs along the advancing border both in order to shore up defences and to promote settlement along the frontier.[53] As well as new economic models and social structures, cultural and linguistic transformation would also transform these territorial additions. By the end of the eleventh century, there is an increasing quantity of texts produced that bear ever closer resemblance to something we can call the Catalan language. These are mostly documents of a legal kind that contain instances of phrasing that is clearly Catalan. Given the prominent role of the religious in the maintenance of a literate culture, the first texts fully written in the Catalan language are associated with the Bishop of Urgell in 1080 and 1095. Catalan noble families also engaged in having family histories written as a mechanism to give their lineage a sense of historical continuity. By the 1150s, Catalonia was united and defined institutionally under a sovereign who was king of Aragon and count of Barcelona. The recent incorporation of vast new terrains was but the beginning in a phase of expansion both by land and by sea that was about to begin.

Notes

1 Halsall, G. (2008) *Warfare and Society in the Barbarian West 450–900*, London: Routledge, pp. 90–91.
2 McKitterick, R. (1983) *The Frankish Kingdoms Under the Carolingians, 751–987*, London: Routledge, p. 88.
3 Latowsky, A. (2013) *Emperor of the World. Charlemagne and the Construction of Imperial Authority, 800–1229*, Ithaca and London: Cornell University Press, p. 215.
4 Chandler, C. (2103) 'Carolingian Catalonia: The Spanish March and the Franks, c.750—c.1050', *History Compass*, vol. 11, no. 9, pp. 739–750.
5 Safran, J. (2013) *Defining Boundaries in Al-Andalus. Muslims, Christians, and Jews in Islamic Iberia*, Ithaca and London: Cornell University Press, 2013, pp. 99–100.
6 Brufal i Sucarrat, J. (2013) 'La medina andalusina de Lleida en el segle XI: Identitat i societat', *Rivista dell'Istituto di Storia dell'Europa Mediterranea*, no. 10, pp. 219–244.
7 Negre, J. and Suñé, J. (2019) 'Territorio, Fiscalidad y Actividad Militar de un Espacio Fronterizo. La Consolidación de Tortosa como límite extremo del Al-Andalus Omeya', *Anuario de Estudios Medievales*, vol. 49, no. 2, pp. 705–740.
8 Catlos, B. (2004) *The Victors and the Vanquished: Christians and Muslims of Catalonia and Aragon, 1050–1300*, Cambridge: Cambridge University Press, pp. 72–73.
9 Campmany, J. (2008) 'El Garraf entre dos imperis. Conquesta franca i reculada sarraïna (900–970)', *V Trobada d'Estudiosos del Garraf*, Barcelona: Diputació de Barcelona, pp. 147–155.
10 Lluch Bramon, R. (2018) 'El Conflicte de Mir Geribert en el marc de la feudalització del Penedès (1041–1058)', *Anuario de Estudios Medievales*, vol. 48, no. 2, pp. 793–820.
11 Backman, C. (2003) *The Worlds of Medieval Europe*, Oxford: Oxford University Press, p. 179.
12 Flocel, F. (2007) *La feudalización de la sociedad catalana*, Granada: Editorial Universidad de Granada, Granada and Barceló, M., Feliu, G., Furió, A., Miquel, M. and Sobrequés, J. (2003) *El feudalisme comptat i debatut. Formació i expansió del feudalisme català*, València: Universitat de València.
13 Feliu, G. (2010) *La llarga nit feudal. Mil anys de pugna entre senyors i pagesos*, Valencia: Publicacions de l'Universitat de Valencia, p. 80.
14 France, J. (2020) 'Armies and Bands in Medieval Europe', in Gordon, M., Kaeuper, R. and Zurndorfer, H. (eds.) *The Cambridge World History of Violence*, vol. II 500–1500, Cambridge: Cambridge University Press, pp. 79–99.
15 Wilson, S. (1998) *The Means of Naming. A Social and Cultural History of Personal Naming in Western Europe*, London: UCL Press, p. 133.

16 Glick, T. (2005) *Islamic and Christian Spain in the Early Middle Ages*, Lleiden: Brill, pp. 157–158.
17 Cortada i Colomer, L. (1998) *Estructures territorials, urbanisme i arquitectura poliorcètics a la Catalunya preindustrial: De l'antiguitat al segle XVII*, Barcelona: Institut d'Estudis Catalans, pp. 96–97.
18 Wickham, C. (2009) *The Inheritance of Rome. A History of Europe from 400 to 1000*, London: Penguin, pp. 530–532.
19 Tünde Mikes, T. (2017) 'Leglislació Històrica de la Família Catalana Medieval i Moderna', *Butlletí de la Societat Catalana d'Estudis Històrics*, no. 26, pp. 163–196.
20 Cuadrada, C. (2017) 'Dones i terres catalanes medievals (segles X-XIII)', *Studis d'Història Agrària*, no, 29, pp. 35–63.
21 Anderson, P. (1996) *Passages from Antiquity to Feudalism*, London: Verso, pp. 168–169.
22 To Figueras, L. (1993) 'Señorío y Familia: Los Orígenes del "Hereu" Catalán (Siglos X-XII)', *Studia Historica-Historia Medieval*, vol. 11, pp. 57–79.
23 Salrach, J. M. (1997) 'Orígens i transformacions de la senyoria a Catalunya (segles IX-XIII)', *Revista d'historia medieval*, vol. 8, pp. 25–55.
24 Masferrer i Domingo, A. (1999) 'La Influència dels Usatges de Barcelona en l'ordenament jurídicopenal dels municipis de la Catalunya Nova: Notes per a un estudi', in Serrano Daura, J. (ed.) *El Territori i les seves institucions històriques*, Lleida: Pagès Editors, pp. 809–838.
25 Barton, T. (2019) *Victory's Shadow. Conquest and Governance in Medieval Catalonia*, Cornell: Cornell University Press, p. 30.
26 Sabaté, F. (2010) 'The Catalonia of the 10th to 12th Centuries and the Historiographic Definition of Feudalism', *Catalan Historical Review*, vol. 3, pp. 31–53.
27 Salrach, J. M. (2000) *Catalunya a la fi del primer mil·lenni*, Vic-Lleida: Eumo, pp. 80–86.
28 Kleinschmidt, H. (2000) *Understanding the Middle Ages. The Transformation of Ideas and Attitudes in the Medieval World*, Woodbridge: Boydell Press, p. 156.
29 Soler Sala, del M. (2015) 'Forum Granate a la fira de Vilafranca. Origen, creació i articulació d'una xarxa de mercats al Penedès feudal (segles ix-xii)', *SVMMA*, no. 6, pp. 67–86.
30 Torra Fernández, L. (2014) 'Origen i Desenvolupament de les Fires a Catalunya', *La Resclosa*, no. 18, pp. 75–88.
31 Pèlachs, A., Nadal, J., Soriano, J. M., Molina, D. and Cunill, R. (2009) 'Changes in Pyrenean Woodlands as a Result of the Intensity of Human Exploitation: 2,000 Years of Metallurgy in Vallferrera, Northeast Iberian Peninsula', *Vegetation History and Archaeobotany*, no. 18, pp. 403–416.
32 Bolòs i Masclans, J. (2014) 'L'arqueologia del Paisatge de la Catalunya Medieval', *Butlletí de la Societat Catalana d'Estudis Històrics*, no. 25, pp. 101–170.
33 Bolòs i Masclans, J. (2004) *Els orígens medievals del paisatge català: l'arqueologia del paisatge com a font per a conèixer la historia de Catalunya*, Barcelona: Publicacions de l'Abadia de Montserrat, pp. 242–243.
34 Bolòs i Masclans, J. (1998) 'Els masos al'edat mitjana. Historia i arqueologia in El mas medieval a Catalunya', *Quaderns*, no. 19, pp. 95–111.
35 Mallorquí i Garcia, E. (1998) 'El mas com a unitat d'explotació agrària. Repàs dels seus orígens, El mas medieval a Catalunya', *Quaderns*, no. 19, pp. 45–64.
36 Salvadó i Montoriol, J. (2003) *Història medieval d'un territori, Sant Fruitós de Bages segles X-XVI*, Barcelona: Publicacions de l'Abadia de Montserrat, pp. 375–376.
37 Vilaginés, J. (1988) 'El fenòmen parroquial en la societat del Vallès Oriental a l'Alta Edat Mitjana', *Acta historica et archaeologica mediaevalia*, no. 9, pp. 125–142.
38 Freedman, P. (1991) *The Origins of Peasant Servitude in Medieval Catalonia*, Cambridge: Cambridge University Press, pp. 38–40.
39 Miró i Tuset, C. (2016) 'L'adopcionisme, una excusa de Domini Polític i Cultural dels Carolingis sobre Septimània i la Marca Hispànica. El Cas D'Urgell (788–798)', *Institut d'Estudis Comarcals de l'Alt Urgell*, pp. 67–82.

40 Torras i Ribé, J. M. (1984) 'Aproximació a l'estudi del domini baronial del monestir de Ripoll (1266-1711)', *Primer Congrés d'Història Moderna de Catalunya, Actes*, vol. 1, p. 204.

41 Gonzalvo i Bou, G. (2010) 'Les Assemblees de Pau i Treva', *Revista de Dret Històric Català*, vol. 10, pp. 95–103.

42 Gonzalvo i Bou, G. (1996) 'Els Jueus i Els Usatges de Barcelona', *Barcelona Quaderns d'Història*, nos. 2–3, pp. 117–124.

43 Bramon, D. (2013) *Moros, jueus i cristians en terra catalana: Memòria del nostre passat*, Lleida: Pagès, p. 63.

44 Bensch, S. (2002) *Barcelona and Its Rulers, 1096–1291*, Cambridge: Cambridge University Press, pp. 60–61.

45 Bisson, T. (1986) *The Medieval Crown of Aragon. A Short History*, Oxford: Oxford University Press, p. 31.

46 Kennedy, H. (1996) *Muslim Spain and Portugal. A Political History of al-Andalus*, London: Routledge, p. 120.

47 O'Callaghan, J. (2003) *Reconquest and Crusade in Medieval Spain*, Philadelphia, PA: University of Pennsylvania Press, p. 209.

48 Villegas-Aristizábal, L. (2017) 'Spiritual and Material Rewards on the Christian-Muslim Frontier: Norman Crusaders in the Valley of the Ebro in the First Half of the Twelfth Century', *Medievalismo*, no. 27, pp. 353–376.

49 Menchón i Bes, J. (2010) 'De l'ager Tarraconensts a la marca extrema d'Al-Andalus. Algunes reflexions entorn al (des)poblament del Camp de Tarragona, la Conca de Barberá i el Priorat entre l'antiguitat tardana i la conquesta feudal', in Prevosti i Monclús, M. and Guitart i Duran, J. (eds.) *Ager Tarraconensis, Paisatge, poblament, cultura material i història*, Barcelona: Institut Català d'Arqueologia Clàssica, pp. 57–73.

50 Virgili, A. (2001) *Ad detrimentum Yspanie la conquesta de Turtusa i la formació de la societat feudal (1148–1200)*, Barcelona: Universitat Autònoma de Barcelona, Servei de Publicacions, pp. 73–75.

51 Virgili Colet, A. (1995) 'Conquesta i feudalització de la regió de Tortosa 1148-1200', *Recerca*, no. 1, pp. 33–50.

52 Carles, V. (2006) '*Abdalà és un nom català? La presència sarraïna a Catalunya a l'Edat Mitjana*', *Mot so razo*, vol. 5, pp. 52–62.

53 Backman, C. (2003) *The Worlds of Medieval Europe*, Oxford: Oxford University Press, p. 199.

4

ARAGON AND THE MEDITERRANEAN EMPIRE 1150–1410

A trans-Pyrenean culture

The Catalan historical tradition traditionally terms the post-Carolingian lands Old Catalonia with the southern conquests referred to as New Catalonia. This tends to suggest that a true Catalonia existed in the north and a Catalan identity was incorporated into the lands liberated from Islam. A similar process occurs with the conquests of the Balearic Islands and Valencia which are deemed to form the Països Catalans, the Catalan (speaking) countries. Yet our sense of modern borders and boundaries was not shared at this time.[1] It is unlikely that anything approaching national identity existed in the middle ages. Identity expressions found were rudimentary and superficial. Fluid allegiances were inevitable in a period where identity was not constructed in a national sense.[2] At best we can speak of a dynastic sense of identity at the upper levels of society but this was also limited by attachment to a transnational sense of Christendom. A shared sense of religiosity is perhaps the only meaningful expression of identity that was shared across social classes. At a popular level, we cannot speak of national identity. Rather, beyond the religious expression, identity was mostly expressed in terms of attachment to locality. The state boundary that today divides France and Spain was not one known at this time. The rulers of Aragon and Catalonia held possessions north of the Pyrenees as well as relations of vassalage and commitment to an extensive territory on both sides of the Pyrenees remained strong. What in time will become the kingdom of France was still divided into a number of rival territories and there was little that was inevitable about its final formation. Equally Spain did not yet exist but by 1150, the number of kingdoms in the Iberian peninsula had fallen to five.

This period is also marked in general by ever-growing military rivalry and the dynamic of medieval Europe was expressed by a pattern of territorial conquest and expansion.[3] For the emerging kingdom of Aragon, it seemed clear that in the future

DOI: 10.4324/9781003218791-5

some kind of clash with a rapidly growing Castile was likely. Both kingdoms were in expansionary mode as was the kingdom of France which controlled over half of future French territory and shared a border with Aragon. This raises once again the continuation of a theme we have noted previously and which will continue to mark development, of Catalan territory found in an intermediate space between emerging powers, now France and Castile. In one sense, the story of Catalonia is that of compression by two greater powers. For now, however, the Catalan lands, part of the kingdom of Aragon, were in the ascendant. Catalan ambitions for territorial expansion in the southern French zone clashed with those of the territory of Toulouse. Control of the neighbouring Provence region was key to this rivalry.[4] Both sides sought and obtained support from other powers, an indication that the Catalan realm was seen as a growing rival, both in terms of the acquisition of territory and in the Mediterranean. International alliances were increasingly forged.

As well as territory held across the Pyrenees, Languedoc and Provence were in the Catalan sphere of influence. The Occitan zone in particular was a centre of textile production which was an industry that gradually emerged in the greater Barcelona areas.[5] In the thirteenth century, Catalan merchants traded in Languedoc and Provence. The most common trade routes were by land from Barcelona through the Pyrenees to Montpellier, and by sea from Barcelona to Marseille. The main imported product was French fabrics, of higher quality than those made in Catalonia and which were resold throughout the Mediterranean.[6] Linkages between Occitania were also cultural and by means of trading where linguistic closeness facilitated communications. Cultural activity was changing and more existed outside of the Church. Occitan became the language of a new innovative musical form, of the troubadours, which introduced emotional expression in music and became popular at court and all levels of society. This form extended from northern Italy to most of the Iberian peninsula and represented a major change as being a popular cultural form that was non-religious in content.[7] In the late twelfth century, this style of musical innovation was found in the Catalan lands producing Raimon Vidal, a prolific troubadour of the early thirteenth century and the most prominent of many exponents of the art.[8]

Occitania and the Cathars

Consolidation and indeed potential Catalan expansion in this zone saw major difficulties develop when the region became the focus of a variant of Christianity that the official Church rapidly deemed a heresy. Its participants and followers referred to themselves as Good Men and Women but their legacy has come down to us as that of the Cathars or Albigensians. Catharism greatly influenced Catalan society, especially from the second half of the twelfth century to the end of the thirteenth century. Cathar doctrine described Jesus as an angel sent by God to show the path to goodness. The assertion of Jesus's earthly nature and rejection of the Old Testament particularly affronted traditional religious opinion. Catharism tended to divide ruling elites, with local lords supportive as it eroded church influence and power. Catharism was also influential amongst the growing merchant community as it was a doctrine which encouraged trade. In fact, it seems that the doctrine found support amongst all social classes.[9] The areas most influenced by the new doctrine were the lower Pyrenees, being the zone with the closest proximity to Occitania. The western Pyrenean Catalan area also became a refuge and centre of Cathar activities. Refugees from persecution and sympathisers could move freely amongst the scattered villages, circulating texts and ideas.[10] The movement spread south, reaching as far as Barcelona and Lleida.

The established Church grew ever more concerned and Pope Innocent III launched a military crusade against the doctrine in 1209, which was supported by the establishment of an Inquisition. This Inquisition lasted some 50 years against a movement deemed to challenge the traditional authority of the Church. The Albigensian Crusade, which repressed Occitan Catharism, and was pursued with brutal violence, profoundly impacted Catalonia. Given the international character of Christendom, the Cathar conflict placed the kings of Aragon-Catalonia in a position where they required to choose between supporting the Papacy and their own vassals. In the first phase of the repression, the king of Aragon, Jaume, submitted to papal pressure and collaborated in the anti-Cathar policy. The next monarch Pere II (1196–1213), adopted a more pro-Cathar policy because of the position of his vassals in the Cathar area. Pere II fought against the pro-Papal forces but in 1213, not only was his army defeated but also the monarch was killed in the Battle of Muret. The defeat at Muret brought to an end a possible continuation of Catalan-Aragonese expansion in southern France.[11] A later treaty saw the Aragonese-Catalan kingdom accept the abandonment of any wider claim in this zone. Whilst Catalonia retained an important zone beyond the Pyrenees, which would be held until 1659, the prospect of trans-Pyrenean expansion had to be abandoned. The monarch of Catalonia-Aragon had to look elsewhere to expand. With the north closed off for further expansion, and the west clearly dominated by Castile, Catalan expansion was reduced to southwards within the peninsula. The northern defeat also gave an impetus to imperial ambitions in the Mediterranean.

Southern Expansion

Parallel to the latter phase of the Cathar dispute, and a year before Muret, the Christian kingdoms of the peninsula combined forces and launched a large-scale offensive against the Almohads. Armies from Castile, Aragon, León and Navarre met the Almohad army at Las Navas de Tolosa in July 1212 and won an overwhelming victory. That battle marked the end of major Muslim power in the peninsula.[12] This victory produced the impetus for the carve up of Moslem Spain. Both Mallorca and the southern territories such as Valencia were increasingly vulnerable due to the fragmentation of Islamic power. Territorial accumulation allowed the monarchy to buy off its nobility and assert its own dominance through new revenue accrued. The Church was also active in the process of acquisition, which allowed it to expand its zone of influence and the reach of Christendom. The Church was central to the construction of the conflict as a religious crusade.

For Aragon-Catalonia, before southern conquest could begin in earnest, the Balearic Islands were attended to. Ruled by Islam, there were seen as an impediment to Mediterranean expansion and a source of piracy and raiding on the coast. What began with Mallorca became part of a new expansive wave. Medieval warfare was often brutal and the conquest of Mallorca is a particularly notable example of extreme violence. Much of the native Islamic population was slaughtered whilst the few remaining fled to the mountains.[13] The killing in the capital of the island was so great that thousands of corpses could not be buried and the victorious troops were decimated by a plague epidemic. Those not killed but captured were sold into slavery and the ultimate result was the wiping out of the native Mallorcan population.[14] The previous population was substituted by colonists from Catalonia. Yet the king who carried out this ruthless conquest is seen as one of the great Catalan kings, Jaume I, who reigned for some 60 years. Due to his role in the expansion of Catalan territory and conquests, his exploits continue to be venerated and for many he remains a heroic representation of Catalan nationhood. King Jaume framed some of his own mythology of the conquest in a volume known as the Llibre dels Feyts (Book of Deeds). Written or dictated by the king, the text, written in Catalan, is likely to have been authored no earlier than 1240, some 11 years after the conquest of Mallorca in 1229 but coinciding with that of Valencia. The Llibre dels Feyts is framed today as the one of the foundational texts of medieval Catalonia.[15]

Conquest of Valencia

By the end of the thirteenth century, Catalan colonists formed the majority of the population of all of the Balearics, and these islands became a separate kingdom. The ruler was a member of the royal dynasty and there were even occasions of revolt against the wider kingdom. In general, however, with the position now safe along the Mediterranean coast, Catalonia pursued expansionary policies along its southern border. The ultimate outcome was the conquest of the kingdom of Valencia, known in Arabic as Sarq al-Andalus, which was one of the wealthiest southern kingdoms. The horta (market gardens) of this region was an extensive irrigated zone and the main source of wealth. The conquest of Valencia took 13 years to complete and it was framed as a religious crusade and formally proclaimed as such by the papacy.[16] Following the intense violence of the taking of Mallorca, the city of Valencia chose surrender. One consequence was, unlike in Mallorca, where no Islamic population remained, in the zone of Valencia a substantial minority population of Moslems continued, lasting until its expulsion in the early seventeenth century. As in other colonial enterprises, a Christian minority was able to impose itself on a Moslem majority population and proceed towards their economic exploitation. Marriage between Christians and Moslems was prohibited and the two religious communities co-existed in an uneasy relationship with the Christians now dominant in all areas.[17] Anxiety at the potential for Moslem rebellion remained a constant concern and these fears were realised at times. The Christian settlers maintained a military culture and ethos.[18] Catalan became the principal language, though some of the inner zone was conquered by the Aragonese, where Catalan did not impinge. Jaume I subsequently collaborated with his Castilian counterparts in the conquest of Murcia, and Castile secured control of the conquered kingdom, according to the terms of the Treaty of Almizra of 1244, designating Murcia as future Castilian territory. Whilst this resolved for a time the frontier, and any potential clash between Castile and Aragon, armed conflict would break out in the future.

Jaume I and Catalan authority

Connections were growing between monarchies across Europe with marriage alliances increasingly common. Catalan monarchs established bonds with territories such as Hungary and the kingdom of Naples. European polities began to develop institutions starting in the medieval period, though use of the term 'state' should be used with care as the reach of these institutions, and associated bureaucracy, was tiny compared to that of modern states. The principal activity of these states was war and defence. Revenue raising was overwhelmingly devoted to these purposes. It was during the thirteenth and fourteenth centuries that Catalan institutions and its early state order took solid shape. Whilst noble rebellions had not come to an end, breaking out twice in the 1270s, the institution of monarchy was increasingly stabilised. The culmination of the reconquest contributed to the concentration of power into royal hands. With vast lands and privileges to award, royal power was strengthened. Jaume enforced his authority throughout his kingdom. The monarch acted as protector of the Church and enhanced its power to offset that of local lords.[19] Under Jaume I, the monarch held extensive power in Catalonia and delegated his authority over the territory through local representatives such as mayors and officials known as veguers. One distinctive feature of the Catalan realm was a modest sharing of power between the king and the upper levels of the elites. The Catalan medieval regime was governed by a form of shared power. This has become known as pactisme. As with Magna Carta in England, this pactisme is often considered as a form of proto-democracy, but it was simply a system where the monarch was required to consult with the upper nobility and highest ranks of the Church.[20] Though a natural and often ruthless authoritarian, Jaume was required to accept these modest measures and the monarchy had to rely on the Cortes to pass new laws. This pactisme occurred in other places in Europe, but it was in Catalonia (and also in England with Magna Carta) where it was more explicitly conceptualised. The Girona native Francesc Eiximenis, in his treatise Lo Crestià, outlined the moral and legal basis of shared power.[21] Thus, the Catalan system was based on the cooperation between the main sectors of the ruling class, at the head of which was the king. Whilst the notion of a proto-democratic Catalonia has been exaggerated for political purposes, shared power amongst the ruling class did give a different inflection to the organisation of rule compared to that of Castile, where elites were more clearly subordinated to the monarch.

One consequence of the vast expansion of the Catalan-led realm was not just war abroad but increasing resentment in other regions at policies that seemed only to benefit Catalonia itself. Whilst monarchical power was growing, it could not be said that the nobility was fully subdued and the expansion of the kingdom produced new tensions amongst elites. Conflict emerged not only within Catalonia but also with lords in Aragon over newly acquired Valencia. Against the wishes of the Aragonese nobles, who wanted to apply to the whole kingdom of Valencia the law of Aragon, the king promulgated a new and specific one, the law of Valencia, and was the first important legal text written in Catalan. The frequent outbreaks of war became ever less popular after the completion of the Reconquest as potential beneficiaries were fewer. Simply put, there was no further land to distribute. For many in Valencia and Aragon, war was seen as being a profitless exercise which did not benefit their regions. The nobility and citizens responded by forming the Union of Aragon in 1287 where a series of demands were made to the king. The Cortes demanded a limit to the taxes the king could impose and the removal of Catalan and foreign administrators. This was a reflection that Catalonia and Aragon, in spite of their union, represented distinctive and not always compatible political traditions.[22] The nobility and towns in Valencia, seeing an opportunity to expand their freedoms, formed the Union of Valencia and demanded the same privileges.

Frequently during the period from 1150 to 1400, Catalonia was at war. The waging of war, whether through conquest or expansion by sea, was a constant drain on revenue. To facilitate its collecting, a range of organisations were devised, which in time became a permanent delegation in 1359 and was called the Diputació del General or Generalitat. Contemporary Catalan identity attaches great symbolic import to the Generalitat, which is the seat of the regional government and repository of historical continuity. This new body could collect taxes and recruit soldiers in the event of an invasion of Catalan territory. These institutions and their ideological formulation are increasingly expressive of a Catalan dynastic consciousness and differentiation with evidence of a proto-national awareness amongst ruling elites. The Catalan aristocracy will become firm defenders of their privileges and potential encroachment by any ruler.

Empire

With the peninsula no longer offering new lands to conquer and with the Occitan zone now lost, the only path to growth was the sea. By the mid-fourteenth century, the Crown of Aragon became a powerful and at times feared power in the western Mediterranean. Expansion happened in phases. The acquisition of Sicily was a key development in this process. The kingdom of Naples and Sicily was in a privileged strategic position that gave it control of trade routes between the eastern and western Mediterranean, and with North Africa and the Balkans. Sicily had been under the authority of the French crown, which produced ever greater local resentment. In 1282, an event known as the Sicilian Vespers occurred and the locals massacred their French rulers in a bloody revolt. The Aragonese king, Pere III was able to claim the island by force. The initial conquest was fairly easy, but the subsequent war with France lasted for 20 years before the pope and the French monarch rec-ognised Sicily as belonging to Aragon. It forced the Aragonese monarchy to fight continuously against a major rival and strained the Catalan economy. Over the fol-lowing 150 years, the Crown of Aragon added Sardinia and the Greek duchies of Athens and Neopatria, in the fourteenth century, and of the kingdom of Naples, in the fifteenth century. Trading bases were established in North Africa, Egypt and Syria. In addition, it had its own fleet, destined to protect the Catalan coast. The Kingdom of Aragon had become a major sea power and developed a greater politi-cal and economic projection of the Crown. This expansion required the military defeat of other powers.

The rise of the mercenary

As an indication of the changing political regime, we find the use of mercenary not vassals forces for military engagements. This the monarchy found greater suited its purposes, by reducing reliability on the nobility. These paid for hire forces appeared in varying roles in wars waged over the next century. They emerged as a consequence of war with France over Sicily. France invaded Catalonia in 1285 with a force of some 20,000, yet the nobility of the provinces of Valencia and Aragon withheld military support. Girona was besieged. The situation was saved only by the arrival of Roger de Llúria, who headed the Sicilian fleet which forced a French retreat. Relentless harassment of the retreating forces was carried out. A chronicle of the time claims that 300 French prisoners were thrown into the sea. A separate group of mercenary soldiers, the Almogávars, some 6,000, under the command of the Italian Roger de Flor, were the main body of the Companyia Catalana d'Orient (Catalan Grand Company), which was contracted to support the Byzantine Empire against the Turks. However, partly due to their reckless violence and plundering, their hirers refused to pay them and the Grand Company began to conquer Byzantine territory, ending up with two duchies in Greece, includ-ing Athens which lasted some 70 years, until 1387. The fact that most settled was unusual for this type of force.[23] Their conquests were independent actions and not officially under the auspices of the Aragonese kings, but they nonetheless had close ties with the Crown of Aragon. The mercenary forces of the Company and Catalan eastern expansion would be rehabilitated in the nineteenth century as a period of Catalan glory.[24]

Cultural splendour

With territorial expansion and conquest came the influence of Catalan high cul-ture in Europe. For contemporary Catalonia, the thirteenth century and much of the fourteenth is seen as a golden age. Catalan led a vast colonial expansion and reached its greatest ever territorial extent. However, we should be aware that most cultural production continued to be conducted in Latin and there was little or no sense of writing in Catalan as being an act of nation making. The Catalan literary revival of the nineteenth century tended to prioritise those works written in Catalan, even if they may not have been that important at their time of writing. Certainly, important works were written by Catalans in the period, though most were not written in the Catalan language as Latin remained the form of expression of cosmopolitan literary culture shared in much of Europe. Within those caveats, we can note that Catalonia was one of the great centres of creativity including religious musical expression.[25] What became known as the Catalan Atlas of 1375 was one major consequence of a sophisticated school of map makers, mostly made up of Catalan settlers in Mallorca.[26]

Innovation was evident in a range of thought, particularly theology and philosophy. As with all imperial projects, empire produced intellectual justification. The medieval Catalan tradition is centred on the chronicle form. The most prominent examples after the volume written by Jaume I, are by Bernat Desclot and Ramon Muntaner, who provided elite reportage of conquest and expansion. Desclot's chronicle is centred on the conquest of Sicily and the defence of Catalonia against French invasion. Ramon Muntaner focuses on the eastern Mediterranean, events which he also witnessed. It is Ramon Llull who stands out as the most prolific and original figure. Llull, from a family of Catalan colonists in Mallorca, wrote over 200 works. He wrote some of his philosophy in Catalan though most of Llull's work was disseminated in Latin. After claiming he had received divine visitations, Llull became a mystic, philosopher, a missionary for the conversion of Muslims and Jews, and one of the founding figures of Catalan literature. He wrote the Libre qui es de l'ordre de cavalleria (The Book of the Order of Chivalry), probably between 1279 and 1283. It reached a wide readership in its original Catalan and was translated into French and English in later periods. Llull's Llibre de contemplació en Déu (Book of Contemplation of God) was first written in Arabic and its themes range from scholasticism to mysticism. Like many other preachers of the time, he was also eager to convert all unbelievers, heretics, Arabs and Jews to Christianity.[27] Arnau de Vilanova was another visionary figure who wrote on the arrival of the anti-Christ and the apocalypse. As well as by figures such as Francesc Eiximenis, moralist and theologian, the Catalan language was used in legal texts. From the 1320s, a poetry festival had been held in Toulouse in Occitania which in time became the inspiration for the Jocs Florals (Floral Games) held in Barcelona in 1393. This form lasted until the mid-fifteenth century. Their revival took place in the 1850s as part of the Catalanist cultural flowering.

Agriculture and the economy

In this period, over 80 per cent of the population lived tied to the land under varying obligations and were subject to the arbitrary power of the feudal lords. As the economy was growing, particularly from around 1200 to 1340, class tension between lords and peasants was mostly kept in check. This did mean that the burdens on the peasantry, whilst resented, were accepted due to a relatively benign wider context of development. The consolidation and extension of taxation was key to the development of the existing economic order.[28] However, coercion also played an essential role in the economy. Laws passed in 1202 and 1283 intensified the power of the nobility over their land, to which not even the king was permitted to interfere.[29] Within the Catalan and Aragonese feudal world, vassal services had spread called Mals Usos and they affected over quarter of rural communities. They outlined a range of payments and obligations ranging from compensating the lord if the peasant home burned down, dowry taxes, fees on wills and permission for the lord to appropriate land in the case of female adultery. The most contentious of all was that the farmer could not leave the land he cultivated at will. Rather if he wished to do so, a substantial fee, the remença, was required. This was a deliberate mechanism to prevent the free movement of peasants.[30] This situation continued as the monarchy was unwilling to intervene as the nobility provided the revenue for ever more costly foreign wars. The peasantry was also subject to ecclesiastical authority. As the Church consolidated its authority, a range of financial obligations fell upon the peasantry, from payments in foodstuffs, donations expected for religious holidays as well as payments for rites of passage such as baptisms and funerals. These were invariably defined as 'gifts' to the Church.[31] Even a commodity as basic as water was not free and incurred payment costs to the lord or in some cases to the monarch.[32] Even so, for most of this period, there is growing trade and the exchange of products. Annual fairs and weekly markets are held in all the medium-sized cities and towns in the country and became ever more important to economic development.[33]

Rise of Barcelona and urban growth

Political and economic power had been consolidated under the feudal order. Though the higher and lesser nobility was unlikely to be ever more than 5 per cent of population, for hundreds of years, they had been the main owners of wealth, together with the Church. This was beginning to change as towns proved able to provide increased revenue, particularly as Catalonia projected itself overseas. The end of an era of the domination of the lordly castle was approaching. We find a growing influence of urban centres, including their capacity to impact on the rural areas surrounding them.[34] The monarchy increasingly utilised the growing influence and wealth of the urban zones as a counterweight to the nobility. Previously, the two main estates, church and nobility, had been unchallenged, but increasingly the merchant class asserted their interests. In Barcelona, a new forum for elite interests was created, the Consell de Cent (the Council of One Hundred), the municipal governing body of Barcelona. Urban inhabitants had much greater autonomy and when economic conditions worsened, cities became attractive locations to escape obligations to both lords and the church. The city becomes the main place of social change whilst developments in the countryside were more halting.

In this period, we find much greater social complexity with the emergence of social actors such as guilds, artisans and merchants. It is a period when surnames are widely adopted either by trade Martell (Smith) or by locality.[35] Women's roles, however, were circumscribed by the wider context. Church narratives spoke of women as figures of danger which was combined with the evocation of Mary. Devotion to Mary became deeply embedded in Catalan culture and a way of crafting an idealised and subordinated view of women. Marriage occurred at a young age with the only real alternative for women being the convent.[36] Amongst those people in the town for whom a craft can be identified as an occupation, a significant proportion were women.[37] With social change came more attempts at social control. The influence of trade led to an increase in the luxury of clothing that in some cases came from Italian cities. Laws defining clothing that could be worn by social status: the sumptuous laws. Between 1345 and 1376, they were updated and each time they became ever more restrictive, especially for women, who were forbidden to wear striped, plaid or painted dresses even inside their home. Civil and ecclesiastical authorities could not allow the clothing of the lower class to match those of their social superiors and these measures even extended to merchants who were not permitted to dress as lords, no matter how wealthy they were. These laws also extended to the consumption of luxury goods and regulations on what could be worn on social occasions and festivities.[38] The inhabitants of the cities had achieved independence from the lords. The urban walls that were built served as a defence, but they were also a symbol of the city's freedom. Towns tended to benefit their residents but exclude outsiders. In 1269, for instance, Barcelona banned foreigners from settling, let alone obtaining citizenship in the city.[39]

Barcelona had consolidated its role as the most important of Catalan cities, its wealth based on its port status and increasingly financial role. Shipbuilding was centred in the city and expanded in line with Catalan expansion overseas.[40] Before the Black Death, the population of Catalonia may have been as high as 500,000. Barcelona, the largest city by far, was approaching 40,000. This ever-growing capital and its pivotal trading role gave a special character to Catalonia and contrasted with the structure of both Castile and Portugal.[41] The cities were undergoing a virtuous circle of expansion, particularly due to the rise of maritime trade, centralised in Barcelona although other lesser ports such as Roses, Sant Feliu de Guíxols or Salou also benefitted. The support of the monarchy for these activities resulted in the creation of Catalan lodges or consulates throughout the Mediterranean. The Catalan taula de canvi, founded in 1401, is now believed to be Europe's first public bank.[42] This new banking and financial system permitted the expansion of credit and spread the use of the bill of exchange which allowed for credit and other transactions. The Barcelona merchant, in contrast to the cult of individualism of the Italian city states, maintained a high degree of religiosity.[43] Even so, war and commercial expansion went hand in hand. In further contrast to the culture that emerged in the case of the Italian city states, the Catalan merchant maintained a close relationship with the rural world.[44]

Merchants

The gradual expansion of money was one element that began to erode the feudal system.[45] The expansion of the merchant class posed a challenge to the traditional order and served as a useful device for the monarchy to keep the nobility in check. Over the thirteenth century, Catalan merchants were active in Constantinople and traded in slaves, wax, copper and cotton. This trading regime was facilitated by collaboration between the monarchy and the Catalan merchant class. Trade with Morocco intensified in the late thirteenth century as it did with Egypt and Syria, in the latter case particularly focussed on spices.[46] Catalonia also maintained trade relations with Bruges, London and many of the Italian city states. As early as the late twelfth century, some merchants became permanently stationed and acted as consuls to facilitate trading relations, particularly in North Africa. The consulates were a kind of small permanent embassy in various countries, intended to support Catalan expeditions. Trade of this magnitude would not have been possible without the existence of an institutional and legal infrastructure. The Consolat de Mar (1282) was a high court created in Barcelona in charge of arbitrating on maritime and commercial issues. This institution brought together the city's shipowners and leading merchants, gradually acquired jurisdiction over the port area of the city, which it exercised it until 1714.[47] Such was the status of Catalonia in this period that the Book of the Consolat del Mar became adopted through much of the Mediterranean.

Wars with Castile and internal revolts

One of the continuing goals of the Crown of Aragon was control of the western Mediterranean. To achieve this, it was also necessary to control the entire Mediterranean coast of the Iberian Peninsula. With expansion came increasing tension with Castile. Furthermore, given the growing status of both powers, their rivalry also had international dimensions. Castile was usually allied with France, as well as Rome, Genoa and Naples, territories that all had sought to control Catalan expansion in the Mediterranean. Whilst as early as the Occitan war, Catalonia had tended to align with England. This relation with England deepened through trade in the following two centuries. The first major war between Aragon and Castile took place in the context of the acquisition of Sicily in the 1280s where Castile aligned with France against Aragon. Dynastic conflict and instability within Castile contributed to war between both kingdoms breaking out in 1296. The clash within the peninsula was over the region of Murcia which was a frontier zone between both kingdoms. By 1300, internal dissension within Aragon over the conduct of the war led to peace. The Kingdom of Murcia was divided and peace between Castile and Aragon was maintained for the next 50 years.

The costs of overseas war also saw tensions due to repeated financial contributions to Mediterranean expansion. Once again both Aragonese and Valencian elites felt they were financing a conflict that seemed only to benefit the Catalan part of the kingdom. Rebellion broke out in Valencia under the auspices of the Union of the Kingdom of Valencia. Its purpose was to strengthen Valencian institutions against what was perceived as increasing royal authoritarianism. Tension within Valencia had been growing in the 1330s and a full-scale revolt occurred in 1347, which coincided with the outbreak of famine in the region. However, in contrast to the region of Aragon, this movement divided Valencian society giving the conflict the aspect of civil war. In the end, the king aided by Aragonese and Valencian troops entered the city of Valencia victorious in December 1348, after defeating the Union. Rebellion against monarchical power meant that the repression was harsh. Twenty-two leading figures of the Unionists were cruelly executed. The leading rebel Joan Sala was forced to drink molten bronze from the Union bell which had been used to call supporters.[48] Though the Valencian revolt had been defeated, its harsh repression left a lingering anti-Catalan sentiment and legacy.

Internal peace had been restored but rising tensions between Castile and the Catalan monarchy, embodied in two authoritarian kings, gave the name to war between the two kingdoms as The War of the Two Peres (Peters), which lasted between 1357 and 1369. On one level, it was a personal conflict between the respective monarchs Pere el Cerimoniós of Aragon and Pedro the Cruel of Castile.[49] This war was also partly an offshoot of the conflict between France and England in the Hundred Years War and occurred in a context of major societal disruption due to the ravages of the Black Death. This conflict saw the greatest losses in the territory of the kingdom of Aragon where it was mostly fought out and Castilian forces engaged in vast destruction. Whilst the end result was defeat for Castile, this was barely a victory for Aragon given the extensive material damage the war produced. Living conditions were worsened for much of the population and impact was felt in reduced Mediterranean trade. The position of the nobility was strengthened in relation to the monarchy as the king required their approval for a range of financial measures.[50] The nobility remained unwilling to cede its power as the events of 1410–1413 attest.

Crisis and plague

At the end of the middle ages, Catalonia experienced, like other European countries, a sustained period of crisis. In cities there was increasing poverty, unrest and popular revolts, whilst tensions rose greatly in the countryside. This is likely to have been caused by the emergence of a colder climate that began in the 1300s. It was a period of social instability, frequent poor harvests and resultant food shortages.[51] Disruption to agricultural production began from around the 1330s and continued until the 1370s, with varying degrees of intensity. Agricultural crises caused widespread hunger and a weakened condition for many. A poor harvest of 1346 was followed soon after by the arrival of the Black Death. This epidemic of bubonic plague, followed by new outbreaks in 1362 and 1371, caused a devastating impact. Population decline is likely to have been in the region of 40 per cent overall with a figure around 500,000 in 1300 declining to not much more than 293,000 by 1380. A town such as Vic, in the interior, provides an indication of the scale of loss as it did not recover its pre-plague population until the early sixteenth century.[52] The consequences of greatly deteriorated economic conditions caused societal conflict in both urban and rural areas. Declines in lords' incomes saw increased pressure on the condition of the peasantry, which some responded to by fleeing to the cities which could not cope with the influx. Those that remained sought improved conditions to their tenancy which was fiercely resisted by the lordly class. The following decades were marked by repeated conflict between lord and peasant. Reprisals and means to ensure social control were carried out against peasants seeking to break free from their domination. The seeds were being laid for peasant rebellion.

All social classes were affected by the economic consequences of the plague. As we have seen, the cost of foreign wars were but one further layer to make the situation worse. City and royal treasuries were under pressure with shortages leading to price rises. A negative spiral ensued and internal migration contributed to rising conflict in the urban areas. Revolts broke out in Barcelona and other towns in 1334 with frequent riots between 1339 and 1343. The monarchy is at the centre of a crisis and is under such severe financial stress it is unable to repay loans. The once growing banking sector began a spiral of default which affected the three main Catalan cities of Girona, Perpinyà and Barcelona over the course of the 1380s. Crisis in foreign trade saw merchants experience bankruptcy. Within the three main territories of the kingdom of Aragon, Catalonia was the region that was most affected by a combination of crises, whilst the Aragonese and Valencia regions were much less impacted. These latter two regions became increasingly important within the overall dynamic of the wider kingdom.

Anti-Jewish pogroms

The Jewish population in medieval Catalonia was concentrated in the urban zones and in towns where Jews lived, they may have been up to 15 per cent of the population. Separate quarters for the Jews were established in districts known as the Call. For a period, the monarchs of Catalonia maintained senior Jewish officials in advisory roles and even on occasion as diplomats. Following the conquest of Valencia, its Jewish inhabitants were given the same rights as the population of Barcelona.[53] However, from around 1300, this benign environment for the Jewish population began to erode which had a number of causes. Anti-Jewish sentiment was increasing in many European societies. Jews had been the main merchants but their role in trade began to be challenged by the rise of a new mercantile class in the city of Barcelona. Catalan merchants came to see the Jewish traders as their direct rivals and a threat to their profits. City councils even issued proclamations that expressed public hostility to the Jews.[54] The changing and worsening economic context followed by the Black Death produced a major change in attitudes towards the Jewish population. The church led a culture of persecution and priests were often the first to blame the Jews for the plague.[55] In the town of Tàrrega, tensions and the search for scapegoats saw the population turn on its Jewish population in 1348. Assault on the Jewish quarter in the town led to the slaughter of possibly as many as 300

Jews. Assaults on other Jewish populations had also taken place but not on the scale of Tàrrega. Decades of relative calm now returned which was broken in the early 1390s. The crisis we have noted earlier included the collapse of banks which began to heighten popular tensions. Jewish financiers were often the most likely to see loans defaulted on. In July and August 1391, a number of assaults were attempted on the Jewish quarter of Barcelona, the largest in Catalonia. The first major attack killed up to 200 Jews, whilst the worst led to the deaths of over 400 in a series of daily assaults which the authorities were unwilling or unable to halt. Those not killed experienced public-forced conversion to Christianity. Other minor assaults on Jewish quarters in Girona and Besalú also occurred. Some modest recovery in the Jewish population did occur in later decades but in a dramatically changed context, in 1492, the Jewish population was given the choice of conversion or exile.

Martí I and the end of the Catalan dynasty

Medieval regimes usually made use of the principle that the eldest male of the royal line was first in place for the succession. The members of the house of Barcelona had succeeded each other without interruption since the founding of the dynasty by Guifré in the late ninth century. Where no male heir had been available, a brother of the dead king might be found as a replacement or another very close relative. Thus, the arrival of a son or a clear successor was pivotal to monarchical stability. Given the context, we have noted of generalised crisis of varying degrees of intensity over the course of the fourteenth century, the death of Martí l'Humà (the Humane) in 1410 with neither issue nor a clear successor led to the end of the House of Barcelona as ruling dynasty. A political crisis was now added to those of the economy and society. Two main candidates emerged: Jaume d'Urgell, who made a claim as a distant family member and last potential male heir of the house of Barcelona and Ferdinand of Antequera, member of the Castilian Trastàmara family. There are two elements to this crisis: firstly, the internal developments themselves and secondly, how they have been framed in later centuries. In one sense there was a Catalan candidate, Jaume and a Castilian one, Ferdinand. However, most Catalan elites, whether rural or urban, supported the Castilian claimant as a better candidate for their interests. The local elites saw Ferdinand as a guarantor of their privileges and the preservation of their dominant role within the Cortes and the Diputació del General. This was resolved by the convening of the rural and urban elites who chose to elect the Castilian Ferdinand as King of Aragon, in June 1412, in the so-called Compromise of Casp. The Catalan candidate Jaume d'Urgell was so unpopular that even Mallorcan representatives who supported his claim were prevented from attending. The compromise prevented civil war.[56] Thus, in one sense, a blood line even if tenuous was over-ruled by a Catalan ruling class that prioritised its interests over attachment to the dynasty. A short-lived revolt by Jaume d'Urgell against Casp was unsupported by the Catalan aristocracy. This is a further confirmation that political and economic interests at the upper levels of society were not interpreted in terms that we might call national or patriotic.

Within the wider historical development of Catalonia and once the actual events became a distant memory, Casp became symbolised and ingrained as an emotional trauma. A narrative grew and was repeated of a Catalonia that might have been had not the last representative of the dynasty died without a son. Casp became interpreted as the first stage in a process of the losing of national sovereignty that would be completed by the defeat of 1714. The Catalan national revival in the nineteenth century constructed a story of medieval glory. We see this pattern in many European societies.[57] This framing of Casp is also linked to the story of Catalan decline as though this decision was the precipitator of all subsequent losses, in particular, the gradual incorporation within Castile/Spain. Whilst nineteenth-century Spaniards evoked the reconquest and the era of the Catholic Monarchs as representing a glorious period in Spanish history, in Catalonia, it was the glory of the Catalan-led kingdom of Aragon at its greatest extent that was reimagined as a golden age of Catalan glory. This was a mostly sanitised version of empire though at times even the exploits of the mercenary Almogavers were celebrated as examples of Catalan heroism.

Notes

1 Barrio Barrio, J. A. (2013) 'El concepto de frontera en la Edad Media. La frontera meridional del reino de Valencia. Siglos XIII-XV', *Sharq al-Andalus*, no. 20, pp. 41–65.
2 Pounds, N. (1973) *An Historical Geography of Europe 450 BC to AD 1330*, Cambridge: Cambridge University Press, pp. 228–229.
3 Teschke, B. (1998) 'Geopolitical Relations in the European Middle Ages: History and Theory', *International Organization*, vol. 52, no. 2, pp. 325–358.
4 Fernández-Cuadrench, J. (2014) 'L'Estat que no va ser catalans i occitans entre els segles VIII i XIII: A propòsit del vuitè centenari de la Batalla de Muret', *Butlletí de la Societat Catalana d'Estudis Històrics*, no. 25, pp. 47–85.
5 Reglà i Campistol, J. (1952) 'El comercio entre Francia y la Corona de Aragón en los siglos XIII y XIV y sus relaciones con el desenvolvimiento de la industria textil catalana', in *Actas del Primer Congreso Internacional de Estudios Pirenáicos*, San Sebastián: Instituto de Estudios Pirenaicos, vol. 6, pp. 47–65.
6 Ashtor, E. (1988) 'Catalan Cloth on the Late Medieval Mediterranean Markets', *Journal of European Economic History*, vol. 17, no. 2, pp. 227–257.
7 Anglès, H. (1935) *La música a Catalunya fins al segle XIII*, Barcelona: Institut d'Estudis Catalans, pp. 312–313.
8 Riquer, I. de (1996) 'Presencia trovadoresca en la Corona de Aragón', *Anuario de Estudios Medievales*, no. 26, pp. 933–966.
9 Mestre i Godes, J. (1994) *Els càtars problema religiós, pretext polític*, Barcelona: Edicions 62.
10 Graham, E. (2016) 'Heresy, Doubt and Identity: Late Medieval Friars in the Kingdom of Aragon', *Studies in Church History*, vol. 52, pp. 135–149.
11 Marvin, L. (2008) *The Occitan War. A Military and Political History of the Albigensian Crusade, 1209–1218*, Cambridge: Cambridge University Press, p. 195.
12 Martín Alvira Cabrer, M. (2014) 'El rey de Aragón Pedro el Católico y sus batallas. Del triunfo de Las Navas de Tolosa al desastre de Muret', in Cressier, P. and Salvatierra, V. (eds.) *Las Navas de Tolosa 1212–2012, miradas cruzadas*, Jaén: Universidad de Jaén, Servicio de Publicaciones, pp. 229–242.
13 Rosselló Bordoy, G. (1989) 'Notes sobre la conquesta de Mallorca (1229-1232): El testimoni dels vençuts', *Mayurqa: revista del Departament de Ciències Històriques i Teoria de les Arts*, no. 22(2), pp. 541–550.

14 Ferrer, A. (2019) 'Captives at the Conquest of Mallorca. September 1229-July 1232', *Imago Temporis. Medium Aevum*, no. 13, pp. 151–176.

15 Barceló Perelló, M. (2005) 'Enganya-l'ull: el guerrer, el comerciant i la noble causa en la història medieval de Catalunya', *L' Espill*, no. 21, pp. 6–26.

16 Burns, F. (2013) 'The Many Crusades of Valencia's Conquest (1225–80): An Historiographical Labyrinth', in Perry, M. (ed.) *Warrior Neighbours. Crusader Valencia in its International Context, Collected Essays of Father Robert I. Burns, SJ*, Turnhout: Brepols, pp. 103–113.

17 Torró, J. (2010) 'Els camperols musulmans del regne de València. De la conquesta a la conversió', *La Rella: anuari de L'Institut d'Estudis Comarcals del Baix Vinalopó*, no. 23, pp. 201–212.

18 Torró Abad, J. (2006) *El naixement d'una colònia: dominació i resistència a la frontera valenciana (1238–1276)*, València: Publicacions de la Universitat de València, p. 99.

19 Pladevall i Font, A. (2013) 'Les iniciatives de l'Esglesia catalana durant el regnat de Jaume I, Jaume I: commemoració del VIII centenari del naixement de Jaume I', in Ferrer i Mallol, M. (ed.) *Jaume I: commemoració del VIII centenari del naixement de Jaume I*, vol. 2, pp. 212–225.

20 Baydal Sala, V. (2015) 'Los orígenes historiográficos del concepto de «pactismo»', *Historia y Política*, no. 34, pp. 269–295.

21 Brines i García, L. (2006) 'La Filosofía Social y Política de Francesc Eiximenis (1ª part)', *Estudios franciscanos: publicación periódica de Ciencias Eclesiásticas de las Provincias Capuchinas Ibéricas*, vol. 107, no. 440, pp. 41–232.

22 Ladero Quesada, M. (1994) 'El ejercicio de poder real en la Corona de Aragón: Instituciones e instrumentos de gobierno (siglos xiv yxv)', *En la España Medieval*, no. 17, pp. 31–93.

23 Jacoby, D. (2015) 'The Catalan Company in the East: The Evolution of an Itinerant Army (1303–1311)', in Halfond, G. (ed.) *The Medieval Way of War Studies in Medieval Military History in Honor of Bernard S. Bachrach*, Farnham: Ashgate, pp. 153–182.

24 Espadaler, A. M. (2007) 'Els Almogàvers, les cares d'un mite', *Butlletí de la Societat Catalana d'Estudis Històrics*, no. 18, pp. 35–51.

25 Bell, N. (2011) 'The Iberian Peninsula', in Everist, M. (ed.) *The Cambridge Companion to Medieval Music*, Cambridge: Cambridge University Press, pp. 161–170.

26 Galera Monegal, M. (2015) 'Estudi raonat de les fonts documentals de l'Atles català de 1375. Des del seu inici fins a l'actualitat', *Treballs de la Societat Catalana de Geografia*, no. 80, pp. 9–66.

27 Badia, L., Santanach, L. and Soler, A. (2013) 'Ramon Llull', in Broch, A. (ed.) *Història de la Literatura Catalana. Literatura medieval (I). Dels orígens al segle XIV*, Barcelona: Enciclopèdia Catalana/Editorial Barcino, pp. 377–476.

28 Gost, P. (2001) 'La primera articulación del estado feudal en Cataluña a través de un impuesto: el bovaje (SS. XII-XIII)', *Hispania*, vol. 61, no. 209, pp. 967–997.

29 Lluch Bramon, R. (2013) 'Tot pensant en el conflicte remença: reflexions i propostes', *Estudis d'història agrària*, no. 25, pp. 29–46.

30 Lluch Bramon, R. (2008) 'Les Viles medieval franqueses i mals usos', *Butlletí de la Societat Catalana d'Estudis Històrics*, no. 19, pp. 9–28.

31 Mallorquí, E. (2011) *Parròquia i societat rural al bisbat de Girona, segles XIII-XIV*, Barcelona: Fundació Noguera, p. 251.

32 Fernández Trabal, J. (2004) 'Les indústries rurals', in Salrach Marés, J. M. and Giralt i Raventós, E. (eds.) *Història agrària dels Països Catalans*, Barcelona: Universitat de Barcelona, vol. 2, pp. 361–394.

33 Font Rius, J. M. (1985) *Estudis sobre els drets i institucions locals en la Catalunya medieval*, Barcelona: Universitat de Barcelona, p. 345.

34 Cuadrada, C. (1997) 'Senyors i ciutadans, les senyories catalanes a la Baixa Edat Mitjana', *Revista d'Historia Medieval*, no. 8, pp. 57–77.

35 Mallorquí, E. (2011) 'Masos medievals i cognoms endèmics a les terres de Girona', *Quaderns de la Selva*, no. 23, pp. 11–55.

36 Vinyoles, T. and Varela-Rodríguez, M. (1998) 'Vocacions femenines del segle XV', *Analecta Sacra Tarraconensia*, vol. 71, pp. 889–906.

37 Milton, G. (2012) *Market Power: Lordship, Society, and Economy in Medieval Catalonia (1276–1313)*, Basingstoke: Palgrave Macmillan, pp. 112–113.

38 Wunder, A. (2019) 'Spanish Fashion and Sumptuary Legislation from the Thirteenth to the Eighteenth Century', in Riello, G. and Rublack, U. (eds.) *The Right to Dress: Sumptuary Laws in a Global Perspective, c.1200–1800*, Cambridge: Cambridge University Press, pp. 243–272.

39 Ogilvie, S. (2011) *Institutions and European Trade. Merchant Guilds, 1000–1800*, Cambridge: Cambridge University Press, p. 54.

40 Riera, R. (2017) 'The Beginnings of Urban Manufacturing and Long Distance Trade', in Sabaté, F. (ed.) *The Crown of Aragon. A Singular Mediterranean Empire*, Leiden: Brill, pp. 201–236.

41 Tilly, C. (1992) *Coercion, Capital, and European States, AD 990–1992*, Oxford: Blackwell, p. 188.

42 Milian, L. (2019) 'La estructura del primer banco público de Europa: la Taula de Canvi de Barcelona (siglo XV)', *Medievalismo*, no. 29, pp. 297–321.

43 Aurell i Cardona, J. and Rubiés i Mirabet, J. P. (1993) 'Els mercaders catalans i la cultura de l'Edat Mitjana al Renaixement', *Anuario de Estudios Medievales*, vol. 23, pp. 221–255.

44 Aurell Cardona, J. (1998) 'La Imagen del mercader medieval', *Boletín de la Real Academia de Buenas Letras de Barcelona*, no. 46, pp. 23–44.

45 Reddy, W. (1987) *Money and Liberty in Modern Europe. A Critique of Historical Understanding*, Cambridge: Cambridge University Press, pp. 114–115.

46 Coulon, D. (2005) 'Barcelona i el gran comerç amb Orientun segle de relacions comercials de Barcelona amb Egipte i Síria (c. 1330–c. 1430)', *Butlletí de la Societat Catalana d'Estudis Històric*, no. 16, pp. 165–170.

47 Ferrer i Mallol, M. (1999) 'El Consolat de Mar i els consolats d'Ultramar, instrument i manifestació de l'expansió del comerç català', in Ferrer i Mallol, M. and Coulon, D. (eds.) *L'Expansió Catalana a la Mediterrània a la Baixa Edat Mitjana*, Madrid: Consejo Superior de Investigaciones Científicas, pp. 53–80.

48 Furió, A. (2001) *Història del País Valencià*, Valencia: Tres i Cuatre, pp. 110–112.

49 Ferrer i Mallol, M. (1987) 'Causes i antecedents de la guerra dels dos Peres', *Boletín de la Sociedad Castellonense de Cultura*, nos. 63–4, pp. 445–508.

50 Kagay, D. and Andrew Villalon, A. (2021) *Conflict in Fourteenth-Century Iberia. Aragon Vs. Castile and the War of the Two Pedros*, Leiden: Brill, pp. 409–412.

51 Pérez Moreda, V. (2017) 'Spain', in Alfani, G. and Ó Gráda, C. (eds.) *Famine in European History*, Cambridge: Cambridge University Press, pp. 48–72.

52 Vila i Bover, M. (1993) 'La pesta negra del segle XIV a Vic', *Gimbernat: Revista d'Història de la Medicina i de les Ciències de la Salut*, vol. 20, pp. 165–172.

53 Baer, Y. (1961) *A History of the Jews in Christian Spain: From the Age of Reconquest to the Fourteenth Century*, Philadelphia: Jewish Publication Society, p. 140.

54 Tov Assis, Y. (2012) 'The Jews of Barcelona in Maritime Trade with the East', in Ray, J. (ed.) *The Jew in Medieval Iberia, 1100-1500*, Brighton, MA: Academic Studies Press, pp. 180–226.

55 Cuadrada, C. (2012) *El llibre de la pesta*, Barcelona: Rafael Dalmau Editor, p. 303.

56 Sesma Muñoz, J. A. (2014) 'Parlamentarismo y sucesión al trono en la Corona de Aragón: el compromiso de Caspe', *Hidalguía: la revista de genealogía, nobleza y armas*, no. 362, pp. 55–84.

57 Evans, R. J. and Marchal, G. (2011) *The Uses of the Middle Ages in Modern European States History, Nationhood and the Search for Origins*, Basingstoke: Palgrave Macmillan.

5

DECLINE AND REVOLT 1415–1660

The instability and turbulence produced by the Black Death continued in the following century, culminating in peasant rebellions and a civil war in the 1460s. In this period, Castile expanded and formed a joint monarchy with Aragon. By the sixteenth century, a new kingdom of Spain became the greatest power in Europe. Catalan fortunes were now inextricably linked to that of its much more powerful neighbour. Whilst the Compromise of Casp brought to an end a ruling Catalan house on the throne of Aragon, it did not mean a dramatic rupture in policy or strategy of the monarchy. There is little evidence that contemporaries saw developments in terms of terminal decline or political rupture. The period after Casp and until probably the 1520s is characterised by the fact that the Catalan language reaches its maximum political and cultural expansion. There was certainly nothing inherently anti-Catalan about these new Castilian monarchs who had strong degrees of popular support at various times, particularly against the native aristocracy. Although Alfonso the Magnanimous read in Spanish at his first Cortes, in Barcelona in 1416, this was so heavily criticised that the rulers did not make this mistake again and hereafter accepted the primary role to the Catalan language. It should be noted that Catalan was, throughout this time, the near universal language. Catalan retained its public religious presence as sermons were delivered in the language of the parishioners. However, in one concrete area, Catalan will lose status and this is as a courtly language as the century develops. This linguistic shift in the upper echelons of Catalan society is related to social prestige, not a policy of discrimination.[1]

Some issues such as economic pressures and class conflicts had already emerged in the previous century, so disputes to come should not be simply read as being caused by a change of dynasty. Whilst historians speak of this period as partly transitional to the early modern period, most of life was still in most respects medieval.[2]

DOI: 10.4324/9781003218791-6

This society remained governed by strict hierarchy and its social ordering was maintained by lord and church. Women had little autonomy or choice beyond marriage or the convent and were subject to the authority of their father which was substituted for that of the husband after wedlock. Modest autonomy might be obtained as a nun but the religious orders were strictly hierarchical and lesser in status than the male monasteries. The female population was described by one prominent writer Jaume Roig in 1460 as being sinful in their very nature.[3] The church as a whole maintained an extensive system of social control and women in particular were subject to its dictates. Whilst the record testifies to the occasional instance of transgression in all social classes by individual women, these instances were clearly exceptional. The population was still predominantly rural and agricultural, and the village structure had been consolidated centuries earlier. The urban pattern of Catalonia was firmly established and Barcelona was pre-eminent, with the city of Perpinyà, beyond the Pyrenees, the second city of Catalonia. Patterns of life, including the question of religious influence, only slowly changed until the emergence of the Inquisition in the 1490s and later the Protestant Reformation. Catalonia did not waver in its loyalty to Catholicism throughout the rise of Luther and Calvin, but rather continued its own development which remained firmly within Catholic orthodoxy. Monasteries expanded and that of Montserrat increasingly came to have an important symbolic role due to its Black Madonna. The cult of Mary continued to be closely adhered to in Catalan religious culture.[4]

The priorities of the new Castilian dynasty of the throne of Aragon represented continuity with what had come before, including consolidating and extending territory in the Mediterranean. The imperial project of the previous century remained central. However, one pattern we have previously noted, as consequence of expansion, continued. As the realm expanded territorially and in international projection, the centrality of Catalonia and its weight within it was frequently challenged. We have noted these trends in terms of both Aragon and Valencia, and they had also occurred with revolts and pressures from Mallorca. The vast Mediterranean expansion was a further factor in this process. New territory was added, in this case the kingdom of Naples, which required lengthy conquest and was not achieved until 1442 after ten years of struggle. Alfonso proceeded to create a highly professional army which was directly loyal to him. As an indication of changing priorities, King Alfonso made Naples his capital, and from there he would deal with all peninsular affairs. Even so, the Catalan language remained the principal means of administrative and court communication under his reign.[5] Yet the costs of empire placed greater strain on Catalonia than anything since the Black Death in the 1350s.[6] Catalan opposition now joined with that of the Aragonese about ever-increasing military expenditure in Sicily and Italy. Catalonia was now financing a lengthy war and occupation where the only beneficiaries were the richest sectors of the merchant class, who remained a small contingent in society. New pressures emerged with an economic downturn and, with an absent dynasty, control of Catalonia was fought out between distinctive economic sectors.

Problems of Empire

Conflict with the Italian city states of Pisa and Genoa over Sardinia lasted for over 80 years, with peace not achieved until 1420. However, the Aragonese attempt to expand further into Naples reignited conflict with Genoa which was backed by the Papacy. Both saw their interests threatened by potential Aragonese domination of southern Italy. A period of brutal warfare occurred which included defeat for the Aragonese and capture of their king. In 1436, a new phase in the conquest began and in February 1443, the Aragonese king paraded through Naples as conqueror.[7] The conquest of Naples was a high point of overseas expansion as ten years later Ottoman Turks took Constantinople in 1452, putting an end to the 1000-year-old Byzantine Empire. The trading opportunities in the eastern Mediterranean and much of North Africa came to an end for the Crown of Aragon and no further territory would be added. With the loss of these eastern markets, Italian territories became central though they required strong military pressure to subdue potential and real rebellions. Their cost placed strains on political stability. Peak empire had been reached and contraction of overseas holdings began.

Growing social conflict

From the late fourteenth century, tensions in the countryside intensified and on occasion led to violence and revolts against the nobles and those who supported them. This conflict occurred because the lordly class tried to halt reduction in income by intensifying demands on the peasantry.[8] As an indication of their advanced consciousness, in the late fourteenth century, the remença union was created, a highly unusual organisation across Europe and testimony to a high level of peasant organisation.[9] A further distinctive feature of the Catalan situation was that, in the conflict between the remença peasants, the monarchy tended to side against the lords.[10] The support of the Trastàmara dynasty to peasant demands was partly out of self-interest. The peasantry was a source of income for the crown and it suited the monarchy to have a weakened lordly class.[11] Given that the peasantry was by far the largest social grouping in society, there were important differences within it, with an affluent minority and a majority group of landless peasants. The landless joined the revolt, which was led by the affluent peasants, who were the most well-organised. The first wave of remences revolts took place during the second half of the fifteenth century and were initially centred in the Girona region. In 1448, King Alfons recognised the Remença Union, which was highly rare in a European context. The monarchy tried to arbitrate between the demands of the peasants while trying to also maintain the traditional social structure of society. Peasant organisation and collective revolt obtained results. In 1455, the king suspended the collection of the greatly resented mals usos, which as we have seen placed a whole range of burdens on the peasantry. Yet the major institutions of the Catalan ruling elites, the Generalitat, and the Council of One Hundred of Barcelona, interpreted the decision as an affront to their social standing. This was a deeply hierarchical society and ruling class contempt for their social inferiors was near universal. The remença conflict is one element within the Catalan Civil War (1462–1472) and peasant/lord dispute and violence both preceded it and occurred again at the war's close.[12] Conflict was not, however, confined to the countryside.

Urban conflict

The city of Barcelona had seen intermittent violent outbreaks against the city rulers throughout the medieval period but social order overall had not been challenged. The European crisis of the fourteenth century saw intermittent conflict and in time, the city of Barcelona became deeply divided into two factions. The grouping that became known as the Biga brought together the richest merchants, bankers and the landlords, including those who held rural holdings but lived within the city walls. They deemed themselves the ciutadans honrats (honest citizens) and believed they ruled by right. Their social basis had begun to change as they became increasingly proto-capitalist and invested in land, though remained urban in culture. This elite controlled not only Barcelona but also the other Catalan cities. Social tensions were rising with the vital textile sector increasingly pressured by a severe drop in prices in the 1420s. With deteriorating finances affecting the lower echelons of the city, protests of the lesser merchants and artisans began to have more force and increasingly sought to challenge the monopoly of the upper class. Thus emerged the faction opposed to the Biga that was known as the Busca. This was formed by small merchants, skilled tradesmen and artisans and sectors of the general populace. In simple terms, the class positions in both blocks were clearly demarcated. The Busca sought political reform and for the sectors it represented to be given a voice within the institutions.[13] One of the main accusations of the Busca against the Biga was the mismanagement of the city's finances and simple corruption. The Busca also sought protectionist policies for its small traders which was opposed by the Biga as the latter benefitted from free trade.

Once again, the monarchy tended to side with the less powerful, partly out of self-interest, as the urban elites together with the rural lords were the greatest potential threat to a consolidated monarchical power. The king's hostility towards the Catalan elites was evident from the beginning of his reign when he clashed with them on countless issues.[14] This ideological hostility between the king and the privileged classes became most evident in the Cortes over questions of taxation. In 1453, Galceran de Requesens, the king's representative as lieutenant of Catalonia, suspended elections and directly appointed a new city council dominated by the Busca. This was interpreted by the ruling elites of the Biga in Barcelona as a tantamount to a coup and overthrow of the natural order. The Biga began to organise and allied with the rural aristocracy. Thus, a challenge by the middling and lower sectors of the city of Barcelona spiralled into a major institutional conflict, leading to determined resistance by the traditional order. A major fracture was opening up across Catalan society. By now, the dominant social forces in both the countryside and the cities were deeply alienated from the monarchy. In spring 1462, several leading Busca figures were executed in Barcelona. These executions and the counter-revolt by the Biga against monarchical attempts to moderate their influence created a breech between monarch and elites that now seemed unresolvable. The Biga and the rural aristocracy were now determined to remove a dynasty that did not respect their privileges. In February, a new peasant revolt had broken out in Girona. Three months later, the major institutions of the Catalan elites proclaimed the king and his queen enemies of the principality of Catalonia. They began to search for a new monarch. Thus, social conflict in both city and countryside and hostility towards the monarchy on the part of both rural and urban elites triggered civil war.

The Catalan Civil War

The Catalan Civil War of 1462–1472 was a multi-layered conflict, with urban clashes between the Biga and Busca, the remences against the landowning class and the elite-dominated institutions against the king. The war included participation by other realms including Castile and Portugal on the side of the Catalan institutions. The king of Aragon sought assistance from France and offered in exchange remaining Catalan possessions beyond the Pyrenees, the counties of Rosselló and Cerdanya. This was a fifth of the Catalan population and although it was later returned, it suggested that this zone could be bargained with. The implication of other powers was an indication that the question of Catalonia could be used to challenge Castile as became evident in other periods. The civil war was a long slow one of attrition with the monarchy gradually accumulating victories. During the conflict, what we can term a form of national sentiment at a level of ruling elites emerged. This was not only the defence of economic interest and privilege but also in a gradually emerging sense that they were acting in the defence of local Catalan institutions against a non-Catalan monarchy. As we have noted earlier, national sentiment did not exist at a popular level in this period in most of Europe, but it was increasingly evident at elite level. In contrast to the modern period of nationalism, the peasants and the lower classes did not see the conflict in national terms and sided with the monarch, who was Castilian. In 1472, after ten years of struggle, peace was signed. Catalan elites which had rebelled against the monarchy was now a greatly diminished force.[15]

The aftermath of civil war

In 1472, the civil war ended with the Peace of Pedralbes. The monarchy had survived the challenge to its authority and could proceed to the accumulation of greater power, as was occurring in other European monarchies. Though the Catalan elites had sued for peace, that the war had lasted ten years testified to their organisational strength. The victorious monarchy had no wish to see the social order upturned. The peace agreement saw the monarchy betray its own peasant supporters. The concessions made to them in the 1440s were withdrawn and most of the lordly privileges were restored. This was cemented by the awarding of further privileges to the lords by the new monarch Ferdinand in 1481. The royal privileging of its former enemies directly led to a new peasant rebellion in 1484 known as the Second Remença Revolt, led by Pere Joan Sala. After an initial peasant victory, this second revolt was crushed. The main leaders were executed, including Pere Joan Sala, who was hung, drawn and quartered. Yet the revolt disturbed the monarchy and in a new policy change, King Ferdinand promulgated the Guadalupe Arbitral Award. This sought to balance the opposing class interests of peasant and lord. Many former rights of the lords were abolished but the peasantry was required to provide compensations to the feudal lords. Formal legal servitude was abolished.[16] This is believed to be the first document issued in Europe on the release of serfs. The main beneficiaries were the most affluent sectors of the peasantry who had financial surpluses that enabled them to pay costs and purchase their own farm. The majority sector of the peasantry emerged in a worsened condition and Guadalupe meant a reinforcement of the feudal domination.[17]

However, whilst Guadalupe only benefitted a minority of the peasantry, it still remained an exceptional document in comparative European terms. Between the French jacqueries, the English peasants revolt and the German peasants war, the usual pattern was repressive violence and defence of the existing order. Furthermore, this partly successful rebellion fed into a narrative of Catalan liberty that would become deeply ingrained.[18] The notion of the Catalan peasant increasingly became associated around a hard-working individual, inherently conservative and deeply attached to the land. In later centuries, the Catalan small farmer became representative of the virtues of the country as a whole which were claimed to be industrious and natural to commercial exchange. Here of course was a contrast to Castilians who had squandered the vast wealth of overseas conquest and were to be plunged into centuries of poverty and marginalisation. The outcome in the long term of the reforms to land entailed a major transformation in the Catalan countryside, where the small farm centred on the traditional mas-type farmhouse became the focus of development. A market in land emerged and marriage alliances were conducted as opportunities to expand and consolidate holdings.[19] A more complex system of social stratification emerged with the richer peasants able to consolidate their gains. These sectors could now hire wage labour, whether impoverished day labourers, and increasingly immigrants of Occitan origin.[20] A virtuous cycle now began as prices rose and the population grew.[21]

Catholic Monarchs

The accession to the throne of Ferdinand the Catholic and Isabella of Castile in 1479 as joint monarchs did not mean the fusion of two different realms. This was a marriage and alliance between two separate kingdoms. They never used the title of kings of Spain. It was a union that adopted the decentralised structure of the Crown of Aragon but on a wider scale.[22] Catalonia retained its own institutions, currency and customs and was not required to provide soldiers except for the defence of its own territory. This joining of two kingdoms was neither conquest nor assimilation. In 1479, the office of viceroy was created, to act as a liaison between local elites in Barcelona and the monarchy. The viceroy was the direct symbol of the authority of the monarch and the character of an individual viceroy might be key to preventing local alienation.[23] As the role became normalised, viceroys increasingly came from non-Catalan regions and became a source of resentment. Rather than there being a point of rupture between Catalonia and the rest of the kingdom, we see the gradual erosion of previous privileges. Some might be reversed after local protests but we can view a broader pattern of standardisation of practices within the wider kingdom. New institutions were devised to administer a vastly expanded kingdom including changes to the selection of local officials. The Supreme Council of Aragon, created in 1494, was devised as an advisory body to the monarchy. Provided it was perceived to respect local traditions, it was broadly accepted amongst Catalan elites. However, as well as potential clashes around legal domains, a royal court established Castilian Spanish as the language of the monarchy, courtiers and diplomatic relations. The Spanish language rose in status and became the form of communication amongst the nobility and those entering military service. A similar process at the highest levels occurred with the church, with the gradual appointment of Castilian-speaking officials. However, the ordinary priesthood and the parishioners remained overwhelmingly Catalan speakers. Learning and using Spanish became the indispensable means for political and social ascent. Thus, important sectors of Catalan society accepted the new dispensation and married into the Castilian nobility. Whilst Catalan was not abandoned, social advance usually required the knowledge of Castilian. The two main Catalan institutions, the Generalitat and the Consell de Cent, had seen their status across society greatly damaged by the civil war and the new strategic alliance between Catalan and Castilian elites seemed to offer a degree of social stability to this stratum.

Inquisition

In 1493, King Ferdinand obtained the return of the last remaining territories beyond the Pyrenees, Rosselló and Cerdanya, to Catalonia from France. However, the fact that these territories had been ceded once meant they became the centre of renewed conflict and were invaded again in the 1520s. War between France and Spain became a near constant in the following century and Catalonia was inevitably impacted by its frontier zone status. Whilst the return of Rosselló and Cerdanya to Catalonia was welcomed, resentment was greatest over the role of the Inquisition under the new monarch. This was not necessarily a religious opposition to the search for heresy. The Inquisition in Catalonia dates from the end of the twelfth century. From the thirteenth century, the Inquisition became institutionalised in the Crown of Aragon, always under papal control to repress heresy, including that of the Cathars, as we have seen.[24] A particularly repressive period occurred under the Dominican inquisitor Nicolau Eimeric (1356–1399), a cleric from the city of

Girona, who even questioned the Catholicism of Ramon Llull and his followers.[25] Eimeric wrote a manual for inquisitors which established a range of signs that indicated the presence of the Devil. This manual was adopted in the conquered territories of Latin America, though in Catalonia the Inquisition became largely inactive after his death.

Under Ferdinand, a new Inquisition was introduced throughout the kingdom. Previous Inquisitions had been administered by the church but this new version was directly subordinated to the monarchy. This Inquisition thus became a powerful political tool. Opposition to the introduction of the new Inquisition was intense in the Crown of Aragon, especially by the Catalan institutions, which resisted the introduction of the Holy Office because they considered it a tool in the service of monarchical authoritarianism.[26] The medieval period where a monarch was only moderately higher in status but not able to fully control the aristocracy was now over. This new modern centralising monarchy sought to accrue ever greater powers. Thus, the issue of the new Inquisition was a conflict over jurisdictions between the monarchy and local institutions. The Holy Office was thus established in Barcelona in 1487 and the autos-de-fé began. As elsewhere, this initial role of the Inquisition was the persecution of Jewish converts to Christianity though many were simply tried in absentia.[27] Between its introduction and 1505, the Barcelona court tried more than a thousand people, more than half of whom had already gone into exile in previous years. It is unlikely that the Jewish population of Catalonia even reached 5 per cent in this period as the pogrom of 1391 had made many leave. In May 1492, the expulsion of the Jews was promulgated in Barcelona. Five centuries or more of residence of Jewish populations came to an abrupt end and Jewish expertise departed with them. Only within the Jewish communities were there minor opportunities for women and this was now brought to an end. Catalonia barely had a Moslem or Protestant population and subsequently Catholicism was central to the making of Catalan identity, or at least its conservative variant.

Even so the Inquisition in Catalonia had a comparatively modest impact. We now know that the institution as a whole was surprisingly cautious and slow moving and, together with local reluctance to collaborate, the Holy Office in Catalonia could not be termed a success. In over 90 per cent of the urban areas, during more than three centuries of existence, the Holy Office never once even appeared.[28] Reluctance to collaborate was greatest when inquisitors were Castilian in origin, though it would have been impossible for the institution to function without substantial support at the middling levels. For a brief period between 1507 and 1518, with the appointments as inquisitors of the native Bishop of Vic and Lleida, and of Tortosa tensions eased. However, new measures were passed in 1518 that essentially meant the form of the Inquisition was common to both Castile and Aragon. A pattern of harmonisation that was followed in other areas produced ever greater resentment. As we have seen, privileges and appointments to those from other areas of the kingdom continued to be a slow burning source of discontent.

Internal development

Within the new expansive and expanding kingdom, the territories of the King-dom of Aragon were not directly involved in the project of American colonial conquest, as Castile had funded the initial enterprise. The kingdom of Aragon was neither participant nor beneficiary, which was further reflection of both realms' autonomous development. For later Catalan historians and in popular memory, this has often been interpreted as discrimination against a Catalonia that was excluded from the vast wealth of American conquest. However, in the same way that Cata-lonia did not benefit from the proceeds of conquest and empire, Catalonia avoided the later negative consequences. Spanish decline after the exhaustion of silver and other mineral deposits was dramatic and continued for hundreds of years. Impe-rial overstretch, near constant warfare on a range of fronts, ultimately produced the collective impoverishment of Spain. By the eighteenth century, Catalonia had begun a period of rapid economic advance and much of Spain remained behind until well into the twentieth century. In time a narrative of Catalan industriousness compared to Castilian backwardness would be constructed and which still has reso-nance today. More important for future relations between Castile and Catalonia was the ever-growing disparity between the kingdoms, in terms of population and size. By 1520, the Catalan population was unlikely to be more than 250,000.[29] The overall population of Castile may have been six million placing it within the largest European kingdoms of the time and more than double that of England. In terms of territorial extent, the Crown of Castile was triple that of Aragon, excluding its new Latin American holdings. Certainly, after civil war and social conflict, the Catalonia of the sixteenth century embarked on a period of modest growth and recovery. In particular, Barcelona and Girona were slowly growing as were areas inland. Whilst agriculture as yet provided little in terms of surplus and the lords were reluctant to support innovation in this period, for a few decades a period of decline was gradually halted. However, a new plague arrived in 1588. This epidemic was the most devastating since the Black Death and spread throughout Catalan territory. This was once again a bubonic plague. Whilst the epidemic of 1588–1590 reduced population, it was not comparable in scale to the Black Death. Both the population and the economy recovered quite rapidly.

Occitan immigration

Immigration filled the demographic gap caused by plagues and crises. It is likely that population decline reached its low point around the time of the Catalan civil war in the 1470s.[30] Population rose overall in the early sixteenth century by some 20 per cent, but the rate accelerated to about 75 per cent between the 1550s and the 1620s. As an indication that Catalonia was recovering, a major role in popu-lation growth has been attributed to substantial immigration.[31] The French wars of religion had created enormous disruption and instability and through the lin-guistic closeness of Occitan and Catalan, and the comparative ease in crossing the

Pyrenees, new arrivals were facilitated. The religious conflict was compounded by a more or less continuous state of war between the kingdom of France and the Spanish monarchy. Tensions did exist with the newcomers. An overwhelmingly Catholic population was suspicious of anything that smacked of Calvinism and at times the French were simply the enemy that ravaged Catalan territory. However, more important was the fact that a growing Catalan economy could accommodate the immigration. Furthermore, much of Catalonia was under-populated. The Occitan immigration was vast in scale and by the 1620s, Catalonia had increased its population to around 475,000, a more than doubling in a hundred years.[32] Some zones had Occitan populations of around 20 per cent, with cultural and linguistic affinity facilitating integration.[33] Occitan surnames survive but in time little cultural or linguistic legacy was left behind.

Barcelona and urban stagnation

By the 1520s, the population of Barcelona was unlikely to be over 25,000 and the city had long ceased being a dominant power in the Mediterranean and had lost markets in North Africa. Trade was no longer a major source of revenue and land became the centre of attention, even for urban-based elites. This was a form of proto-capitalist profit seeking in land which laid the basis for later development. Within the Iberian peninsula, the city of Barcelona was only eighth in terms of size and be described as at best a small- to medium-sized city. As we have seen, the Catalan city had lost its status as the capital of the kingdom and court was transferred to Naples. The gradual process of fusion of Castile and Aragon further reduced the importance of the city. The two other main Catalan cities, Perpinyà and Girona, had also been negatively affected by war with France and were subject to periodic sieges and the plundering of the surrounding countryside. Barcelona faced a long period of stasis and the city ceased for a period to be a dominating presence across the geography of Catalonia. The city was further disrupted by the arrival of plagues. With a Catalan aristocracy increasingly integrating with that of Castile, we can term this period an intermediate phase before the emergence of new social sectors engaged in trade in a new capitalist form. By the 1580s, we can begin to discern urban revival and the emergence of new elites engaged in cultural patronage.[34] However, greater potential expansion was limited by the constant piracy along the coast. Usually based in North Africa, these pirates took advantage of conflict between Spain and France to attack the Catalan and Valencia coast. Major actions included the sacking of towns such as Cadaqués and Palamós, as well as Badalona, which was just 10 miles from Barcelona. Catalonia had still not obtained a form of stability that would allow for sustained economic growth.

Catalonia and the Habsburgs

Over the course of the sixteenth century, the monarchy of the Crown of Aragon and the Kingdom of Castile was unified under a single monarch under the

Habsburg dynasty. This was a new and distinctive form of monarchy and entailed the construction of new narratives of kingship. Spain became the world's leading power, administering the largest European territory since Charlemagne. Across Europe, whether in England under the Tudors, France or Portugal, monarchies were engaged in processes of creating state administrations and centralisation. This period is marked by the decline of feudalism and transitions to a capitalist form of economy. We also find that European territories are the most dynamic centres of social and economic change, processes that contributed to and facilitated the early form of the nation state. It is in this context that we can discern the increasing integration of Catalonia within Spain and its empire. The comparative size of Catalonia compared to a greater and ascendant Castile gave a degree of inevitability to these trends. Madrid, established as capital of Spain in 1561, accumulated power and centrality, becoming the sole court. Amongst Spanish ruling elites, the ancient rights and privileges of the territories of Aragon, including Catalonia, and local attachment to them, were seen as archaic.

Each monarchical regime has its own distinctive character, and in part depends on the person of the monarch. Some Spanish monarchs exhibited a degree of recognition and understanding to their territories, whilst in other reigns, Catalonia was barely visited at all. We have noted the sources of tensions, including that of the Inquisition. With the emergence of the Protestant Reformation, Spain became the embodiment of religious orthodoxy and central to the European defence of Catholicism. Philip II became the personal incarnation of the Counter-Reformation, his reign lasting 40 years. Philip was determined to crush Protestantism in his dominions and embarked on a lengthy war against the Netherlands. This decades long conflict had major negative consequences for the Spanish economy. As part of the Catholic counter-attack, the Inquisition was expanded and study outside of Spain was prohibited, to prevent access to Protestant heresy. Whilst Protestantism barely impinged on the Catholic orthodoxy of Catalonia, in 1569, inquisitors in Barcelona arrested representatives of the Generalitat in a dispute over jurisdictions. This was one instance of many that contributed to growing fracturing in relations between the local institutions and a remote monarch who only visited Barcelona twice in 40 years. Whilst the broad trends were pointing towards absolutist monarchy in Spain, the king, at war on a range of fronts declined to pursue full political centralisation at this time.[35]

Bandits

Spain's imperial project had been funded by the largest deposit of silver yet found in the world. This silver was usually transferred from South America to Spain via the well-secured ports of the Netherlands. However, the revolt of the Netherlands against Spanish rule, in the second half of the sixteenth century, led to a change in policy and the Mediterranean now became the preferred route for the transfer of bullion. Thus was born the route through Barcelona. Royal convoys also passed through Lleida, as well as Zaragoza to reach Barcelona. Small-scale banditry had long been an issue in the territory due to reduced opportunities on the land and plague. The vast wealth now being transferred throughout Catalan territory changed the dynamic of banditry into something new and highly organised. This new banditry was distinctive because it included the involvement of nobles.[36] The potential riches were so great that the new banditry, which co-existed with the old form, became a lord-led form of private warfare. Banditry became a new tool of feudal rivalry and by the late sixteenth century, two main groupings had emerged known by the nicknames of nyerros and cadells.[37] As an indication that this form of bandit was an unusual social formation, religious opinion aligned with both groups. The bishop of Vic even dedicated a sonnet in 1609 to one leading bandit.[38]

Thus, when we speak of banditry in this period we are speaking of two distinctive forms. One variant which had deep roots was that of the small grouping usually defined as the outlaw. As elsewhere such as with Robin Hood, some bandits obtained both local support and social prestige.[39] This tradition of banditry created its own myth-history through individuals such as Perot Rocaguinarda, or Joan Sala Ferrer, known as Serrallonga, who was executed in 1634. Catalan topography, containing within some of the most mountainous areas within the Iberian peninsula, was ideally situated to provide refuge as were other areas which were inaccessible to those without local knowledge. The second larger form of banditry became not only a means to accrue vast wealth but also a source of institutional conflict between Catalan elites and the monarchy. Repressive measures by the king's representative caused bitter conflicts of jurisdiction with the Catalan authorities.[40] As well as aristocratic involvement in the banditry, higher Catalan officials declined to participate in the persecution and often provided protection to the bandits. In this sense, what was deemed crime in the eyes of Castile found protection amongst the higher strata of Catalan society.[41] Catalonia became strongly associated in Spanish and other eyes as one of Europe's leading zones of banditry. This issue became one more symptom of a growing estrangement between the Catalan ruling elites and the Spanish Empire.

From the late sixteenth century, the social order provides increasing evidence of social fluidity. Population recovery and growth produced new societal pressures. Whilst a few are able to improve their social status through trade or land consolidation, others now fall into an extreme poverty. We move away from the medieval form of social structure into a hybrid model that contained medieval continuities with features that we can term proto-modern. Changes in ownership forms of property meant the building of a new legal infrastructure. Reduced opportunities on the land meant options for many only included seasonal work as farm labourers and we find a rise in begging and vagrancy. We see the construction of the categories of the deserving and undeserving (idle) poor with only the former entitled to charitable assistance, particularly on the part of the organisations of the Church.[42] Charity was overwhelmingly organised within a religious context. In a society in flux, crime adopted an increasingly violent character.[43] The emergence of a precarious form of existence outside of the feudal tradition of mutual assistance led to a clear escalation of robbery and other means of survival.[44] In this context, we see increasingly the social construction of crime. A distinctive criminal category emerged which only impacted on women.

Witches

For around a hundred years from the late sixteenth to the late seventeenth century, the witch-hunt was particularly intense and affected all of Europe. In a collective wave of persecution mostly centred in the German lands, parts of France and Italy, and Switzerland, at least 60,000 executions were carried out. The wave of repression affected both Catholic and Protestant zones. In general terms, the Spanish monarchy was an exception to the witch-hunt as issues of heresy came within the control of the Inquisition and mass hysteria around witches was subordinated to its procedures. Even so what became by far the worst witch-hunt in early modern Spain broke out in Catalonia. It began north of the Pyrenees in 1614, in the Rosselló zone and continued until 1622. It marks the worst episode of witch-hunting that Catalonia has ever experienced. This craze for persecution began from below and occurred outside of the auspices of the Inquisition.[45] The repression against women accused of being witches spread producing between four hundred and a thousand accused. Leading Catalan theologians and jurists called witches a 'plague'.[46] Although the total number of those executed remains unclear, it seems likely that there were at least 150 executions in 50 different locations, mostly found in the central zone of Catalonia.[47] Those accused in Catalonia were charged with crimes similar to other persecutions in Europe, being accused of a range of relationships with the devil, including sexual relations. Witches were believed to be part of a universal sect which was presided over by the devil, and whose main aim was to attack the Christian world. All ills befalling communities from the birth of a disabled child or animal to poor harvests were attributed to a witch in a persecutory cycle. The floods of 1617 were given a religious inflection and interpreted as divine punishment. The wave of trials and executions was brought to an end in 1622, when the royal authorities decreed that all accused of witchcraft were to be transferred to the jurisdiction of the local court. Most were soon released and the collective hysteria that had appeared in these years gradually abated.

Towards rupture and revolt

From around the 1580s, the modest recovery of previous decades accelerated producing a general pattern of economic growth until around 1630. The population grew further, and economic activity diversified, though this was an economy geared for export. Surpluses were small but the absence of major shortages was an improvement on previous periods. Barcelona finally embarked on a sustained period of revival, in particular through the textile industry. Rural aristocrats increasingly moved to the Catalan capital as it developed. In parallel, the fusion of the old nobility with the merchant class gave rise to a new urban class formation. However, the fact that major roles were increasingly given to Castilians produced local tensions.[48]

For a variety of reasons, many of the territories of the vast Spanish kingdom had accumulated grievances by the early seventeenth century and we should situate developments in Catalonia until 1660 within a wider crisis of the Spanish Empire.[49] In time Spain would lose the Netherlands, Portugal, Naples and it nearly lost Catalonia. The decline of Spain has long concerned historians with the causes usually attributed to relentless spending on war as well as the exhaustion of silver supplies from the Americas placing the finances close to breaking point. The recovery that Catalonia had begun to experience stalled in the 1630s.[50] Economic conditions became grave in much of Spain and although Catalonia was less dramatically impacted, a deteriorating economic context fed into a growing political distrust. In 1617, Catalonia had been subject to the worst torrential rain and flooding known, which can be situated within a more general period of climatic instability.[51]

As we have seen, some sectors of Catalan society had become politically integrated with the Spanish realm, whilst those based within the local institutions continued to see themselves as representing a native political tradition. In this latter sector, loyalty to the wider institutions of the monarchy was particularly weak.[52] The new ruling class that was being forged again prioritised their dominant role in the local institutions over any abiding loyalty to the monarchy. By the 1620s, Catalonia seemed so marginal to the concerns of the wider empire, that the king of Spain no longer felt it necessary to visit the region to carry out the traditional oath to uphold local privileges. Local discontent had been growing due to a perception that these rights were no longer respected by officials, who were usually of non-Catalan origin. With the outbreak of renewed war between France and Spain in 1635, the situation reached breaking point as the geographical location of Catalonia placed it again on the front line. We have noted the ever more explicit trends towards monarchical absolutism, part of a pattern exhibited in other European countries. It was the long-standing exemptions of contributing to military costs that caused a dramatic change in policy led by the king's advisor, the Count-Duke Olivares. A Catalan contribution was sought repeatedly in the parliaments held between 1626 and 1632. The new demands of Olivares were interpreted as a naked power grab by Madrid. A centralising political administration was resisted by the Catalan institutions.

1640

The revolt of 1640 emerged through two distinct strands: the institutional rebellion of local elites and a popular rebellion led by the peasantry. Early in the war with France, Catalan territory was the battleground with repeated French incursions. Large numbers of Castilian forces were increasingly stationed in the region, and their billeting fell upon the peasantry. We have noted the deteriorating economic conditions, and the housing and feeding of troops became a major source of grievance. It is in this context that Olivares launched what was called the union of arms, meaning that all the territories of the monarchy contributed to the imperial army and required Catalonia to contribute 6,000 soldiers. In the Catalan case, this clashed with its long-standing exemption, which only provided for forced recruitment to defend the territory of the Principality. However, the other two main regions, Aragon and Valencia, supported the new measures and did not rebel. These territories continued their independent political development. The indiscipline of Castilian troops, resentment at another war with France and the attempted erosion of a long-standing political exemption produced the Catalan revolt of 1640.[53] Rebellion began with a peasant uprising in June 1640 which the increasingly alienated Catalan elites chose to support, though they remained fearful that it might turn against them. In one sense, these elites had little choice after peasants entered Barcelona and attacked those associated with the monarchy. Catalonia broke with the Spanish monarchy and became a protectorate of France. Catalan forces thus aligned themselves with the French in the war against Spain.

This conflict not only had purely political connotations but was also a class and social war. For over ten years, Catalan territory became subordinated to France though local traditions were upheld. The Generalitat, initially led by the cleric Pau Claris, embodied the political revolt, including a short-lived Republic. Initially, elite interests aligned with those of the peasantry but Catalan rulers became increasingly divided and fearful of the popular war of the peasantry. Peasant grievances now centred on the lodging and feeding of French troops, who had simply seemed to displace one force for another. Anti-French sentiment became as common as that against the Spanish monarchy and institutions. Thus, the revolt saw the peasantry find new oppressors to turn against.[54] In 1650, in the final phase of the conflict, the Mediterranean plague (1647–1651) arrived in Catalonia. It decimated the population in a number of areas and reached Girona and Barcelona. This event contributed to the end of Catalan resistance and Barcelona submitted in 1652, bringing to an event the revolt of the Catalans. Whilst Catalonia was restored to the monarchy, Portugal achieved its separation from Spain, which contributed to the general pardon issued by the Spanish monarchy. A renewed commitment to respect Catalan traditions and institutions was made.

Territorial rupture

In parallel to the revolt of the Catalans and the Portuguese, the Thirty Years War came to an end in 1648 and further confirmed the greatly diminished status of Spain. France intervened in both the Portuguese and Catalan revolts and saw them as opportunities to weaken their Spanish rival. The peace agreement between France and Spain of 1659 had major implications for Catalonia. French troops had remained in the zone of Rosselló and Cerdanya. We saw earlier how this zone had been bargained during the Catalan civil war but was returned in 1493. Now in the context of an ascendant France and greatly weakened Spain, this zone was demanded by the French as the price of peace. A new permanent frontier was now imposed between Spain and France in the peace treaty of 1659. This represented a dramatic loss, as Perpinyà had continued to be the second most important city of Catalan territory. Revolts took place against French rule on several occasions, the most serious in 1470. Repression was harsh, with land confiscated and summary executions. In 1672, the Catalan language was displaced by French in both schooling and the church. Further restrictions followed and by the mid-eighteenth century, the language had been largely displaced by French for all public uses. This loss of this area has remained a part of Catalan historical memory and the zone is still called today Catalunya Nord (northern Catalonia). For Catalans, this has further significance in that this territorial loss has been accepted in Spanish political culture whilst that of Gibraltar continues to be a source of contention and resentment. In the Catalan civil war of 1462–1472, we have seen how the conflict had little that could be termed a national conflict, with the mass of the Catalan peasantry siding with a Castilian monarch against Catalan elites. Yet the revolt of 1640, complex and with distinctive positions in Catalan society, can be partly framed within a national context.[55] Thus, whilst 1640 was not a nationalist rebellion in the modern sense, neither was it simply a popular revolt absent of a national component.[56] Yet the war was later remembered and is still framed by some as a nationalist revolt and the short-lived appearance of the first Catalan Republic is still honoured. Once again, in historical memory, it is the framing of events that matters.

Notes

1 Marfany, J. L. (2001) *La llengua maltractada*, Barcelona: Empúries, p. 237.

2 Phillips, C. (2007) 'Family and Community in the Spanish World', in Parker, C. and Bentley, J. (eds.) *From the Middle Ages to Modernity: Individual and Community in the Early Modern World*, Lanham, MD: Rowman & Littlefield, pp. 71–90.

3 Roig, J. (1988) *Llibre de les dones*, Barcelona: Laertes, p. 132.

4 Alanyà i Roig, J. (2005) 'Culte i devoció a la Puríssima al bisbat de Tortosa (segles XIII-XXI)', *Analecta Sacra Tarraconensia*, vol. 78, pp. 159–308.

5 Soler, A. (2018) 'El català i altres llengües en concurrència a la cort i a la cancelleria napolitanes d'Alfons el Magnànim', *Caplletra*, no. 65, pp. 43–67.

6 Ferrer i Mallol, M. T. and Coulon, D. (1999) *L'expansió catalana a la Mediterrània a la Baixa Edat Mitjana*, Barcelona: CSIC, Institució Milà i Fontanals, pp. 341–359.

7 Ryder, A. (1976) *The Kingdom of Naples Under Alfonso the Magnanimous: The Making of a Modern State*, Oxford: Clarendon Press, pp. 303–305.

8 Feliu i Montfort, G. (1996) 'El règim senyorial català als segles XVI i XVII', *Pedralbes: Revista d'historia moderna*, no. 16, pp. 31–46.

9 Freedman, P. (1991) *The Origins of Peasant Servitude in Medieval Catalonia*, Cambridge University Press, pp. 179–180.

10 Parareda, A. and Sala, P. J. (2003) *Via fora, lladres! la revolta dels remences contra la servitud feudal*, Barcelona: Barcanova, pp. 33–34.

11 Sobrequés, S. (1973) 'La política remença de la monarquia en temps d'Alfons el Magnànim', in Sobrequés i Vidal, S. and Sobrequés i Callicó, J. (eds.) *La guerra civil catalana del segle xv. Estudis sobre la crisi social i econòmica de la Baixa Edat Mitjana, vol. 1: Causes i desenvolupament de la crisi*, Barcelona, Edicions 62, pp. 11–39.

12 Lluch i Bramon, R. (2000) 'Els pagesos medievals: els remences', *Revista de Girona*, no. 202, pp. 63–66.

13 Femández Trabal, J. (1999) 'De Prohoms a ciudadanos honrados. Aproximación al estudio de las elites urbanas de la sociedad catalana bajomedieval (s. XIV-XV)', *Revista d'Historia Medieval*, no. 10, pp. 331–372.

14 Sentañes, E. M. (2006) *Lleida a les corts. Els síndics municipals a l'època d'Alfonso el Magnànim*, Lleida: Edicions de la Universitat de Lleida, pp. 91–92.

15 Ryder, A. (2007) *The Wreck of Catalonia. Civil War in the Fifteenth Century*, Oxford: Oxford University Press, pp. 262–265.

16 Fernández i Trabal, J. (2002) 'El conflicte remença a la Catalunya del segle xv (1388–1486)', *Afers*, nos. 42–43, pp. 582–624.

17 Serra i Puig, E. (1980) 'El règim feudal català abans i després de la sentència arbitral de Guadalupe', *Recerques: història, economia, cultura*, no. 10, pp. 17–32.

18 Freedman, P. (1999) *Images of the Medieval Peasant*, Stanford: Stanford University Press, pp. 117–118.

19 Ribas, P. G. (2011) *Delmes, censos i Lluïsmes. El feudalisme tardà a la Catalunya vella (Vegueria de Girona, S. XVI-XVIII)*, Girona: Documenta Universitària.

20 Gual, V. (2008) 'El punt de partida de l'agricultura moderna. De la Sentència arbitral de Guadalupe i les Germanies a la crisi de finals del cinc-cents', in Giralt, A. (ed.) *Història agrària dels Països Catalans. Vol. 3. Edat moderna*, Barcelona: Universitat de Barcelon, pp. 13–30.

21 Dantí i Riu, J. (1986) 'El Vallès Oriental a l'època moderna: el creixement demogràfic i econòmic als segles XVI i XVII', *Pedralbes: Revista d'historia moderna*, no. 6, pp. 197–207.

22 Serrano Daura, J. (2019) 'Una aproximación a la Corona de Aragón de Fernando el Católico', *Revista de Dret Històric Català*, no. 18, pp. 35–97.

23 Serra i Puig, E. (2003) 'Poder polític: municipi, Generalitat i virrei', *Barcelona: quaderns d'història*, no. 9, pp. 25–50.

24 Baraut, C. (1996) 'Els inicis de la inquisició a Catalunya i les seves actuacions al bisbat d´Urgell (segles XII-XIII)', *Urgellia: Anuari d'estudis històrics dels antics comtats de Cerdanya, Urgell i Pallars, d'Andorra i la Vall d'Aran*, no. 13, pp. 407–438.

25 Cuscó i Clarasó, J. (2005) *Els beguins, l'heretgia a la Catalunya medieval*, Barcelona: Publicacions de l'Abadia de Montserrat, pp. 78–79.

26 Vicens Vives, J. (1936) *Ferran II i la ciutat de Barcelona*, Barcelona: Universitat de Catalunya, vol. 1, p. 374.

27 Bada i Elias, J. (2009) 'L'Expulsió dels jueus, 1492', *Butlletí de la Societat Catalana d'Estudis Històrics*, no. 20, pp. 51–68.

28 Kamen, H. (1993) *The Phoenix and the Flame. Catalonia and the Counter Reformation*, New Haven and London: Yale University Press, p. 436.

29 Simon i Tarrés, A. (1992) 'La població catalana a l'epoca moderna. Síntesi i actualització', *Manuscrits*, no. 10, pp. 217–258.

30 Feliu i Montfort, G. (1999) 'La demografia baixmedieval catalana estat de la qüestió i propostes de futur', *Revista d'historia medieval*, no. 10, pp. 13–44.

31 Capdevila Muntadas, M. A. (2004) 'La inmigració francesa un factor decisiu de la recuperació demogràfica de la comarca del Maresme a l'època moderna?' *Estudis d'història agrària*, no. 17, pp. 231–242.

32 Simon i Tarrés, A. (1992) 'La població catalana a l'època moderna. Síntesi i actualització', *Manuscrits. Revista d'història moderna*, no. 10, pp. 217–258.

33 Millàs i Castellví, C. (2005) *Els altres catalans dels segles XVI i XVII. La immigració francesa al Baix Llobregat*, Barcelona: Publicacions de l'Abadia de Montserrat, p. 85.

34 Narváez Cases, C. (2005) 'El patronatge de les noves oligarquies urbanes a l'art català dels segles XVI i XVII', *Recerques: Història, economia i cultura*, no. 51, pp. 5–25.

35 Anderson, P. (1974) *Lineages of the Absolutist State*, London: New Left Books, pp. 75–77.

36 Torres i Sans, X. (1985) 'Les bandositats de Nyerros i Cadells a la Reial Audiència de Calalunya (1590-1630) Policia o Alto gobierno?' *Pedralbes: Revista d'historia moderna*, no. 5, pp. 147–174.

37 Corteguera, L. (2018) *For the Common Good Popular Politics in Barcelona, 1580–1640*, Ithaca, NY: Cornell University Press, p. 105.

38 Plaza, C. and Fuguet, J. (2020) *Història de la Conca de Barberà. Cultura tradicional i cultural*, Tarragona: Publicacions URV, p. 270.

39 Reglà, J. (1965) *El bandolerisme català del barroc*, Barcelona: Edicions 62, pp. 187–188.

40 Carrió Arumí, J. (2014) 'La política militar hispànica i la persecució de bandolers a Catalunya en els segles XVI-XVII', *Recerques: història, economia, cultura*, no. 69, pp. 99–130.

41 Torres i Sans, X. (1998) 'Les bandositats de "nyerros" i "cadells": bandolerisme català o "feudalisme bastard"?' *Pedralbes: Revista d'historia moderna*, no. 18(1), pp. 227–242.

42 Solà i Colomer, X. (2016) 'Petits hospitals rurals: caritat, misèria i supervivència en els segles XVI i XVII. Alguns exemples de pobles de la Garrotxa i la Selva', *Annals del Patronat d'Estudis Històrics d'Olot i Comarca*, no. 27, pp. 99–133.

43 Cabruja i Vallès, E. (2008) 'Inestabilitat i conflictes socials. La baronia de la Conca d'Òdena en el transcurs dels segles moderns', *Pedralbes, Revista d'historia moderna*, no. 28, pp. 505–520.

44 Ibars, T. (1994) *La delinqüència a la Lleida del Barroc*, Lleida: Pagès editors, pp. 133–136.

45 Castell Granados, P. (2012) 'La persecución de la brujería en el Pirineo leridano (ss. XV-XVI)', in Villanueva, C. (ed.) *Estudios Recientes de Jóvenes Medievalistas*, Lorca: Universidad de Murcia-Sociedad Española de Estudios Medievales, pp. 25–38.

46 Knutsen, G. W. (2009) *Servants of Satan and Masters of Demons: The Spanish Inquisition's Trials of Superstition, Valencia and Barcelona, 1478–1700*, Valencia and Barcelona, 1478–1700, Turnhout: Brepols Publishers, pp. 85–86.

47 Alcoberro i Pericay, A. (2008) 'Cacera de bruixes, justícia local i Inquisició a Catalunya, 1487-1643: alguns criteris metodològics', *Pedralbes: Revista d'historia moderna*, no. 28(2), pp. 485–504.

48 Casey, J. (1999) *Early Modern Spain. A Social History*, London: Routledge, pp. 120 and 172.

49 Belenguer Cebria, E. (1993) 'La monarquia hispànica i la Corona d' Aragó. El progressiu qüestionament del pactism a Catalunya', *Pedralbes: Revista d'historia moderna*, no. 13(1), pp. 207–216.

50 Serra i Puig, E. (2013) 'La crisi del segle XVII i Catalunya', *Butlletí de la Societat Catalana d'Estudis Històrics*, no. 24, pp. 297–315.

51 Roma i Casanovas, F. (2017) 'El magne diluvi de 1617 en les seves fonts', *AUSA*, no. 179, pp. 213–231.

52 Amelang, J. (1992) 'Distribució social i formes de vida', in Sobrequés, J. (ed.) *Història de Barce-lona. Vol. IV*, Barcelona: Enciclopèdia Catalana, pp. 165–211.

53 Elliott, J. H. (1984) *The Revolt of the Catalans: A Study in the Decline of Spain (1598–1640)*, Cambridge: Cambridge University Press.

54 Elliott, J. H. (1997) 'Revolution and Continuity in Early Modern Europe', in Parker, G. and Smith, L. (eds.) *The General Crisis of the Seventeenth Century*, London: Routledge, pp. 109–127.

55 Simon i Tarrés, A. (1999) 'Ideologia i identitat nacional a la Revolució Catalana de 1640', *Cercles: revista d'història cultural*, no. 2, pp. 10–23.

56 Torres i Sans, X. (1995) 'Pactisme i patriotisme a la Catalunya de la Guerra dels Segadors', *Recerques: Història, economia i cultura*, no. 32, pp. 45–62.

6

1660–1830 POLITICAL INCORPORATION, ECONOMIC ADVANCE

Until the nineteenth century, transport and communications continued to occur at the same pace as much of the middle ages. Even so we find much greater movement of population than in previous centuries, in particular through migration from the countryside to urban areas. Throughout Europe the state form was also undergoing rapid change. A shift in which Castile, its political culture and language increasingly became synonymous with Spain. The Spanish regime sought to emulate the centralising model of France yet much of the history of Spain from the 1660s is a failure to do so. The Hispanic Monarchy was immersed in a profound crisis. Spain lost most of its European dominions becoming much more oriented to Spanish-America than previously. This is a Spain that is no longer a great power and enters a long spiral of decline, lasting until late into the twentieth century. The Spanish state was virtually bankrupt and was negatively impacted by the new European land power: France. The strategic position of Catalonia, straddling most of the Pyrenees frontier with France and with extensive access to the Mediterranean, deepened the determination of the rulers of Spain to control the territory. The peace treaty between France and Spain also concerned itself with issues of trade and smuggling. Whilst France assimilated the northern Catalan territory acquired in 1659, the Spanish administration was so weakened it was required to be accommodating with local regional elites. The end of conflict in 1652 had led neither to reprisals nor the abolition of the Catalan institutions. Traditional rights (furs) were largely upheld and respected and this became known as a neo-foralist policy. Whilst many of the upper echelons were content to obtain privileged roles in the new post-1652 regime, it did not mean that they had abandoned their political culture wholesale. The defence of regional institutions remained ingrained. When the possibility of a French Bourbon monarch taking the throne of Spain in 1705 took place, we find anti-French hostility and attachment to a confederal political system in Spain a part explanation of the Catalan revolt that leads to the dramatic events of 1714.

DOI: 10.4324/9781003218791-7

A new revolt

War between France and the Spanish monarchy was near constant between 1659 and 1697. Catalonia developed its strong anti-French sentiment as a result of repeated French occupations of Catalan territory which were marked by abuses and harassment of the population. In 1675, Louis XIV asserted the permanence of the new frontier with Spain by the completion of the defensive system of the Pyrenees. During the Nine Years' War (1689–1697), French troops occupied much of Catalonia and held Barcelona for four months. Barcelona submitted after a lengthy siege with substantial civilian casualties.[1] War with France entailed the constant presence of Spanish soldiers. The Catalan revolt of 1640 had many causes, yet one we noted was that of the forced billeting of troops. Defeat in 1652 had negative consequences for the Catalan peasantry, including increased indebtedness and pressure from local lords.[2] Just 20 years after resolution in 1659, the same issue produced a new outburst of popular rebellion. The stationing of the Spanish army incurred great costs on rural areas and discontent grew with the casual indiscipline of the troops. The economic situation had itself deteriorated in 1687 after a locust plague had damaged crops. A soldier who sought to take a hen from a peasant woman was the spark that led to a new revolt.[3] The Revolt of the Barretines, as it became known, was both social protest movement and popular uprising in the countryside.[4] The situation worsened when a new system of taxes was decreed to be collected by the nobility. The revolt proper broke out in the Llobregat plain and insurgents blockaded the city of Barcelona.[5] The revolt required harsh repression to subdue but was achieved as peasants had no support from Catalan elites as they had seen how the previous peasant revolt of 1640 had rapidly turned against them. Left to stand alone, the peasantry was defeated though concessions on billeting costs accrued were made. Conflict between lord and peasant was also evident with a series of revolts in 1688 where again the lordly class aligned itself with the viceroy and government authorities.

Economic revival

Economic recovery in the Catalan economy contrasted with developments in Castile, where stagnation and decline was evident. For Catalonia, a new period of the expansion of the land under cultivation occurred, with processes of forest clearing and new methods of cultivation being introduced. Farming that usually only supplied basic subsistence needs became increasingly productive providing surpluses. With new sources of income, some sectors now had opportunities to consolidate or invest in early industry. Even so, these advances remained modest as Catalonia, as we have seen, continued to be affected by a state of near permanent war with France. Later in the century, during the period of the French revolutionary and Napoleonic wars, major disruption will occur. Yet for now, changes were underway leading to a reconfiguration of the social structure in the countryside with the consolidation of an elite peasantry.[6] Throughout the second half of the eighteenth century, objects that were previously unknown appeared in modest homes, such as napkins, spoons and forks.[7] Differentiation between those able to buy these basic commodities and those too poor to do so indicated changes underway in the social structure. These changes then represented a shift from a medieval system of mostly self-sufficiency though in most cases, the farmhouse remained the main locus of production.

Access to land was a fundamental requirement for marriage, where the eldest son inherited the whole estate of his father.[8] The figure of the hereu (heir) prevented the fragmentation of smallholdings that occurred in other zones in Spain. Male figures in the family who did not inherit were those most likely to leave the land and migrate to the urban zones. Marriage had a clear social function in the countryside allowing the transfer of property to the next generation. Where landholdings between families were concerned, agreements were established where those to be married were simply pieces in the negotiation.[9] The situation became ever more pressured for poorer indebted peasants. Common lands were subject to privatisation, with access to woods and forests limited, leading to increased social conflict.[10] This conflict over the commons was increasingly common in many areas of Europe. Land that had been abandoned was brought into use and devoted to wheat, olives and vines. Changes in land owning led to increased concentration in fewer hands, produced growing numbers of day labourers, some of whom migrated to the cities. At certain times of the year, large numbers moved around in search of temporary work, whether on the land or in search of other forms of work. Landless day labourers were numerous and survived with difficulty.[11] Many of them began to emigrate to the cities which in time would form a new industrial urban working class. Thus, society was becoming much more complex than had been known in previous eras.

The city of Barcelona began to experience sustained economic revival and growth. What was distinctive about this period was the growing inter-connectedness of Barcelona with other urban zones.[12] By the early eighteenth century, Barcelona was developing an increasingly sophisticated political culture.[13] In this context, economic ideas flourished amongst an emerging merchant elite. The leading figure to emerge for the framing of an early Catalan capitalism was Narcís Feliu de la Penya who crafted a strategy for economic progress.[14] He sought to devise an economy policy where Catalonia could emulate English and in particular Dutch commercial economies. The Dutch Republic achieved notable advances in agriculture and trade, partly enabled by wealth obtained in the slave trade. Feliu de la Penya attached great importance to the textile industry as a lever of economic growth. He was also deeply anti-French. He took part in the defence of Barcelona during the siege of 1697 and campaigned for protectionist measures against the entry of French manufactures into the country. With much of Spain in a pessimistic cycle of decline, it was significant that Feliu de la Penya advocated greater Catalan involvement and leadership in the economic development of Spain, a notion we will return to.

War of the Spanish Succession

By 1700, Spain had ceased to be a major power in Europe and the evidence of the weakness of Spain was the outbreak of the War of the Spanish Succession (1701–1713). This war has its origins in the struggle to obtain European dominance fought out between the two great European powers of the period, the Austrian Habsburgs and the French Bourbon dynasty. The death of King Charles II of Spain without an heir in 1700 led to an attempt by both European powers to place their preferred candidate on the Spanish throne. The war that broke out in 1701 had complex European entanglements and shifting alliances, with the conflict itself testimony to the diminished status of Spain as it was other powers that decided who would be Spain's ruler. Spain split internally with much of the kingdom of Castile, including the Basque zones, supportive of the French Bourbon claim, whilst the territories of the kingdom of Aragon (including Catalonia) supported the Austrian Habsburg claimant. The War of the Spanish Succession can also be seen as a type of civil war within Spain, with the country split from west to east over its preferred pretender. Catalans generally believed that the French Bourbon tradition would erode their traditional privileges. Amongst the privileged sectors of society, the French were also their commercial rivals. When the Habsburg pretender visited Catalonia he was warmly welcomed.[15] This was not though a war of secession, but rather a defence of a type of monarchical regime.

The war began to be fought out in the Iberian Peninsula and in 1707, with the victory of Almansa in Valencia, Philip V conquered the regions of Aragon and Valencia. The king immediately suppressed the autonomous institutions of both territories, making it very clear that he did not intend to forgive the disloyalty of his rebellious kingdoms. Thus, defeat would mean the annihilation of Catalan institutions. At the beginning of 1711, with the fall of Girona, only Vic, Cardona, Tarragona and Barcelona remained for the cause of Archduke Carles. The wider European conflict was officially brought to a close by the Treaty of Utrecht of 1713, with the French candidate victorious. Britain received important concessions from France in Canada and Gibraltar from Spain. Thus satisfied, the British abandoned their previous allies in Spain, including the Catalans. Yet the Catalans did not accept the result of the Treaty even though they stood alone after Habsburg and British forces left Spain in July 1713. Catalans hoped that the constantly shifting international alliances that had been a feature of the whole war since 1701 might change again, providing them with new allies. However, this was not to be. Furthermore, early eighteenth century Barcelona was already a dynamic and wealthy city that no ruler would allow to fall into others hands.[16]

1714

The new Spanish Bourbon rulers first sought to pacify the Catalan countryside leaving only the city of Barcelona still resisting. During this rural pacification, reprisals against the peasants were brutal with hundreds of summary executions.[17] There was little to prevent Bourbon domination. By this time, there were over 85,000 Bourbon troops in a Catalan population not totalling more than half a million. Society fell under military occupation. By 1713, most of Catalan territory was in Bourbon hands leaving just the city of Barcelona and the town of Cardona still willing to resist. The harsh repression of much of the Catalan countryside only strengthened the willingness of the city of Barcelona to continue resistance. In June 1713, the Barcelona authorities met and initially decided to capitulate. However, the decision to surrender was overturned by popular and guild pressure. The defence of Barcelona was now organised. Repeated bombardment over the course of the year 1713–1714 was largely ineffective. Well-organised local forces allowed the city to hold out for over a year, and morale within the city mostly remained high. To break the deadlock, new French reinforcements arrived in July 1714. The final assault took place in the early morning of 11 September. Over 18,000 troops took part. Even so, the defenders remained capable of intense resistance and great losses again occurred. The final hours of the siege saw fierce hand to hand fighting, house by house, street by street, resulting in terrible destruction to the city. Estimates of the total losses amongst the defenders are around 7,000–8,000 dead and wounded, whilst losses for the besiegers are believed to total at least 10,000 with an upper figure at a high of 15,000.[18] Barcelona was conquered.

Post-1714

In contrast to the former territories of the crown of Aragon, Navarre and the Basque Country retained significant autonomy until well into the nineteenth century as they had not backed the Austrian side. For those who had been defeated, however, a different policy was pursued. The defeat of Catalonia and the wider territories of the former Kingdom of Aragon led to the abolition of the traditional local rights and privileges maintained since the middle ages. The Spanish Bourbon victors of 1713–1714, inspired by the model of France, began a process of centralisation which included the standardisation of linguistic and cultural differences. Unlike the outcome of 1652, this time there was no forgiveness for the vanquished. The new ruling system for the defeated regions was militaristic. The traditional figure of the civilian viceroy was also replaced by that of a military Captain-General. The whole population was banned from carrying weapons, including sharp knives. This policy extended to the small university sector. The then existing universities of Lleida, Barcelona, Girona, Tarragona, Tortosa and Solsona were closed and their activity transferred to a new location of Cervera, a town seemingly rewarded for its loyalty to the Bourbon king. This remained the only Catalan university until the 1830s. Even in this period of conquest, a number of small-scale revolts broke out on several occasions in the 1720s and 1730s. To ensure that resistance from the city of Barcelona might never be possible again, an enormous military fortress, the Ciutadella, was built overlooking the city, being completed in 1725. Over 6,000 Bourbon troops were permanently stationed in Barcelona, with some 20,000 more remaining in Catalan territory.[19] Most of the new high-ranking posts were held by Castilians, though sufficient numbers of local nobility were content to assist in their rule. 1714 has become embedded in Catalan historical memory as the moment when Catalan political identity was destroyed. Yet in 1814, there was no marking of this event and the re-interpreting of the meaning of 1714 is something that is constructed later in the nineteenth century. As elsewhere in Europe, it will be the rise of nationalism that will craft a narrative of difference and national revival.

The Church

Catholicism in Catalonia retained its centrality throughout this period, though most of the bishops during the War of the Spanish Succession supported the Bourbon dynasty. The parish network of the middle ages retained its structure and permanence in everyday life.[20] The theology of the counter-Reformation contributed to religious fervour and in a city such as Girona, the continued dominance of the church held back both cultural and economic development.[21] The locust plague of 1687–1688 saw clerics leading a campaign of prayer. Where necessary religious buildings were subject to repair, religious processions became an almost weekly event. The religious brotherhoods were one of the key expressions of popular religiosity. Just between 1650 and 1702, there are 37 new approved brotherhoods.[22] Church-run hospitals expanded, administering a form of social welfare to the poor, homeless and marginalised.[23] The Catalan language became more used, where it substituted Latin in preaching and administration.[24] However, the new post-1714 regime saw increasing use of Spanish and at the level of bishop, these appointments were frequently from other areas of Spain. Spanish became increasingly used in the seminaries in Catalonia. However, in the local parish, Catalan continued to be used with complete normality and the increasing use of documentation in Spanish had little impact on a population with at best limited literacy. The church, however, remained a wealthy landowner and organisation. The church was deeply embedded in the power structure and the new century would bring an increasing anti-clerical culture.

Population growth

By the end of the seventeenth century, there was, in general terms, a decline in mortality and an increase in the birth rate, with earlier marriage than other areas of Spain.[25] Early marriage suggested confidence in the future. The eighteenth century represented a demographic revolution in terms of population growth. Between the census of 1717 and 1787, the Catalan population grew by 70 per cent. Although the population earlier in the century was greater than once believed, this is still a remarkable increase.[26] This also represented an important increase in the proportion of the Catalan population within Spain from 7.25 per cent to 9.5 per cent. This growth occurred throughout the territory, in urban, rural and mountainous zones.[27] These changes impacted on increased marriage rates, even in the cases of those who had little to inherit, which also led to the building of new homes. Where the land could not cope with population growth, the outcome was migration.[28] In spite of periodic shortages and the return of plagues at times, the birth rate rise was able to overcome disruption. The ever-increasing efficiency of the agricultural sector was key to ensuring that food shortages were infrequent. To avoid the potential of shortages and even famine, more land was brought into cultivation.

Economic and social recovery

As in most areas of Western Europe, the eighteenth century is a century of economic expansion. It is widely accepted that whilst the war and siege of 1714 represented political defeat, the medium- and long-term economic consequences were much more favourable in the Catalan case. As part of its project of harmonisation and modernisation, the new Bourbon regime removed trade barriers within Spain which rapidly gave Catalonia economic advantage in much of the peninsula.[29] The country was beginning to develop an internal market. During this century, trade improved, both within Catalonia and abroad. Philip V issued a series of decrees banning the import of cotton fabrics and that preference be given to domestic products in the purchase of military supplies. This meant that the cotton industry in Spain, which was essentially synonymous with Catalonia, was given an unusually high degree of support.[30] Printed cotton was imported from India and the first textile factories were established between 1736 and 1738. At the end of the century, there were a hundred textile companies in Catalonia and the foundations of the modern cotton industry were already in place. Britain's war with America in the 1770s permitted a new opportunity for Catalan cotton.[31] By 1790, Catalan cotton production was second only to that of England. Types of production varied with home-work being one form. This provided an extra source of income to both middling and poorer sectors. This was a type of industry that impacted on the countryside through the transfer to rural areas of textile activities.[32] Women's role in society was increasing through the putting out system of the textile industry. Women, in spite of the long days of work, with shifts normally at least 12 hours, also moved to the new factories and became, though subject to factory discipline, relatively autonomous through acquiring their own income. Child labour of those aged between 9 and 14 was already in evidence in these early factories.[33] The textile industry was joined by expansion in the agricultural sector, particularly of brandy and wine production. These products became increasingly lucrative meaning that land growing of cereal was much reduced. Abundance of olive trees generated a production of oil important enough to dedicate it to export. This was increasingly a commercial agriculture.[34] Their export allowed the import of essential products for domestic consumption, such as wheat, salt or plants for dyeing.[35] Thus, we can increasingly speak of a new capitalist agrarian model in the second half of the eighteenth century.[36]

End of the Seville monopoly

The contours of Catalan economic expansion were greatly facilitated by the end of what was known as the Seville monopoly, meaning that all Spanish exports were required to first pass through this port. In 1765, this trade was liberalised for nine Spanish ports, a list which included Barcelona. The port became increasingly important to the city's expansion. Trade in a range of goods, imports and exports could be conducted via the port and at greater speed than land routes. It was the industrialising Catalan urban areas that produced a commercial class that crafted trading networks with other areas of Spain.[37] Thus, new markets were being added both internationally and within Spain. Trade liberalisation led to rapid economic growth, providing sales opportunities to wine and brandy and in particular intensifying production in the textile trade. Other industries such as paper, iron and shipbuilding were stimulated due to demands from overseas. In the latter decades of the century, about 20,000 people worked in the cotton industry in Barcelona alone whilst Mataró, Olot, Manresa, Vic and Vilanova also benefited. We can see the impact on growth in a small town in the Girona region, Tortella, whose population constantly expanded until the 1830s.[38] Reus became Catalonia's second city, growing from some 4,000 to 16,000 inhabitants by 1802 and was a magnet for the surplus rural workforce. Barcelona was increasingly an industrial city and was now polluted by coal and fumes from the dye factories.[39] These elements, agricultural expansion, growing overseas trade and emergent industry, combined to produce a virtuous cycle of growth until the French Revolution.

Popular protest

Conflict in the countryside never entirely ceased, but most incidents remained of a local character. The growth of an agriculture designed for profit meant anti-lord struggles intensified as the century proceeded. From mid-century rent increases were the catalyst for greater protest.[40] Catalonia's rebellious culture was evident in a series of riots in towns including such as Mataró, Vic, Tarragona, Lleida and Girona and Cervera.[41] In 1773, what became known as the revolt de les quintes broke out against an attempt at forced military recruitment which impacted on the poor disproportionately. Communities organised to prevent a forced call-up and assisted those who fled to the mountain areas. Growing discontent led to revolt in Barcelona in May 1773. Troops fired on the crowds and relative peace was restored. However, the measure was withdrawn. Food shortages and clashes with the authorities occurred with frequency throughout the century, though rarely large in scale. Three months before the outbreak of the French Revolution in France, on 28 February 1789, Barcelona experienced a popular uprising. There had been a series of poor harvests, and on the day the protest broke out, basic foodstuffs like bread had seen a price rise of 50 per cent. For those who financial situation was always precarious, price rises which meant basic commodities such as bread could not be afforded produced collective outrage. A deep-rooted popular culture of revolt was finding new forms of expression. Women played a major role in the revolt and a leading figure was Josepa Vilaret, who was later executed. Until this point, the family remained the place that decided women's role in society. Women were permitted to be single, married or widows with the only alternative being the nunnery. The bread revolt and women's part in it indicated that a new political subject was emerging: woman as rebel.

Organising modernisation

As the Catalan economy continued its development, new ideas and organisations appeared to direct what was increasingly a commercial revolution. As an indication that previous political conflicts were of lesser importance, relations tended to improve between trading elites in Catalan cities and their rulers in Madrid.[42] In 1758, the Junta de Comerç de Barcelona (Board of Trade) was created with a view to influencing economic policy and as it developed, it launched technical schools as well as science-based vocational training.[43] This organisation then can be seen as part of the emergence in Europe of civic engagement with learning and development, or what was termed at the time as improvement. The Junta acted as a lobby in Madrid and sought to promote innovation and modernisation in all areas and was supportive of measures to remove internal trading barriers. This body acted as an institution that communicated the interests of a new business class. In parallel to this scientific and economic strategy, the Junta also engaged in cultural patronage and the key figure to emerge from this policy was Antoni de Capmany. In 1779, the first part of Capmany's Memorias históricas sobre la marina, comercio y artes de la Antigua Ciudad de Barcelona (Historical Memoirs on the Navy, Commerce and Arts of the Old City of Barcelona) was published in Barcelona, with the final volume in 1792. This work of economic history represented a model of history writing in the rationalist mode, supported by great empirical data. Capmany also produced material on contemporary economic issues, and as with his predecessor earlier in the century, Feliu de la Penya, he too looked to Holland and Britain as models for capitalist and commercial development. As an indication of the growing differentiation of Catalonia from most Spanish regions that did not develop economically, Capmany formulated the notion of an increasingly advanced and productive Catalonia.[44] Capmany's ideas had a long-lasting influence and he can be considered as a leading figure of a new intellectual tradition.

Language

Since the end of the war in 1714, Spanish had been established as the sole language of the administration, although this had a relatively limited impact on the public life of the Catalan language. This process would also be applied to Latin which had been the language normally used in the education sector. This policy was not necessarily linguistic persecution and should be situated with a wish amongst Spanish rulers for the political and cultural harmonisation to be established in its territory. In reality, however, it could only mean the diminution of status of the Catalan language. As the century proceeded, a clear shift was evident in terms of the Spanish language as one holding prestige and status, with legislation ensuring its dominance. This process was intensified with a policy of primary education to be delivered in

Spanish of 1768 and a number of proscriptive measures around publishing books in Catalan passed in the 1770s.[45] This meant that works on history, science and political economy produced in Catalonia were invariably written in Spanish in this period.[46] The higher status of Spanish would not be reversed until well into the nineteenth century. We see a differential process at work depending on social class. For the upper echelons of Catalan society, the adoption or use of Spanish had clear utility, whether easing trading encounters, reaching a wider audience or achieving social advance. However, amongst most of the population who were outside of the structures of power and formal education, the Catalan language remained their everyday means of communication. Beyond the key centres of power or urban residence, a process of linguistic substitution advanced little. However, by the end of the century, Catalan barely existed as a language of high culture and it ran the risk of being marginalised and becoming simply a patois associated only with the rural world. Yet as we will see, this did not happen. The decades to come will also see a gradual reversal of the diminished status of the Catalan language, first indicated by the publishing of the Gramàtica i Apologia de la Llengua Catalana (Grammar and Defence of the Catalan Language) in 1813 by the cleric Josep Pau Ballot.

The French Revolution and Catalonia

The French Revolution of 1789 inevitably impacted greatly on Catalonia due to its proximity. More important of course was that this was a revolution that sought to spread its ideology, if necessary through force of arms. Catalonia had long been an entry point for French ambitions in Spain and it became so once again. The rebellious tradition of Catalonia seemed to make it an ideal terrain for the activity of revolutionary committees and distribution of propaganda. The committee established in the former Catalan city of Perpinyà, since 1659 in France, seemed to make it an ideal point for the launch point of revolution. The popular revolt that had taken place in Barcelona just a few months before the French Revolution also seemed to indicate that Catalan society would embrace the revolutionary cause. However, French revolutionaries rapidly discovered that Catalan society was not only deeply anti-French but it also retained profound attachment to the Catholic church.[47] The outcome was strong hostility to the new French revolutionary regime. The church in Catalonia became one of the centres of counter-revolutionary ideology, which continued into the Napoleonic period.[48] French religious escapees were welcomed by the Catalan church and it became, as elsewhere in Spain, hostile to the liberal and anti-religious culture promulgated by the French Revolution.[49] Political exiles in Catalonia organised the counter-revolution and created local forces willing to assist European reaction in the assault on the Revolution.

In 1793, Spain declared war on France, a period which lasted until 1795, becoming part of the European anti-revolutionary coalition. This period of conflict was fought out above all in the former Catalan zone of France, the Rosselló, which Spanish forces sought to occupy. 20,000 permanent troops stationed in Catalonia were increased to over 30,000, and together with Navarre and the Basque Country, were the key zones of war with France. By late 1794, a mass French revolutionary army began a counter-offensive, sweeping all before it. Over 60,000 forces were sent to fight a now outnumbered Spanish force. Spanish troops were expelled from the Rosselló and the French army began its counter-offensive. French conquest of the frontier fortress of Figueres in 1794 was a major blow to the Spanish forces, with heavy losses. The surrender of some 9,000 Spanish troops without much resistance being offered was a minor scandal at the time. French forces now entered Spanish Catalonia and distributed revolutionary material in Catalan. Whilst there were sectors in Catalan society supportive of the revolutionary agenda, for the mass of the population, the French forces were simply deemed an invading army rather than being seen as radical in political terms. French attacks on religious buildings and executions of prisoners ensured that popular resistance quickly emerged. After the Peace of Basel was signed in 1795, Spain undertook to fight alongside France against Britain. This period of changing alliances represented increasing turmoil in the ruling order in Madrid at the posture of Spain, with the Prime Minister Godoy becoming the embodiment of anti-French resentment. As a consequence of the new alliance with France, the British blocked trade with the Americas, which directly harmed Catalan trade interests.

Catalonia and Napoleon

In October 1807, Spain and France signed the Treaty of Fontainebleau, which authorised French troops to cross Spain to attack Portugal. It soon became clear that the French not only intended to traverse Spain but also to occupy Spanish territory militarily. Brutal sieges ensured the conquest of major cities such as Tarragona and Girona. Massacres of civilians such as that in the case of Lleida contributed to rapid popular alienation. With the French installing Napoleon's brother as king of Spain, patriotic sentiment rallied around the Spanish monarch Ferdinand, even though he embodied the absolutist political tradition. French forces occupied Catalonia between 1808 and 1814. However, from the very beginning, attacks were launched against the invaders with rural Catalonia being the principal centre of resistance. This became a sustained war of attrition against French occupation with often extremely harsh responses by French forces on the ground. Confiscation of produce and harvests added to popular grievances. It is perhaps significant that whilst in Spain, the Napoleonic wars is known as the War of Independence, in Catalonia, it is remembered simply as the French War. In popular memory, hostility to France had been formed over the eighteenth century from resistance to the French Bourbon claimant in 1714, to the loss of a fifth of Catalan territory in 1659 and to the frequent wars with France, most recently in 1793–1795. As the century developed, there was a generalised Catalan acceptance of the Spanish monarchy, and former pro-Austrian sentiment gradually faded. Hostility as expressed in Catalonia in the period 1789–1815 was in fact directed at forces in Madrid and locally that supported accommodation with France. The pro-French sectors in Catalan society were mostly made of the upper echelons including some landowners, merchants and manufacturers, and bishops who felt it was necessary to align with the new power. However, at the popular level, hostility to the French occupiers was the dominant sentiment and was usually combined with defence of traditional religion. Only in the city of Barcelona was a notable divergence evident. With a distinctive urban culture, the city broadly accepted the new French rulers and their promise of citizenship.

After the conquest of most of the country, the French sought to win over the general population with an accommodationist policy. Marshal Augereau, the first Napoleonic governor in Catalonia, made the Catalan language, which had been banned from the public sphere since 1714, official and its usage was permitted within the administration. The daily Diari de Barcelona was published in Catalan and French. In 1812, two months before the proclamation of the Constitution of Cádiz, Catalonia was annexed to the French Empire. Four new administrative regions were created: Ter, Segre, Montserrat and Boques de l'Ebre, each with their departmental capital. Catalonia now became a French province. Over 2,000 French officials were sent to organise and harmonise Catalonia according to the French administrative and legal tradition. This attempted pro-Catalan policy did little to change the reality on the ground with a situation of near permanent guerrilla war in the interior of the country. A popular uprising which began in Madrid on 2 May 1808 and was severely repressed, led to a near revolutionary situation in much of the country. The traditional order seemingly collapsed and popular committees, known as juntes, took charge of the situation. The events of 1808 also disrupted the feudal order as peasants refused payment to their landlords. Catalan resistance to the French occupation, as in the rest of Spain, began spontaneously. Priests, landowners and educated sectors joined together in the organisation of the juntes in order to organise the anti-French struggle. The first to be created in Catalonia was that of Lleida, significantly presided over by the bishop. Whilst it became ever more evident since the 1790s that the value systems of countryside and city were diverging, those who would become post-war known as liberals and absolutists were temporarily united in the collective goal of removing the French occupiers. Whatever position Catalans held in terms of their status within Spain, this did not prevent Catalonia being part of the wider Spanish opposition.[50] All evidence points to the Catalans as sharing the same position as other areas of Spain throughout the conflict. No claims for the separation of Catalan territory from Spain were made.

1812 and the Constitution of Cadiz

What became for Spaniards the war of independence had a dramatic impact on the country's political culture. In 1810, the Central Supreme Junta convened the Cortes in Cádiz to draw up a Constitution, which was agreed in 1812. The Constitution established the basic parameters of a liberal and democratic regime including a separation of powers, universal male suffrage, individual rights and equality of all Spaniards before the law. The Constitution of 1812 was one of the most enlightened of Europe of the early nineteenth century. The political programme was broadly supported by an emergent bourgeois class, professionals as well as artisans and workers. However, the Catholic church and a range of conservatives throughout society remained hostile to its content. Twenty representatives from Catalonia attended Cádiz but they were a mostly a conservative cohort and sought to defend ancient privileges and resist the abolition of feudal dues. The 1812 Constitution of Cádiz was also an expression of Spanish national sovereignty which produced a centralisation of government and administration. The division of Spain into provincias followed the model initiated by France in the creation of the département and ended the official recognition of areas such as Catalonia and Galicia. The Constitution of Cadiz came to symbolise the dream of a liberal and modernising Spain and it would be invoked repeatedly in the decades to come. For its opponents, however, Cádiz represented an assault on tradition and conservatism.

Impact of the wars

The French revolutionary and Napoleonic wars were the most devastating conflict Catalonia experienced until the Spanish Civil War. Population losses numbered some 70,000, around 7–8 per cent of the population. War impoverished Catalonia, factories ceased production and trade was paralysed. Agriculture and livestock suffered very serious losses, with labour shortages meaning harvests were uncollected or confiscated by French troops. This was combined with dramatic falls in agricultural prices. At least a decade was necessary to re-establish production in sectors such as wine and olive oil. The wars and French occupation produced extensive destruction to the infrastructure of Catalonia. The population experienced the traditional ravages of war as well as brutal reprisals. The church and aristocracy suffered through forced confiscations and erosion to their positions under French rule. The resultant economic crisis brought a temporary halt in the growth of Catalonia.

Liberal restoration and reactionary revolt

In 1814, Catalonia returned to Spanish sovereignty. This was a fractured society due to the consequences of the Napoleonic War. The restoration of Spanish national sovereignty was seized as an opportunity by the monarchy to reverse the political gains at Cadiz. The monarch closed the Cortes of Cadiz and abolished the Constitution signed there. The new Spanish regime, as it sought to restore its authority, was bankrupt. The planned restoration of the Inquisition was not achieved nor was it possible to restore feudal privileges that had been abolished in 1811. Even so an ultra-reactionary political regime was installed which lasted until 1820. Relations were ruptured between the populace and their traditional rulers and the new regime of Ferdinand only maintained power through harsh repression of liberals. The Catalan church and the constituency it represented entered the modern world as deeply conservative and counter revolutionary. Some 3,000 Catalans of a liberal persuasion went into exile as the consequence of a hostile political climate. The militarisation of society meant that both political traditions, liberal and absolutist, now turned to arms to resolve political differences. Liberals carried out military rebellions or pronunciamientos with the aim of restoring the Constitution of 1812. The first attempted coup against absolutist control occurred in Catalonia in 1817 but failed to have much traction, and its leader, the Captain General of Catalonia Luis de Lacy was executed. However, this revolt indicated a new political culture was emerging with the public reading of proclamations and the communication of ideas. This gave a different tinge to events compared to those of the eighteenth century. The expansion of printing and the distribution of pamphlets and newspapers contributed to the building of a new cultural and political public sphere.

Spanish weakness after 1814 was used as an opportunity by independence movements in the American colonies, a process which continued until 1825 with the separation of most of Latin American possessions. Catalonia, had as we have seen become a major beneficiary of the Latin America trade. The process of independence in the early 1820s was a major blow to the Catalan export market.[51] Spain lost most of its former colonial empire in America and only held Cuba and Puerto Rico. The loss of most of the Spanish colonies was initially a major loss but in time Catalan interests made particularly Cuba central to its interests.[52] This was a Cuban economy based on the slave trade and numerous Catalan elites were financial beneficiaries of this servitude. Barcelona established itself as the main Spanish port throughout the nineteenth century. The political instability between 1814 and 1820 hindered economic recovery. The contours of an internally divisive nineteenth century were being laid down. Political disturbance was joined with continuing disruption with the climate one contributing factor. From the latter part of the eighteenth century harsher climatic conditions were evident. The little Ice Age impacted in Catalonia in varying measures including the freezing of the River Ebro at various points in the eighteenth century.[53] Winter lengthened for a period before a new period of gradual warming. As the climate transitioned to a warmer period in 1817, there was a severe drought which left the peasants without most of the harvest. This was one in a series of sustained droughts of varying intensity which occurred between 1812 and 1824, becoming the most severe water shortage in the history of modern Catalonia.[54] The final element in the deadly trilogy of war, famine and pestilence occurred in 1821, when Barcelona and some surrounding areas were hit by an outbreak of yellow fever, which resulted in the deaths of over 18,000.

Malcontents 1827

In 1820, a liberal coup successfully restored the Constitution of Cadiz and a three-year period of reform was renewed. With the return of a liberal administration, it is now the reactionary sectors of society that mobilise against it. The king asked for help from the Holy Alliance, which responding by sending to Spain a vast French force that became known as the Hundred Thousand Sons of St. Louis. This army defeated the liberals and restored the absolute monarchy of Ferdinand VII. The liberal experiment was over after just three years. However, this restoration was deemed too timid by ultra-reactionary sectors and their strength was made evident by the revolt of the Malcontents in 1827, which began in and was mostly centred in Catalonia. A number of factors explain the resort to arms beyond loyalty to an ultra-conservative ideology. Many were ex-combatants from the guerrilla wars against the French whom peace and the poor economic conditions had left many in penury.[55] They were attached to a deeply traditional monarchy in the person of Ferdinand and as well as fervent attachment to Catholicism. The rebellion began in April 1827 in Tortosa and soon spread to the rural areas of Girona. The rebels issued proclamations in favour of the Inquisition, as well as public criticism of the French and liberals.[56] The revolt spreads to other areas and at its peak comprised some 20,000. The rebels were sufficiently strong to lay siege to the cities of Girona and Tarragona. The malcontents used their knowledge of mountain areas to avoid capture and mounted lightning raids. The government seemed to have lost its ability to maintain safe passage through its own land. Only the arrival of the king in person seemed to halt the revolt as well as the intervention of the church. Harsh repression was meted out to those who had rebelled, including the execution of supposed ringleaders, with others exiled to Ceuta. What this conflict symbolised was that counter-revolutionary forces were prepared to resist violently all attempts at accommodation with liberal reform.

The Napoleonic war ruptured the old order and marked the beginning of the transition to a liberal regime. Traditional power relations had been disrupted by the reforms of Cadiz. Yet their power had been temporarily checked but not broken. The church and conservative sectors retained sufficient power to block reform. Equally, the new liberal block seeking the modernisation of the country and the establishment of a capitalist economy remained too weak to successfully push through their reforming ambitions. Thus, the story of Spain and Catalonia for most of the nineteenth century and beyond is an intense political dispute between supporters of ultra-conservative and liberal positions. This conflict between supporters and opponents of a gradually eroding Ancien Régime was resolved in arms on three further occasions in the nineteenth century. Major change in terms of industrialisation, urbanisation and associated changes in values such as secularisation contributed to a growing sense of crisis and anxiety. In the decades to come, the emergence of an urban working class added to the sense of a growing social conflict between urban and rural Catalonia. This had ideological, cultural and religious elements. Entry into the modern world would be particularly tumultuous in the Catalan case.

Notes

1 Albareda i Salvadó, J. (1995) 'L'impacte de la guerra dels Nou Anys a Catalunya. L'ocupació francesa de 1697', *Afers: fulls de recerca i pensament*, vol. 10, no. 20, pp. 29–46.
2 Olivares Periu, J. (1995) 'Plets i endeutament comunal en la immediata postguerra dels Segadors', *Recerques: Història, economia i cultura*, no. 33, pp. 33–52.
3 Camprubí i Pla, X. (2015) 'L'impacte dels allotjaments a Tona: de la Revolta dels Barretines (1687) al pas de l'exèrcit austriacista durant la Guerra de Successió (1711)', *Ausa*, no. 175, pp. 61–87.

4 Espino López, A. (2003) 'El coste de la guerra para la población civil: la experiencia catalana, 1653–1714', *Millars: Espai i historia*, no. 26, pp. 155–184.

5 Albareda, J. (1988) 'Els dirigents de la revolta pagesa de 1687–89: de barretines a botiflers', *Recerques*, no. 20, pp. 151–170.

6 Gifre i Ribas, P. (2003) 'La consolidació d'un grup pagès: els senyors útils i propietaris de masos (1486–1730)', *Revista Pedralbes*, no. 23, pp. 513–536.

7 Mas Ferrer, J. (2020) 'Pautes de consum i condicions de vida dels treballadors de la terra a partir dels inventaris post mortem a Catalunya: el cas de la Selva (1750–1805)', *Estudis d'Història Agrària*, no. 32, pp. 69–96.

8 Marfany, J. (2012) *Land, Proto-Industry and Population in Catalonia, c. 1680–1829, An Alternative Transition to Capitalism?* Farnham: Ashgate, pp. 96–97.

9 Baldor Abril, E., Cáceres, I. and Farràs Royo, N. (1995) 'Els recursos econòmics de la pagesia altafullenca: Segona meitat del segle XVIII', *Estudis altafullencs*, no. 19, pp. 19–38.

10 Badosa Coll, E. (1990) 'Endeutament col·lectiu i desaparició de béns comunals a Catalunya a la segona meitat del segle XVIII', *Pedralbes: revista d'història moderna*, no. 10, pp. 51–66.

11 Moreno Claverías, B. (2004) 'Les condicions materials de vida dels rabassers penedesencs al segle XVIII: treball, mercat i consum', *Estudis d'història agrària*, no. 17, pp. 615–630.

12 Torra Fernández, L. (2001) 'Botigues de teixits, crèdit comercial i crèdit al consum: Xarxes comercials a la Catalunya del segle XVIII', *Recerques: Història, economia i cultura*, no. 41, pp. 5–30.

13 Serra, E. (2016) 'Naixement de la concepció de la ciutadania: el marc històric', in *Dret, conflictes i justícia. Barcelona 1700*, Barcelona: Ajuntament de Barcelona, pp. 51–93.

14 Dantí i Riu, J. (2012) 'Catalunya entre el redreç i la revolta: afebliment institucional i diferenciació social', *Manuscrits. Revista d'Història Moderna*, no. 30, pp. 55–76.

15 O'Reilly, W. (2009) 'Lost Chances of the House of Habsburg', *Austrian History Yearbook*, vol. 40, pp. 53–70.

16 Garcia Espuche, A. (2014) 'Lliçons del setge de Barcelona (1713–1714)', *Gimbernat. Revista d'Història de la Medicina i de les Ciències de la Salut*, vol. 61, pp. 11–22.

17 Fontana, J. (2014) *La formació d'una identitat. Una història de Catalunya*, Vic: Eumo Editorial, pp. 224–225.

18 *Catalunya 1714: la Guerra de Successió: Ruta pels escenaris*, Barcelona: Ohdigital, 2014, p. 116.

19 Cata Tur, J. (2016) 'La repressió després de 1714: execucions, empresonaments i exili', in Puig i Oliver, J. (ed.) *1714*, Barcelona: Institut d'Estudis Catalans, pp. 101–107.

20 Puigvert i Sola, J. (1997) 'Església i territori en els orígens de la Catalunya contemporània', *Treballs de la Societat Catalana de Geografia*, no. 44, pp. 85–111.

21 Boadas i Raset, J. (1986) *Girona després de la guerra de succesió: riquesta urbana i estructura social al primer quart del segle XVIII*, Girona: Ajuntament, pp. 84–85.

22 Bada Elias, J. (1994) 'La religiositat popular al bisbat de Barcelona en la segona meitat del segle XVII: alguns indicadors', *Analecta Sacra Tarraconensia*, vol. 67, no. 2, pp. 259–269.

23 Solà i Colomer, X. (2016) 'Petits hospitals rurals: caritat, misèria i supervivència en els segles XVI i XVII. Alguns exemples de pobles de la Garrotxa i la Selva', *Annals del Patronat d'Estudis Històrics d'Olot i Comarca*, no. 27, pp. 99–134.

24 Agustí i Farreny, A. (1994) 'Els bisbes de Lleida i l'espanyolització (segles XVI-XVIII)', *Analecta Sacra Tarraconensia*, vol. 67, no. 2, pp. 233–245.

25 Muñoz Pradas, F. (1997) 'Fluctuaciones de precios y dinámica demográfica en Cataluña (1600-1850)', *Revista de Historia Económica = Journal of Iberian and Latin American Economic History*, year 15, no. 3, pp. 507–543.

26 Ferrer, L. (2007) 'Una revisió del creixement demogràfic de Catalunya en el segle XVIII a partir dels registres parroquials', *Estudis d'història agrària*, no. 20, pp. 17–68.

27 Vilar, P. (1962) *Catalunya dins l'Espanya Moderna, Vol. III, Les transformacions agràries del segle XVIII català: de l'impuls de les forces productives a la formació d'una burgesia nova*, Barcelona: Edicions 62, pp. 121–141.

28 Palau Elcacho, L. (2020) 'L'evolució demogràfica de la Catalunya interior al llarg dels segles XVIII i XIX: El cas del Pla d'Urgell', *Estudis d'història agrària*, no. 32, pp. 139–172.

29 Martínez Shaw, C. (1981) *Cataluña en la carrera de Indias: 1680-1756*, Barcelona: Crítica, pp. 54–56.

30 Thomson, J. K. J. (1992) *A Distinctive Industrialization: Cotton in Barcelona 1728–1832*, Cambridge: Cambridge University Press, p. 71.

31 Thomson, J. K. J. (2005) 'Explaining the "Take-Off" of the Catalan Cotton Industry', *Economic History Review*, vol. 58, no. 4, pp. 701–735.

32 Solà Colomer, X. (2017) 'Notes sobre la indústria drapera a la Vall d'Hostoles en el segle XVIII', *Annals del Patronat d'Estudis Històrics d'Olot i Comarca*, no. 28, pp. 141–166.

33 Mora-Sitjà, N. (2011) 'El primer proletariat català. Mà d'obra i relacions laborals a les fàbriques d'indianes de Barcelona', *Barcelona: quaderns d'història*, no. 17, pp. 237–252.

34 Capdevila Muntadas, M. A. (2004) 'Pagesos, mariners i comerciants a la Catalunya litoral. El Maresme a l'època moderna', *Butlletí de la Societat Catalana d'Estudis Històrics*, no. 25, pp. 193–203.

35 Congost i Colomer, C. (2008) 'Una societat rural dinàmica i canviant. El segle XVIII', in Salrach Marés, J. M. and Giralt i Raventós, E. (ed.) *Història agrària dels Països Catalans*, vol. 3, pp. 559–583.

36 Congost i Colomer, R. (2015) 'Els canvis en l'Empordà del segle XVIII: la tesi d'una revolució industriosa', *Annals de l'Institut d'Estudis Empordanesos*, vol. 46, pp. 371–388.

37 Lluch, E. (1996) *La Catalunya vençuda del segle XVIII: foscors i clarors de la Il.lustració*, Barcelona: Edicions 62, pp. 109–111.

38 Soler i Simon, S. (2017) 'Tortellà al segle XVIII una època de creixement i transformacions', *Annals del Patronat d'Estudis Històrics d'Olot i Comarca*, no. 28, pp. 113–140.

39 Martí i Escayol, M. A. (2002) 'Indústria, medicina i química a la Barcelona de finals del segle XVIII: el tintatge i la introducció del carbó mineral des d'una perspectiva ambiental', *Recerques: Història, economia i cultura*, no. 44, pp. 5–20.

40 Tello, E. (1997) 'La conflictividad social en el mundo rural catalán, del Antiguo Régimen a la Revolución liberal, 1720–1833', *Noticiario de historia agraria. Boletín informativo del seminario de historia agraria*, year 7, no. 13, pp. 89–104.

41 García-Varela, J. (1997) 'Moviments de protesta i resistència a la fi de l'Antic Règim (1714-1808): cap a una integració de les actituds i les trajectòries socials', in Arnabat i Mata, R. (ed.) *Moviments de protesta i resistència a la fi de l'Antic Règim*, Barcelona: Abadia de Montserrat, pp. 7–36.

42 Vilar, P. (1992) 'Les transformacions del segle XVIII', in Nadal i Farreras, J. and Wolff, P. (eds.), *Història de Catalunya*, Barcelona: Oikos-Tau, pp. 385–420.

43 Roura, L. (2013) 'Il·lustració i projectes per al país', in Albareda, J. (ed.) *Catalunya, nació d'Europa, 1714–2014*, Barcelona: Enciclopèdia Catalana, pp. 178–223.

44 Grau i Fernández, R. (2011) 'Un patriota d'altres temps: Antoni de Capmany i la historiografia racionalista', *Butlletí de la Societat Catalana d'Estudis Històrics*, no. 22, pp. 93–112.

45 Ballbé i Sans, N. (2018) 'La "Real Cédula de Aranjuez" del 23 de juny de 1768: propòsits d' uniformització lingüística en un context de Despotisme "il·lustrat"', *Revista de Catalunya*, no. 303, pp. 43–56.

46 Campabadal i Bertran, M. (2006) 'La Reial Acadèmia de Bones Lletres de Barcelona al segle XVIIIl'interès per la història, la llengua i la literatura catalanes', *Butlletí de la Societat Catalana d'Estudis Històrics*, no. 17, pp. 215–227.

47 Roura i Aulinas, L. (2010) 'Guerra, frontera i absolutisme (Guerra Gran, Guerra del Francès i -de reüll- Guerra de Successió)', *Annals de l'Institut d'Estudis Gironins*, no. 51, pp. 89–108.

48 Riera i Fortiana, E. (1982) 'El estamento eclesiástico catalán en la guerra de la Independencia', *Pedralbes: Revista d'historia moderna*, no. 2, pp. 211–236.

49 Barnosell, G. (2012) 'Guerra i religió a Catalunya: 1792–1840', in Barnosell, G. and Galofré, J. (eds.) *La Guerra del Francès al Pla de l'Estany*, Banyoles: Centre d´Estudis Comarcals de Banyoles, pp. 15–24.

50 Fraser, R. (2008) *Napoleon's Cursed War: Spanish Popular Resistance in the Peninsular War*, London: Verso, pp. 114–115.

51 Valls Junyent, F. (2010) *La Cataluña atlántica: Aguardiente y tejidos en el arranque industrial catalán*, Zaragoza: Prensas de la Universidad de Zaragoza, Universidad de Zaragoza, pp. 286–288.

52 Fradera, J. M. (1986) 'El comerç americà durant el segle XIX', in *El comerç entre Catalunya i Amèrica, segles xviii i xix*, Barcelona: L'Avenç, pp. 109–121.

53 Roma i Casanovas, F. (2014) 'Canvi social i conflictivitat als segles XVIII i XIX. El cas d'Osona', *AUSA*, no. 26, pp. 925–944.

54 Dannecker, A. and Barriendos i Vallvé, M. (1999) 'La sequía de 1812–1824 en la costa central catalana consideraciones climáticas e impacto social del evento', in *La climatología española en los albores del siglo XXI*, Barcelona: Publicaciones de la Asociación Española de Climatología, pp. 53–61.

55 Torras Elias, J. (1970) 'Societat rural i moviments absolutistes. Nota sobre la guerra dels malcontents (1827)', *Recerques: Història, economia i cultura*, no. 1, pp. 123–130.

56 Arnabat i Mata, R. (1999) 'Notes sobre l'aixecament dels malcontents, 1827', *Butlletí de la Societat Catalana d'Estudis Històrics*, no. 10, pp. 107–128.

7

1830–1939 SOCIAL CONFLICT, NATIONAL REVIVAL AND IDEOLOGICAL DISPUTE

Over the next hundred years, there are repeated crises of the Spanish political system. Spain remained trapped in a cycle of decline, falling further behind the major European powers. Economic development was laggardly in most of the country. The education system was poorly developed and funded. The comparative weakness of the Spanish state order also had consequences for Spain's inability to create a collective project of national unity. Spain's minority national questions, in particular those of the Basque Country and Catalonia, continue to be present into the twenty-first century. As we have already seen, Spain experienced extensive internal conflict, the Napoleonic War (1808–1814), the Royalist War (1822–1823) and that of the Malcontents (1827–1828). These three conflicts were compounded by a series of civil wars: the first Carlist war (1833–1840), the Matiners war or second Carlist war (1846–1849) and the third Carlist war (1872–1876). Urban revolts continued to be frequent. In all of these wars or revolts, Catalonia was implicated, since all these wars took place in its territory and two of them almost solely (the Malcontents and the Matiners). The city of Barcelona was central to the development of a range of political cultures. Following the disruption and upheaval of the period between 1790 and 1825, Catalonia embarked on its own route to modernity. Though 1714 had seemed to represent the permanent defeat of Catalonia, by the later nineteenth century, Catalonia had increasingly become the most dynamic part of Spain. Economic differentiation in Catalonia would be key in contributing to a distinctive political tradition in the modern period. The industrialisation underway in Catalonia made the characteristics of Catalan society different from the rest of Spain and closer to that of southern France and areas of northern Italy. The main features of this process, a declining nobility, an emergent industrial class and urban working class gave a distinctive inflection to Catalan society. Migration processes from country to city increasingly became permanent. Mass political consciousness came here earlier as did the processes of urbanisation, industrialisation

DOI: 10.4324/9781003218791-8

and mass political participation. Catalan society underwent rapid modernisation, impacting both sexes. Women encountered new opportunities but were also subject to new mechanisms of exploitation, particularly within the factory system. Whilst domestic service was concentrated amongst younger women, factory labour employed women of all ages. Child labour was increasingly in evidence as industrialisation increased and was not prohibited until 1900. Men, women and children experienced a range of health deficiencies including serious hearing loss in the often deafening factories and greatly shortened lives due to the lengthy working day and dangerous conditions.

Catalonia found itself occupying an intermediate space between the most advanced and least developed European regions. Catalonia consolidated during the late eighteenth century a modern economy, which as the century developed seemed to mark its character from the rest of Spain. Textiles continued to be the most economically important sector. From 1830 onwards, mechanisation became increasingly common and the first steam engine was introduced. The earliest rail links in the Iberian peninsula were located in Catalonia. Economic change naturally impacted on the social structure and Catalonia became the region with the largest number of industrial workers developing numerous workers' associations. Catalonia produced a sophisticated industrial class but this was a class that did not hold political power. Its capacity to hold a degree of influence in Madrid remained paramount. Whilst industrial and agricultural interests were broadly aligned internally, the Catholic church remained the most feudal institution in Catalonia and its economic interests were greatly challenged by economic modernisation.[1]

Carlism

Developments in the countryside led to the emergence of the movement known to us as the anti-modern and ultra-Catholic movement of Carlism. Between 1833 and 1839, the First Carlist War took place. Carlism, opposed to the reigning Bourbon dynasty, also advocated the recovery of Catalonia's own laws lost in 1714. It was a peculiar political formation in its appeal to tradition, deference and hierarchy. The shift to capitalist relations in the countryside was a contributory factor in the development of Carlism as this capitalist modernisation seemed to render all previous traditions with it. Carlism was not a revolt of the poor but rather of those undergoing impoverishment.[2] This was to be the social basis of traditional Carlism. Church alienation towards the liberal political system was compounded by confiscation of land and the resultant eviction of religious orders. The liberal regime forced through these measures to create a capitalist form of property ownership. This was extensively applied without compensation between 1836 and 1842. The Church saw its wealth dramatically reduced though it still remained comparatively rich. The Church found an outlet for the defence of its value system in its association with Carlism. The anti-church riots in 1835 seemed to be a further factor in placing the Catalan church on the defensive. After losing the war through an armistice in 1839, a new war broke out in 1846 which lasted until 1849 and is known as the

Matiners War, or Second Carlist War. This war was different to the first and the third Carlist war which took place between 1872 and 1876. This second conflict, the Matiners War, was only fought out in Catalonia and was a response to worsening economic conditions. This was the only one of the three Carlist wars where urban workers also expressed their discontent against the government in an untypical and unstable alliance with Carlists.[3]

Liberal Catalonia and urban change

In spite of the pattern of repeated warfare and periodic outbreaks of disease, from 1800 to 1860, the Catalan population doubled from 850,000 to 1,700,000. Towns such as Reus, Tarragona, Mataró, Sabadell and Badalona grew dramatically. The cities had generally maintained a physical and architectural structure mostly unchanged since the medieval period. As populations grew, this made cities particularly prone to disease. Barcelona in particular experienced large waves of immigration coming from rural areas in search of work, and industrial growth which was confined within medieval walls. By mid-century, the city was overpopulated and experienced a range of diseases, in particular cholera and yellow fever which killed thousands. As a response, the destruction of the medieval walls began in 1854 and lasted until 1868. In the same year, due to popular rebellion, the Ciutadella fortress built in the 1720s was destroyed. By 1860, the population of Barcelona had risen to 190,000 and 14 Catalan cities had populations over 10,000. By the end of the nineteenth century, urbanisation had reached levels of 40 per cent in Catalonia, which can be contrasted with regions such as Galicia and Andalusia which barely reached levels of 20 per cent. A growing liberal and republican culture was linked to the processes of urbanisation. This was evident in a transformation of the public sphere, where forums for ideas, magazines and newspapers expanded their range. Partly geographical, partly cultural, Catalonia tended to be the first area in the peninsula to receive the latest European intellectual ideas and currents.

Urban protest

During the period of the first Carlist war 1833–1839 and after, we also find expressions of urban violence. Between 1835 and 1843, Barcelona experienced ten popular uprisings and urban riots that in Barcelona took the name of 'bullangues'. The first Carlist war had seen brutal levels of violence, common to civil wars, with reprisals and counter-reprisals common. The first major revolt in Barcelona took place following news of Carlist violence against the inhabitants of Reus, then the second largest in Catalonia. The result was a popular rebellion resulting in particular in attacks on organised religion and the burning of convents. At least 15 religious figures were killed. Factory machinery was also destroyed and the military governor of Barcelona was assassinated. Urban revolts were evident in other Catalan cities, including against attempts to impose the draft on the male populace. Hostility to organised religion was often a component to these revolts. In the early

1840s, policy changes in Madrid which led to the opening of Spanish markets to British products negatively affected Catalan industry. In November 1842, factory owners and workers in Barcelona rebelled. The response from the Spanish government was an indiscriminate bombardment of the city, killing 30. Collective outrage at the bombing and subsequent executions led to the fall of the Spanish government. This government response was even worse in the revolt of 1843 known as La Jamància, when over 12,000 projectiles were launched on the city, killing over 300. This revolt in Barcelona lasted some 80 days and can be seen as pre-cursor to the Paris Comune in terms of its character and the subsequent repression and violence.[4] The turn to political organisation was increasingly evident and over the 1840s, we find the first workers' societies, which initially acted as mutual societies and cooperatives. These became the embryo for militant trades unions, which the city of Barcelona became internationally famous for. As early as 1855, these new workers organisations successfully called the first general strike. This spread to the industrial zone surrounding Barcelona and brought out over 100,000 striking workers. In spite of intensive repressive violence, the strike held and ended following a series of government promises, though these were later broken.

Cultural revival, la Renaixença

The period from the late eighteenth century through the middle of the nineteenth is the time of the development of modern ideas of both the state and of the cultural nation. As we have seen, a Catalan sense of difference had been evident though not fully formed in earlier periods, yet by the time of the Napoleonic wars, political differentiation with other regions of Spain was harder to perceive. Carlism, for example, which mobilised vast numbers, sought an alternative candidate for the Spanish throne. Catalan Catholic culture differed little from that of the rest of the peninsula in terms of its attachment to reactionary theology. The Spanish language was given official status over Catalan in the Church in 1828 and this measure was unpopular because most parishioners were Catalan speakers. The Spanish education laws of 1836 and 1857 asserted that only Spanish could be used in the classroom and with the Church dominant in the education system, these measures too provoked controversy. Whilst the church hierarchy was more accepting of Castilianisation, at the level of the parish, many of these measures meant little to a priest and populace who remained monolingual in Catalan. Teachers posted from other regions of Spain encountered pupils who struggled to understand them. The Catalan cultural renaissance, la Renaixença, emerged amongst elite sectors who had most engaged in the process of the adoption of Castilian Spanish for social advancement. Amongst the urban and rural population this shift had not taken place. This cultural movement had little or no relevance to the majority of the Catalan population and it is significant that it chose the most elitist of literary forms, the epic poem, as its first expression. The publication of Carles Aribau's Oda a la Pàtria (Ode to the Fatherland) in 1833 is usually seen as the beginning of the cultural Renaissance, though other forms of Catalan culture had continued throughout the post-1714 period such as popular and religious festivals. Over the nineteenth century, we find a process of Catalan cultural and literary revival that, later in the century, will form a political expression. The influence of Romanticism was pivotal in the first phase as it provided a ready-made doctrine to re-interpret the past. Catalan intellectuals undertook the study and promotion of the language, the legal tradition and popular customs.

The Romantic movement and its Catalan expression found the true essence of the country in a countryside untainted by modernisation. Observing the rivers, hills and mountains on their visits from Barcelona, writers crafted a new imaginary and eternal Catalonia.[5] Landscape emerged within the literary revivals as subjective reality. The development of cultural projections found political expression with the development of a fully formed Catalan national movement. The revivalist phase led by linguists, poets, etc. found its golden age in the medieval empire of Catalonia. The historical remoteness of this period enabled a simplified narrative of national heroes and villains. The medieval ruler Jaume I was framed as a glorious national king of Catalonia and the mercenary Almogàvers were invoked as virile symbols of Catalan national assertion. The extension of the Renaixença multiplied literary production in Catalan, although language standardisation was some way off and much of this production was produced in an archaic language. From 1842, periodicals in Catalan appeared. As this process deepened, it sought to re-craft a sense of national identity and reverse Catalan cultural decline, which had lasted some 300 years. It would only be in subsequent decades that re-interpretation of the siege of Barcelona in 1714 in the Catalan national imagination began. The siege came to be increasingly important in the Catalan national story. In the mid-1860s, poems were written about the heroic defenders of 1714. In 1872, a popular history of the siege became available to patriotic Catalans via subscription. In 1886, the first organised commemoration of September 11 took place, followed two years later by the building of a monument to commemorate Rafael Casanova, the leader of the civil authorities during the siege of 1714. As the new Catalan nationalist movement grew in the latter part of the century, the story of 1714 became increasingly framed as one of heroic resistance against Spain. Against the odds, the Catalans had held at bay vastly superior opponents. By century's end, we find socially constructed the Catalan people, el poble català, as a political subject. However, other identity expressions challenged this conception, found most explicitly in the organisation of labour.

The labour movement

Industrialisation brought with it vast social change. Time became ordered according to the dictates of the factory system. Artificial light meant factories worked near constantly.[6] Shifts worked by mid-century were often as long as 14 hours. Whilst early death was common, substantial surplus labour was available in the countryside and thus supply easily met demand. However, the concentration of large numbers contributed to the emergence of the Catalan labour movement. Periods of repression and secrecy alternated with those of legality and the expansion of workers societies. Catalonia was in the vanguard of union organisation throughout the peninsula. On 18 June 1870, the first Spanish Workers' Congress took place in Barcelona which led to the creation of Spanish Regional Federation of the First International. Half of the Spanish total membership came from the Catalan region. Following the dispute between followers of Marx and Bakunin, the Spanish federation clearly aligned with the anarchist tradition. The workers movement in Catalonia was the most sophisticated in terms of its political culture and tradition of organisation. This movement was also strongly connected to the emergence of radical republicanism which signified periodic cross-class alliances with the urban middle class. This was pivotal towards the Catalan role in the proclamation of the First Republic of 1873–1874, which was greatly resisted in the countryside by the third and final Carlist war.

The subsequent restoration of the monarchy and the pseudo-democratic settlement of the mid-1870s meant extensive periods of repression of organised labour in the following decades. This resulted in worker radicalisation and employer resistance. However, in this early phase of the organised working class, it had still to find its form of organisation and ideological coherence, with a variety of strands competing. By the 1880s, there were three principal labour organisations in Catalonia and by the early 1890s, working-class organisations were increasingly able to successfully call strikes and demonstrations. This would mean that Catalan-organised labour became one of the most militant in Europe, giving a particular intensity to social conflict before the Spanish Civil War. With the near constant prohibitions, sectors of Catalan anarchism turned to direct action and violence in the 1890s: Propaganda of the Deed. With bomb attacks on the Liceu opera house and a religious procession killing over 30, the authorities and bourgeois Barcelona created a climate of anti-anarchist hysteria. Though the acts themselves were carried out by fringe figures, hundreds of workers activists were arrested and tortured in Montjuïc jail. Barcelona became internationally known not only as a city of bombs but also a city of vicious repression.[7]

Political Catalanism

Between 1868 and 1873, there was a situation of general economic crisis, which contributed to a culture of rebellion culminating in the short-lived First Republic.

In addition, a very powerful republicanism emerged in the cities, starring in an endless series of riots and uprisings, whilst apart from the rural areas, Carlist traditionalism persisted. A further revolt against the military draft occurred in 1870. The final expression of Carlist rebellion was the third Carlist war which broke out in 1872 and lasted until 1876. Caricatured as a revolt of priest and peasant, this final revolt was destined to defeat as the movement was unable to attract industrial workers to its cause.[8] Parallel to this, an initial reformist programme for Spain, led by Catalonia, was federal republicanism. The leading ideologue of Catalanist republicanism was Valentí Almirall, who called for the revival of the political structure of the kingdom of Aragon, which by inclusion of the region of Aragon signified that language was not the primary element for membership. In the Pact of Tortosa of 1869, republican and federalist representatives evoked the territories of the Crown of Aragon: Aragon, Valencia, Catalonia and the Balearics. Following the failures of the First Republic and the installation of the Restoration Monarchy in 1875, Almirall responded by focussing on Catalonia alone. This choice of the principality as the core political space would be shared by all subsequent intellectual contributions in the construction of political Catalanism. The chosen nation was to be Catalonia alone.[9] Thus, Catalanism was subject to a process of constant innovation and change. Simply put, the Catalanism around cultural elites of the 1840s was quite distinctive to that of the later nineteenth century. A significant contribution to political Catalanism came from the federalist publication Diari Català which became the first newspaper of the new era to be written only in Catalan, which attained a circulation of 3,000. In the early 1880s, a number of new Catalanist organisations were created. The first expression of what can be termed a manifesto was the Memorial de Greuges (report of grievances) of March 1885, presented to King Alfonso XII by leading cultural and political representatives. Framed in terms of loyalty to Spain, the grievances raised included the maintenance of a separate Catalan Legal Code and call for a protectionist policy for Catalan industry.

Catalan economic interests were now clearly divergent from most of Spain and though Catalonia was an advanced economic zone in Spain, compared to other European zones, such as northern France or Italy, Catalan industry was poorly equipped to compete. Thus, Catalan industrialists were, in general, in favour of protectionism, whilst most Spanish agricultural interests were opposed. As we have seen, Catalan textiles were particularly challenged by Britain. Spain's market was the natural outlet for Catalonia's output because Catalan industry found no competition there. In 1869, the Fomento de Trabajo National was created by industrial interests and one of its main functions was a protectionist lobbying entity. The Foment became the key political expression of Catalan employers and was closely linked to the organisations of conservative Catalanism. Thus, political Catalanism came to express economic discontent, a relationship it has never entirely lost. Protectionism and Catalanism became almost synonymous. Protection ensured industrial domination of the Spanish national market. The generalised perception of Spanish governmental unwillingness to fully support Catalan industry was equally important to Catalanism as its cultural manifestations. Catalan elites, now organised as a truly bourgeois class, had incorporated aristocratic traditions within their political culture and acquired great wealth which was used for financial patronage of projects such as the Liceu opera house in Barcelona.

Cultures of Catalanism

Catalanism continued its political development, finding expression amongst republicans, federalists and conservatives. The final defeat of Carlism in 1876 saw the church develop a religious Catalanism. This represented a transition from the ideology of Carlism. This process of religious Catalanisation looked to the glories of the Catalan medieval past and became centred around the monastery of Montserrat, and the town of Vic. Montserrat became symbolically represented as the heart of a true and Catholic Catalonia.[10] In 1881, the Black Madonna of Montserrat was proclaimed Catalonia's Queen and Patron. For the conservative leading cleric Torras i Bages, the revitalisation of Catalonia could only come through its return to its Christian roots.[11] Thus, we can observe the construction of a conservative Catalanism centred on tradition, religion, family and identity. This conservative variant evoked the rural world as carrier of the true national essence where property and hierarchy were respected. In 1883, at the Second Catalanist Congress, the call for schooling in the Catalan language was made.[12] As late as the 1880s, the majority of the Catalan population had only a rudimentary knowledge of the Spanish language. In 1902, further discontent was created in the Catalan church when measures were passed requiring the catechism to be taught only in Spanish. The limited state education available in Spain was conducted solely in Spanish though in practice teachers in rural areas continued to often use Catalan.[13] As often happened in movements around language revival, language standardisation was disputed as some advocated a more archaic and traditional model, based on the literary language used until the seventeenth century, and others advocated a model based on a more contemporary Catalan. At the First International Congress of the Catalan Language in 1906 and the Institut d'Estudis Catalans in 1913, a fully modernised Catalan language was defined.

The Unió Catalanista was created in 1891 as a federation of nationalist associations. The Unió called a conference of all persuasions of Catalanists to the town of Manresa in 1892, with the aim of drawing up a document that would help delineate a Catalanist agenda. This conference became the most important political event of this period and culminated in a manifesto titled Bases for a Catalan Regional Constitution. The Bases of Manresa, as they came to be known, was the first formulation of nationalist demands, and they attained a canonical status as a foundational document of Catalanism. The Bases provided a reference point for future autonomous movements in Catalonia and agreed to give to the Spanish state the responsibility for international relations including those pertaining to the economy, defence and the maintenance of a transport infrastructure. By the later decades of the century, Catalanism had developed a range of political cultures, coming to represent the liberal professions, intellectuals and Catholic sectors of society.[14]

1898 and the Lliga

Over the course of the nineteenth century, Catalan business benefitted from the existence of Spain's remaining colonial Empire, and Cuba had become of prime importance to Catalan economic interests. Capital returned from plantation economies in Cuba fed into the expansion of Barcelona.[15] Since the 1870s, Spain had been challenged by a Cuban revolt and it was notable that Catalan conservative support prioritised its important economic ties with the island and felt little sympathy with a nationalist insurrection against Spanish rule. The Catalan business community was not only unsupportive of Cuban demands for autonomy, but it was also equally fearful of a political movement that smacked of radicalism.[16] However, Catalan progressive opinion was supportive of Cuba and political tensions can be traced to the different positions taken on the 'Cuban question'. The 1890s were a pivotal decade in the politicisation and organisation of conservative elites in Catalonia. The shock of Spanish defeat by the United States in 1898 reverberated throughout Spain. In Catalonia, the loss of the colonies of Cuba and the Philippines demonstrated with great clarity to industrialists the failure of the Castilian agrarian-dominated state to protect the overseas markets that were of such importance in Catalonia. Almost 60 per cent of Catalan exports had gone to Cuba.

The loss of the colonies increased the importance to Catalan industry of the Spanish market as a whole, and thus Catalonia became more strongly tied to Spain. The loss of Spain's last remaining colonies in 1898 led to a complete breakdown in relations between Catalan elites and the political system. This situation worsened in 1899. The previous year's defeat had resulted in a substantial financial deficit, which the government sought to balance by raising taxes. The response by the guilds of Barcelona was to close commercial and industrial establishments so as to avoid paying tax without breaking the law. The consequences of this unusual strike, which spread to many medium-sized towns in Catalonia, was the suspension of constitutional guarantees, embargoes and arrests of taxpayers and the resignation of the mayor of Barcelona, who disobeyed orders from Madrid by refusing to embargo the assets of those who refused to pay. Industrialists and shopkeepers, led by the mayor of Barcelona organised to boycott a taxation measure imposed by Madrid which harmed Catalan interests. The government response was severe with non-payers imprisoned. The political consequence was the emergence of a conservative Catalanism that sought to lead the modernisation and transformation of Spain. Partly influenced by the example of northern Italian leadership, Catalan politicians, intellectuals and businessmen wanted Catalonia to become the Piedmont of Spain, the political and economic engine of the new times. In 1901, the Lliga Regionalista de Catalunya was created. The Lliga became a truly modern political party with a sophisticated and well-organised party structure and a leading press organ, La Veu de Catalunya. The modest success of the Lliga in Barcelona in the municipal elections of 1901 broke the dominance of the Spanish liberal and conservative parties. Enric Prat de la Riba emerged as the leading ideologue of Catalanism in this period.

New labour struggles

By 1900, Barcelona rivalled Madrid in population. The city contained within it the political culture of Catalanism, an organised industrialist sector and a sophisticated cultural middle class. However, for most of the following period, Barcelona became known internationally for its deeply rooted revolutionary and anarchist working class culture. The movement developed a culture of anti-clericalism and anti-militarism, and one of worker self-improvement through education. At the beginning of the century, more than 50 per cent of the Catalan population was illiterate. What was underway was the building of a new political identity. This political culture was soon tested by the outbreak of a general strike in 1902 with the demand for a nine hour maximum working day. Catalan employers once again demonstrated their intransigence and sought to break the strike and the labour movement. The general strike brought out 100,000 strikers and paralysed industry in Barcelona. The strike saw intense state repression and imposition of martial law, which was strongly supported and advocated by Catalan industrialists and Lliga politicians. This still remained an overwhelmingly native working class as the first wave of migration from outside Catalan territory did not begin in earnest until the 1920s. The pro-employer position of the Lliga aligned it firmly within the class struggle and had implications for the development of political Catalanism as the regionalist project seemed trapped in positions that could not appeal to workers. The close links between Catalan industry and the Spanish market explains why the political expression of the regionalists and Catalan business, the Lliga Regionalista, did not look for separation from the Spanish state. Their political project remained the reform and modernisation of Spain, which if necessary could be led from Barcelona against a recalcitrant Madrid-based agrarian-dominated political class. Catalan employers frequently ignored the modest social measures passed by Madrid around workplace safety and the Lliga simply functioned as a transmission belt for industrial interests. Thus, the development of the Catalan national movement was handicapped from an early stage by the unwillingness of local elites to consider meaningful social reform.

Social change

For a period from the late 1890s until the Spanish Civil War, Catalan cities continuously expand. Barcelona incorporated surrounding zones which in time became fully part of the city such as the district of Gràcia. Growth is evident in a range of cities including Girona, Manresa, Tarragona as well as the expansion of smaller towns into full city status. Industrialisation continues to deepen bringing with it changes in road and rail links. The population expanded constantly throughout this period and was only briefly impacted by the global flu pandemic of 1919–1921, which killed over 6,000 in Barcelona alone. The character of migration now changed. For most of the nineteenth century, movement had been from country to city and was internal. This was later joined by some migration from Valencia but this brought with no language differences. It was during the years between 1915 and 1920 that the character of migration changes. This is the beginning of a process that lasts until the 1960s of over-increasing numbers of Spanish speakers migrating to Catalonia from the poorer areas of Spain.

New political conflict

Following a Spanish military attack on a satirical newspaper which the Spanish government proved itself to be unable to censure, an attempt was made to fuse

Catalanist traditions in Solidaritat Catalana, which contested the elections of 1907 with a landslide victory, winning 41 of 44 seats in Catalonia. This electoral success raised concerns amongst the Madrid political class and Spanish military at the Catalan problem. However, the movement struggled to maintain this unity beyond 1907 and it was fully broken in 1909 by the events known as the Tragic Week. Spontaneous protests organised by women against the call up became an explosion of anti-clericalism which spread to 22 Catalan towns and cities. During this week, three members of the clergy were killed, some 80 churches, convents and religious establishments were destroyed. This was one of the most violent episodes of the period in Europe and it resulted in 104 deaths and the arrest of over 2,000. The Catalan Church as an institution was viewed as part of the governing elite, and the embodiment of anti-liberal and conservative ideology. The Tragic Week ruptured the brief unity represented by Solidaritat Catalana and the Lliga Regionalist re-emerged from the experience terrified of popular mobilisation. The hope for political reform from Madrid was now shelved. In 1910, the Confederación Nacional del Trabajo, CNT was created, which cemented the adoption of an anarcho-syndicalism influenced above all by Kropotkin and the Italian anarchist Malatesta. Prior to the arrival of significant Spanish-speaking migration, the Catalan anarchist movement expressed an anti-nationalist political posture. This had important implications for the Catalan national movement as the dominant trades union body had little or no interest in anything that it deemed as bourgeois nationalism, represented by a Lliga Regionalista which it deemed simply a representative of Catalan political reaction. The development of political Catalanism was hampered by its direct association with this force. Social tensions in Catalonia had no parallel in any other area of Spain which meant that anarchists and conservative Catalanists remained irreconcilable.

Mancomunitat

Following repeated lobbying by the Lliga and testimony to its political strength, a new administrative body in Catalonia was created in 1914: the Mancomunitat de Catalunya. Though this body only fused powers already existing in the four Catalan regions: Barcelona, Tarragona, Lleida and Girona, the Mancomunitat came to symbolise the first expression of Catalan self-rule since the defeat of 1714 and the Nova Planta Decree of 1716. This was a victory for political Catalanism, and activity was centred in culture including schools, vocational training, museums, archives and libraries. The official status given to the Catalan language prepared the ground for the increase in publications in the language experienced throughout the 1920s, in spite of the persecutions under General Miguel Primo de Rivera. The long-term significance of the Mancomunitat lay in its promotion of Catalan culture.[17] A second area of activity was in the terrain of infrastructure with financing of a range of public works projects including road building and the extension of a basic telephone network. The Mancomunitat thus contributed to the modernisation of the Catalan economy but remained a body that only appealed to the more affluent strata of Catalan society. The existence of this organisation coincided with a particularly tumultuous period politically and socially.

World war and revolutionary flux

The outbreak of European war was an event that greatly impacted even those countries that did not participate, such as Spain. Society in Catalonia was broadly sympathetic to the Allied powers of Britain and France. Catalan employers greatly benefitted from the economic boom war brought with it, being able to sell to and supply both sides in the war. The textile industry performed particularly well, with exports now becoming a major source of sales. The result was an economic boom. However, rising prices was also a consequence and this began to increase social tension as already precarious workers came under sustained financial pressure. Salaries failed to keep up with prices throughout the period 1914–1920.[18] Social antagonism increased as Barcelona's elites embarked on displays of conspicuous consumption. The growing wealth being created was not used to re-invest and the response of the Madrid government was to propose a tax on excessive profits. This negatively affected the Catalan business class which interpreted the measure as economic persecution directed by Spanish landowning interests. Thus, economic grievances were given a nationalist inflection by Catalan elites. In this context of conflict between Madrid and Barcelona, the Bolshevik seizure of power in Russia resonated in the Catalan labour movement, as it did throughout Europe. The first workers' revolution in world history transformed the social context throughout Europe producing optimism and fear depending on class position. Initially, anarchism was strongly sympathetic to the apparent gains but after a delegation sent to Russia reported on the repression by the Bolsheviks against both Russian anarchists and the Mensheviks, anarchism became fiercely anti-Bolshevik. The origin of major political divisions in the Catalan radical left are found here and were not resolved until the 1960s.

The year 1917 commenced with a triple challenge to Restoration Spain. The military were in a rebellious mood and increasingly concerned at the erosion of their own pay, conditions and promotion system. The Lliga sought to lead a parliamentary reform movement from Barcelona, hoping to achieve the long-desired modernisation of Spain's failing political system. This sense of crisis was compounded by a general strike in the summer of 1917. These events produced a crisis of the state. The Lliga became trapped by its attempt to defend private property, law and order, political reform and Catalan identity.[19] Although the general strike was defeated, this was followed by three years of near constant peasant revolt in the southern Spanish countryside. The authorities throughout Spain resorted to increasingly vicious repressive violence. Social conflict now spread to the Catalan factory system and became ever more violent with Catalan employers aided by the military determined to destroy the anarcho-syndicalist trade union movement. The period of class conflict was accentuated by the end of the First World War and the ending of the economic opportunities created by the war. Employers sought to reduce pay and break the trade union movement in Catalonia, above all the CNT. The anarcho-syndicalist union was in a phase of growth and its challenge was met with extreme violence. A thousand died between 1917 and 1923, mostly at the hands of hired gunmen contracted by employers, with a small number of employers also killed as anarchism responded in kind. Barcelona attracted international fame as a city of violence. From 1917 to the outbreak of war in 1936, Spain experienced repeated crises with only short periods of political stability. Catalonia was the most turbulent and destabilising zone in Spain. The Barcelona employer 'lockout' of 1919–1920, involving over 200,000 workers, symbolised the growing capacity of the CNT, and the city experienced periods of power cuts which seemed to symbolise the collective fear and anxiety of the Catalan ruling class. The Lliga Regionalista increasingly sided with the reactionary forces of the Spanish monarchy against the union challenge.[20] The Lliga's prioritisation of the maintenance of social order meant it became supportive of the military coup d'état of General Miguel Primo de Rivera, launched in Barcelona in 1923. Primo de Rivera was the Captain-General of Catalonia and the Lliga saw him as the saviour of Catalonia and Spain. For the Lliga, its commitment to democracy and even home rule for Catalonia was of lesser importance than law and order which was now to be implemented by military rule.[21]

Dictatorship

The military government of Primo de Rivera was part of a wider phenomenon of counter-revolutionary reaction in Europe in the 1920s. Conservative sectors felt that all that had once provided stability in their world view was under threat. Events in Russia seemed to presage their removal from the stage of history. With varying degrees of intensity, these military or fascist type regimes came to power across Europe determined to halt the revolutionary challenge. Thus, one of the early actions of Primo de Rivera was the proscribing of the CNT in 1924, followed by the arrest of its leading activists and the suppression of its publications. Here the dictatorship carried out the agenda of the Lliga Regionalista and Catalan elites. Yet as we have seen, from the point of view of the authorities in Madrid, Catalonia represented both labour threat and regionalist-nationalist challenge. As the Dictatorship consolidated, measures to defend Spanish unity were rapidly approved. On 18 September 1923, a decree was passed to repress separatism, subjecting to military jurisdiction any attack on the unity of the Spanish fatherland. Other decrees prohibited the use of the Catalan flag and the Catalan language in government administration. Within a month, 50 cultural entities had been closed, together with a range of publications. Finally, measures decreed the obligation to teach only the Spanish language in school and the Mancomunitat itself was dissolved in 1925. Thus, this pre-autonomous type of government had barely lasted ten years before its abolition. Catalonia became a source of mobilisation against the dictatorship in its later phase which led to growing strength in republican and Catalanist forces, which increasingly became fused on the parliamentary and reformist left. At times during the dictatorship, radical nationalist and even pro-independence Catalanists attained unprecedented influence, though this would fade post-1931.[22]

Towards republican unity

The cultural repression of Catalanism under Primo de Rivera resulted not only in a growth in national feeling. It also generated sympathy amongst Spanish Republicans and Socialists for the future recognition of Catalan autonomy. The rapprochement between Catalan and Castilian intellectuals had been growing in the final years of the dictatorship and there was a growing Spanish sympathy for the right of Catalonia to defend its own language and cultural identity.[23] Thus, the reformist movement that would launch the Second Spanish Republic in 1931 included in its programme the concession of political autonomy to Catalonia. The political agreement that became known as the Pact of San Sebastián contained the promise to support the establishment of a Catalan regional parliament, with its powers held in the medieval seat of Catalan government, the Generalitat. In time it became apparent that perceptions in Madrid differed as to the scale of Catalan self-rule, which from the perspective of Barcelona represented a restoration and not simply the concession of new powers. The republican Generalitat, despite being managed by progressive Catalanism, resumed and deepened the work of the Mancomunitat that had been interrupted by the dictatorship of Primo de Rivera.

The Second Republic

The 1930s would also come to represent a period of the radicalisation of the workers movement in Spain and the clash between the Catalan working class, mobilised around anarchism, and Catalanism would deepen. Between 1915 and 1930, internal migration from other areas of Spain became a major source of population growth in Catalonia and this gave an increasing ethno-nationalist inflection to political division.[24] By the 1930s, a fifth of the Catalan population had its origins in other regions of Spain and it was particularly concentrated in the greater Barcelona industrial zone. Whilst many of the leading cadres of the Catalan anarchist movement were non-Catalans, the majority of the rank and file were Catalans and felt that the anti-centralist ideology of the Esquerra was the closest (party) political expression to their own radicalism. The political divisions evident in Catalonia and the rest of Spain in the previous decades were not resolved during the period of the Second Republic. Society was deeply polarised between large landowners and landless labourers and peasants, centralisers and those seeking devolution, between Catholics and hardline anti-clericals. The final fracture was between those who opposed and those who favoured republicanism and democracy. Issues around the question of Spanish unity also emerged once the question of devolution to the historic nations of Catalonia and the Basque Country was addressed.

The anarcho-syndicalist CNT re-emerged after the persecution of the Primo de Rivera regime. One consequence was the intensification of social conflict in Catalonia in the 1930s, which had both urban and rural manifestations. Catalan small-holders, the rabassaires, radicalised in the 1930s against the pressures of rent payments to their landlords. This conflict became highly politicised with Catalan landlords defended by the Lliga, whilst the left republican government defended the small farmer interest. The CNT took a radical turn during the 1930s and was also prone to factionalism between moderate syndicalists and radical anarchists, now organised within the Federación Anarquista Ibérica. These were tactical differences in terms of restoring the dominance of the CNT.[25] Whilst other forces emerged to challenge the anarchists, including communists and revolutionary socialists, the CNT maintained its dominance. The Second Republic also represented an important moment in the advance of the collective rights for women, including the right to vote. Both of the two main Catalan parties organised women's sections.[26]

During this period of the 1930s, electoral politics was fought out between the Lliga Regionalista and Catalan republicanism, which now converged around a new formation, Esquerra Republicana de Catalunya. Esquerra would be dominant during the Republic and would be the party that implemented Catalan autonomy, attained in 1932. The populism of the Esquerra, and its domination of Catalanism through its power in the Generalitat, greatly accelerated the diffusion of Catalanism during the Republic. The Esquerra had the support of Catalan intellectuals in their promotion of Catalan language and culture. The Lliga, the force of conservative Catalanism, was damaged by its initial association with the dictatorship, though it revived somewhat as the Republic proceeded, becoming part of the mobilisation in defence of property, order, the family and religion. The achievement of ERC was in giving to Catalanism a new expression, breaking with the long-standing pattern of association of Catalanism with conservatism and the right.[27] As the political situation in the Second Spanish Republic deteriorated, the new right-wing government in Madrid faced a leftist government in Catalonia which, together with the Spanish left, decided to respond in October 1934, in defence of the social gains of the Republic.[28] The president of the Catalan regional government proclaimed the 'Catalan State' within the Spanish Federal Republic. Though later claimed as a form of independence proclamation, this was rather a Catalan commitment to the Spanish Republic and its protofederalist system. The unwillingness of the CNT to support the General Strike ensured its failure in the case of Catalonia. The consequences in the Catalan case was the suspension of autonomy and the imposition of direct rule from Madrid. Leading Catalan officials, including the regional president, Lluís Companys, were imprisoned. The Lliga and Catalan business became increasingly reactionary during the course of the Republic.[29] Elements with this political culture were inspired by the project of Italian fascism. By the time of the February 1936 election, the Lliga had completed its reactionary turn and participated in the election as part of the Front Català d'Ordre. Whilst Madrid experienced the most political violence between February and July 1936, Catalan society was also deeply polarised and the Spanish military revolt of 17–18 July 1936 unleashed its violent expression.

The Spanish Civil War and Catalonia

The military revolt in Catalonia was rapidly defeated by popular mobilisation. Its defeat resulted in a radicalisation of the CNT-led working class and the subsequent outbreak of revolution. Factories were collectively organised according to the principles of anarchism. Land collectivisation was extensive and was often spontaneously introduced at a local level, though there were also times when it was introduced by force.[30] This revolution also had major implications for women who experienced a radical transformation in terms of the permissible within Catalan society.[31] The anarchist Federica Montseny became the first ever female government minister in Spain. The Spanish Civil War as experienced in Catalonia brought to the fore a range of political conflicts that had been partly underway in the previous years. The anarchists and other revolutionary sectors advocated a policy of revolutionary war. This position was challenged by the Esquerra who increasingly allied with the Catalan communists. This new alliance subordinated social gains to victory in the war. As the war proceeded the latter position became widely accepted.[32] The war also produced conflicts between republican governments in Madrid and Barcelona which did not always share the same perspective on how to obtain military victory. Finally, as Nationalist Spain consolidated, it became increasingly evident that the political project being crafted by the rightist coalition led by the military entailed a determination to destroy Catalan and Basque nationalism. With the Spanish fascist party providing a political ideology for the revolt, the unity of Spain was given a talismanic-like quality.

The crushing of the rebellion of 19 July 1936 by workers' organisations and security forces loyal to the Republic created a situation where the elected government of Catalonia ceased to have a monopoly of violence and lacked the ability of the Generalitat to enforce its orders and laws. However, the Catalan government established a tacit understanding with anarcho-syndicalism by which the government gave legal form to the revolution, whilst the revolutionary forces accepted that the Generalitat still had certain prerogatives. This situation of parallel power was only resolved following the May Days of 1937 where the government forces regained both the initiative and political power from the street. This conflict was fought out in the streets of Barcelona between the anarchists, assisted by revolutionary Marxists against the forces of order represented by Esquerra and Catalan communism. The victory of the latter was in one sense the beginning of the end for the Catalan anarchist movement as one holding a near monopoly of working-class organisational power.

The outbreak of revolution in the summer of 1936 had other major consequences. The first was a wave of repressive violence against all deemed to be counter-revolutionary forces, from middle-class Catalanists to the Catholic church. The result was the fleeing from Catalonia of large numbers of conservatives to Burgos, San Sebastián or Rome. This exile was often enabled by the Catalan government itself during the period of shared power with the revolutionary committees. A system of revolutionary justice was introduced, which was initially spontaneous but became more structured as the war proceeded.[33] Once the initial revolt was defeated, a wave of political violence was unleashed on those deemed to be supportive of the coup attempt including businessmen, industrialists and those associated with conservative parties. In rural areas, repression often began with the burning of religious buildings, execution of ecclesiastics and local symbols of power and authority. Between mid-July and December 1936 executions totaled over 6,400.[34] In the first few weeks after July 1936, some 400 members of the Lliga Regionalista were killed. All of the fears of Catalan elites seemed confirmed as expropriation of businesses and their conversion into companies administered by the workers occurred. The promise of the restoration of 'order' by the military-led alliance of the Spanish Nationalists would account for the support given to it by the former supporters of the Lliga Regionalista. Cambó and others raised financial support for the military junta set up to fight against the Republic. Those who survived fled. The result was that large number of the traditional elites in Catalan society departed the country.[35] Perhaps the most dramatic violence was the assassination of over 2,000 priests and members of the religious orders. Though this happened throughout republican Spain, in proportionate terms, the number killed was the highest in Catalonia. This was an unprecedented assault on organised religion.

Defeat and its implications for Catalonia

As the war proceeded, and following Franco's war of attrition, republican-controlled territory contracted. The failure of the battle of the Ebro fought between July and November 1936 represented the death knell for a now isolated Catalonia. By January 1939, Francoist troops entered Barcelona as victors, some three months before the capitulation of the rest of Spain. The victory of Franco in the Civil War resulted in a range of legislation which erased all of the social gains of the 1930s and permanently abolished the Catalan Generalitat.[36] Francoist victory entailed complete defeat for both working-class radicalism and for the culture of Catalanism. For much of the previous hundred years, Catalonia experienced war, violence and conflict, revolution and counter-revolution. We have seen a range of these expressions, from the wars of Carlism, to the Tragic Week of 1909 to the revolution of 1936. A brief experiment in democracy for Spain began in 1931 with autonomy obtained for Catalonia the next year. It seemed that Spanish republicanism had a place for a multi-national conception of Spain. By the 1930s, Catalan culture was in a new phase of social advance that was unmatched since the late middle ages. Over 40 daily newspapers were found, with hundreds of weekly and monthly magazines. Ranging from anarchism to Catholic theology, cinema to sport, this seemed to represent a culture in expansive mode. The construction of a school system imparting republican values delivered through the medium of Catalan was also evidence of a future-oriented cultural project.[37] Catalan was used extensively in the local administration and was found across a range of local and city-based radio stations, with listenership in the hundreds of thousands and growing every year. Catalan and republican defeat in the civil war in 1939 marked an abrupt and traumatic halt to these developments.

Notes

1 Santirso Rodríguez, M. (1994) 'Revolució liberal i guerra civil a Catalunya, 1833-1840', *Butlletí de la Societat Catalana d'Estudis Històrics*, no. 6, pp. 205–212.

2 Anguera, P. (1995) *Déu, Rei i Fam. El primer carlisme a Catalunya*, Barcelona: Publicacions de l'Abadia de Montserrat.

3 Vallverdú i Martí, R. (2019) 'La Guerra dels Matiners en Cataluña. Crisis económica y revuelta social, Aportes', *Revista de historia contemporánea*, no. 100, pp. 99–121.

4 Bou, J. (2004) 'La Jamància: el naixement de l'última bullanga popular (juny-agost de 1843)', *Barcelona, Quaderns d'Història*, no. 10, pp. 171–186.

5 Sanllehy i Sabi, M. À. and Bringué i Portella, J. M. (2005) 'Les muntanyes i els homes: una aproximació a la societat, l'economia i la història', *Estudis d'història agrària*, no. 18, pp. 15–46.

6 Maluquer de Motes, J. (1992) 'Los pioneros de la segunda revolución industrial en España: La Sociedad Española de Electricidad (1881–1894)', *Revista de Historia Industrial*, no. 2, pp. 121–142.

7 Abello i Güell, T. (1992) 'El proceso de Montjuïc, la condena internacional al régimen de la Restauración', *Historia Social*, no. 14, pp. 47–60.

8 Vallverdú i Martí, R. (1995) 'La defensa de Montblanc durant la tercera carlinada. Aproximació sociològica als guerrillers carlins', *Aplec de treballs*, no. 13, pp. 143–170.

9 Dowling, A. (2019) 'When National Symbols Divide: The Case of Pan-Catalanism and the *Països Catalans*', *Journal of Iberian and Latin American Studies*, vol. 25, no. 1, pp. 143–157.

10 Massot i Muntaner, J. (1979) *Els Creadors del Montserrat Modern*, Montserrat: Biblioteca Serra d'Or, p. 35.

11 Torras i Bages, J. (1984) *Obres Completes*, Montserrat: Publicacions de l'Abadia de Montserrat, vol. 1, p. 242. See also Oltra, B., Mercadè, F. and Hernandéz, F. (1981) *La Ideologia Nacional Catalana*, Barcelona: Anagrama, pp. 45–47.

12 Illa, M. (1983) *El Segon Congrés Catalanista. Un congrés inacabat (1883–1983)*, Barcelona: Generalitat de Catalunya, p. 25.

13 Monés, J. (2005) *Formació professional i desenvolupament econòmic i social català (1714–1939)*, Barcelona: Societat d'Història de l'Educació dels Països de Llengua *Catalana*, p. 341.

14 Smith, A. (2014) *The Origins of Catalan Nationalism, 1770–1898*, Basingstoke: Palgrave Macmillan, pp. 204–205.

15 Rodrigo y Alharilla, M. (2015) 'From Periphery to Centre: Transatlantic Capital Flows, 1830–1890', in Leonard, A. B. and Pretel, D. (eds.) *The Caribbean and the Atlantic World Economy Circuits of Trade, Money and Knowledge, 1650–1914*, Basingstoke: Palgrave Macmillan, pp. 217–237.

16 Díez Medrano, J. (1995) *Divided Nations: Class, Politics and Nationalism in the Basque Country and Catalonia*, Ithaca: Cornell University Press, p. 94.

17 Balcells, A., Pujol, E. and Sabater, J. (1996) *La Mancomunitat de Catalunya i l'Autonomia*, Barcelona: Institut d'Estudis Catalans, pp. 441–449.

18 Gabriel Sirvent, P. (1988) 'Sous i cost de la vida a Catalunya a l'entorn dels anys de la Primera Guerra Mundial', *Recerques: Història, economia i cultura*, no. 20, pp. 61–91.

19 Romero-Salvadó, F. (2008) *The Foundations of Civil War: Revolution, Social Conflict and Reaction in Liberal Spain, 1916–1923*, London: Routledge, p. 94.

20 Bengoechea, S. (1998) *El Locaut de Barcelona (1919–1920): Els Precedents de la Dictadura de Primo de Rivera*, Barcelona: Curial.

21 Smith A. (2010) 'The Lliga Regionalista, the Catalan Right and the Making of the Primo de Rivera Dictatorship', in Romero-Salvadó, F. and Smith, A. (eds.) *The Agony of Spanish Liberalism: From Revolution to Dictatorship, 1914–1923*, Basingstoke: Palgrave Macmillan, pp. 145–174.

22 González Calleja, E. (1999) *El Máuser y el Sufragio: Orden Público, Subversión y Violencia Política en la Crisis de la Restauración (1917–1931)*, Madrid: CSIC, pp. 406–407.

23 Tussell, T. and Queipo de Llano, G. (1990) *Los Intelectuales y la República*, Madrid: Nerea, p. 93.

24 Balcells, A. (2015) 'La inmigració i la política catalana durant la Segona República', *Cercles: revista d'història cultural*, no. 18, pp. 21–41.

25 Vega, E. (2004) 'La CNT a Catalunya entre revolució i reforma, 1930-1936', *Butlletí de la Societat Catalana d'Estudis Històrics*, no. 15, pp. 157–168.

26 Duch Plana, M. (2020) 'Els feminismes del segle XX a Catalunya', *Butlletí de la Societat Catalana d'Estudis Històrics*, no. 31, pp. 233–290.

27 Casassas i Ymbert, J. (1990) 'La Catalunya d'Entreguerres, 1917–1936', in V.V.A.A., *Lluís Companys, Trajectòria d'un President*, Barcelona: L'Avenç, p. 79.

28 López Esteve, M. (2013) 'Els Fets d'octubre de 1934 a Catalunya: entre l'acció de govern i la mobilització social', *Butlletí de la Societat Catalana d'Estudis Històrics*, no. 24, pp. 631–649.

29 Muniesa, B. (1985) *La Burgesia Catalana Ante la Segunda República Española*, Barcelona: Anthropos, 2 vols.

30 Puig Vallverdú, G. (2020) 'La terra en comú. La col·lectivització agrària a Catalunya durant la Guerra Civil, 1936-1939', *Segle XX: revista catalana d'història*, no. 13, pp. 51–72.

31 Navarro, N. (2009) 'La inserció de les dones a la vida pública i política durant la Segona República (1931–1939)', *Eines per a l'esquerra nacional*, no. 9, pp. 151–163.

32 Romero Baeza, M. (1996) 'Julio-septiembre de 1936: las guerras civiles de Euskadi y Catalunya', *Historia y comunicación social*, no. 1, pp. 109–130.

33 Pagès i Blanch, P. (2004) 'La justicia revolucionaria i popular a Catalunya (1936–1939)', *Ebre 38. Revista Internacional de la Guerra Civil (1936–1939)*, no. 2, pp. 1–14.

34 Solé i Sabaté, J. M. and Villarroya, J. (1989) *La Repressió a la Reraguardia de Catalunya 1936–1939*, Barcelona: Ediciones Península, p. 179.

35 Doll-Petit, R. (2004) 'Repressió, salvament i fugida a la reraguarda catalana, 1936–1939', *Ebre 38: revista internacional de la Guerra Civil, 1936–1939*, no. 2, pp. 49–60.

36 Vázquez Osuna, F. (21017) 'L'anihilació de la República del general Franco i l'administració de justícia de Catalunya (1936–1939)', *Revista de Dret Històric Català*, no. 16, pp. 297–319.

37 Escribano, D. (2015) 'Política lingüística a la Catalunya autònoma de la Segona República (1933-1938)', *Recerques: Història, economia i cultura*, no. 71, pp. 159–187.

8

FRANCOISM AND THE DEMOCRATIC EXPERIENCE 1939–2008

The establishment of the Franco regime in Catalonia represented the harshest experience of the modern period for much of Catalan society. The Francoist state sought to obliterate dissent, which was pursued with brutal violence, including the violent repression of organised labour and the Republican supporting peasantry. Cultural and linguistic repression was but one additional element in this process. The full incorporation of Catalonia into the Spanish fatherland began with the prohibition of all that marked out Catalonia as culturally and politically distinct. All cultural and political symbols associated with the Republican period were eliminated. This was compounded by a public erasure of the Catalan language. This was the language then used by over 80 per cent of the population. The Franco political project sought to create in years what had taken the French state more than a century to achieve, a culturally homogeneous, monoglot population. The regime's view of Spanish unity was premised on the assumption that there existed a historic Spanish nation which incorporated all within the frontiers of the Spanish state. Recognition could be permitted to regional sentiment on a folkloric level, but any suggestion that Catalonia possessed the attributes of a nation was anathema to those that rallied to Franco.

Local support for the new regime

Yet a view that Francoism was imposed on an overwhelmingly resistant Catalonia is a simplification, as the civil war as fought in Catalonia has already shown. There were important social sectors that remained deeply hostile to Republican ideals. Even so, few Catalans were found at the highest level of the new regime partly because there was a weak Catalan tradition of enrolment in the Spanish military officer corps and because the Falange was weakly rooted. Even those who supported Franco in the civil war were often held in suspicion due to their Catalan origin. In the third component of the new regime, the Catholic church, adherence

DOI: 10.4324/9781003218791-9

to the new regime occurred with almost complete normality, which can be partly explained by the experience of the civil war and the mass executions of the religious within Catalan society. The Francoist victory of 1939 meant not only the destruction of cultural Catalanisation but also the reversal of democratisation that had accelerated in the 1930s. The dictatorship brought with it the return of property, order, an end to working class protest and the restoration of the Catholic religion. There is abundant evidence of extensive collaboration of certain sectors of Catalan society with the Franco regime, with Catholic sectors, landowners and the business elites the most notable examples.[1] Rule at a local level throughout Catalonia would have been impossible without their input.[2] Therefore, social sectors that had been represented by the Lliga Regionalista had been subject to revolutionary persecution in the first year of the war now welcomed the Franco regime. However, the political tradition that represented conservative and traditional Catalanism since 1901 was abruptly ended. Thus, by renouncing all political activity, a certain restoration of their social prestige became possible.

Culture and exile

Franco's dictatorship abolished the main support mechanisms for the language and Catalan culture. This began with the dismantling of institutional support, from regional and local governments to cultural organisations. The Catalan language disappeared from education and from official life, publications in Catalan were limited to religious pamphlets or to the occasional re-edition of an older work, almost always in small print runs and usually in an archaic variant of the language. A new process of the adoption of Spanish on the part of Catalan elites began, particularly in the richest areas of Barcelona. Many workers and most peasants, as well as middling sectors, continued to speak the Catalan language but there began a near universal process of bilingualism. Education was in Spanish alone but Catalan remained the language of the home and was used with a degree of frequency amongst those with a shared familiarity. However, all public and official relations were to be only in Spanish. Large numbers joined the exodus to exile in 1939. This comprised a diverse group from anarchist activists, ordinary soldiers and their families, political and administrative officials and the majority of intellectuals. The number of Catalans who crossed the French border during January and February 1939 has been estimated as being as high as 100,000.[3] Until the mid-1940s, the task of preserving Catalan high culture was a role of those in exile, in particular amongst those based in Mexico. By 1943, there were already 12 periodicals in Catalan. Political unity was much less effective as pre-war and civil war divisions maintained. From the mid-1940s, the exiles play a diminishing role in both oppositional and cultural activity.

Political repression and opposition

The long-lasting Franco regime is marked by distinctive phases. The first of 1939–1944 is marked by extreme violence and mass executions. In this immediate post-war period, the anarcho-syndicalist CNT suffered the most repression in the urban, industrial context and Esquerra Republicana in the rural and small towns of the Catalan interior.[4] ERC remained extremely weak throughout the dictatorship. The anarchist movement was subject to sustained repression and at least 11 CNT organising committees were captured by the regime's secret police. By 1950, the historic anarchist movement as a mass movement was no more. It also failed to adapt to new times and new social forces. Organised protest against Francoism came from two main areas. Firstly, a transformed left led by the Catalan communists of the Partit Socialista Unificat de Catalunya (PSUC). The PSUC became, during the Franco regime, the hegemonic anti-Francoist force in Catalonia. Secondly, the nationalist movement would be rebuilt by a new generation from within sectors of Catholicism. The PSUC was, in 1936, weak and unimportant in the Catalan political spectrum. However, the circumstances of the Spanish Civil War and the role of the USSR and International Communism transformed its status. The PSUC was a Catalan communist party, as it repeatedly demonstrated its commitment to Catalan identity during the course of the dictatorship. Its major publications, Treball and Nous Horitzons, were published in Catalan and it played an important role in the incorporation of Spanish-speaking immigrants into Catalan society. The party structure aided it in conditions of clandestinity, in spite of many of its leading figures being captured and executed by the dictatorship.

Maquis and strikes

In the early phase of the dictatorship, the only meaningful response from sectors of the opposition was to meet regime violence with that of the anti-Franco guerrilla, known from their participation in the French resistance as the maquis. This type of resistance began almost as soon as the civil war ended and was separately organised by anarchists and communists. Catalan anarchists began to take violent action against the new regime from its very beginning, many of whom had their base of operations in the Pyrenees border zone and crossed the border to carry out military action. One of the most significant groups was led by Quico Sabaté, who together with Josep Lluís Facerías became symbolic of the guerrillas of the anarchist movement. Spanish and Catalan communists also organised armed forces and on a much larger scale. The PCE, in 1944, after the liberation of France, set out to carry out the largest post-war action: the military invasion of Spain. The operation consisted of sending about 6,000 armed men through various Pyrenean valleys in Navarre and Aragon. The central action would be played by about 3,000 men in the Aran Valley. But the invasion of the Aran Valley was a complete failure as local people showed no enthusiasm to join the action. Despite this failure, however, small-scale guerrilla warfare increased and was especially intense during the years 1947–1948, at a time when it is estimated that more than 200 guerrillas were acting, in small groups, throughout the territory. From 1952 onwards, the PCE gave the final order for the total evacuation of its guerrillas. From the 1950s onwards, only a small number of anarchist guerrillas continued their struggle in a situation of growing isolation. Ramon Vila Capdevila, another prominent Catalan anarcho-syndicalist, continued the clandestine struggle in the Catalan mountains until he was killed in action by the Civil Guard in 1963.

In early 1946, a strike in the Manresa textile industry began a series of unprecedented labour conflicts. Strikes then spread to all of the towns in the greater Barcelona industrial belt such as Sabadell and Terrassa. The most important labour conflict was in Mataró, with a general strike lasting three days in March 1946. The notable feature of these strikes was the important role of women.[5] The strikes were accompanied by protests against food shortages and rationing, with low wages adding to the poor living conditions of workers. Internal migration to urban areas had also worsened general conditions with the authorities making no provision for new arrivals. As these strikes were interpreted as being non-political and rather simply economic in origin, concessions were made to the strikers. Price increases applied to Barcelona but not to Madrid in early 1951 had a different impact. Popular unrest in Barcelona led to a widely supported boycott of trams followed by an extensive strike in the spring of 1951. The mobilisation lasted two weeks and spread throughout Catalonia, becoming the most extensive popular protest since the civil war ended.[6] Leading regime officials in Barcelona including the city mayor were forced to resign and the price rises were annulled. This was a reminder to the regime that a culture of protest in Barcelona and amongst Catalans had not been destroyed.

Modest changes in cultural policy

The end of the Second World War represented a major blow to the Franco regime as its former allies, Nazi Germany and fascist Italy, were defeated. The regime was forced into making some modest reforms as well as those that there were simply cosmetic. A monolithic political and repressive structure began to allow scope for some local expression. The Catalan national dance, the sardana, was increasingly evident in public and it was invoked as a religious cultural expression.[7] The use of the Catalan language and some cultural symbols in a religious ceremony at the monastery of Montserrat in April 1947 had been allowed, though this permission led to the removal of the civil governor. As an indication of the opening undertaken by the regime after the end of the Second World War, some of the propaganda for the referendum on the Law of Succession of July 1947 was produced in Catalan. A co-option of a Catalan religious culture was underway. It was an indication that pious, Catholic and conservative components in Catalan culture could escape proscription if they embodied regional or local features. Emblematic of the lifting of restrictions imposed at the beginning of the dictatorship was the re-emergence in December 1946 of the Orfeò Català (Catalan Choral Society), most of whose repertoire was sung in Catalan. The previous year had been celebrated as the centenary of Jacint Verdaguer, poet, author and theologian, and 100,000 copies of his works were published during the year. Similar patterns were evident in other areas of high culture. Whilst this did not mean the return to some kind of cultural normality, the Francoist attempt at the complete extirpation of Catalan culture was being slowly abandoned. What remained of course beyond consideration was any political expression or association with this culture. As the regime entered a new consolidated phase, it needed to adapt to prevent the turn to opposition from the lower middle classes and other middling sectors in Catalan territory. Whilst the Catalan language was not recognised, it was tolerated. The process of modest Catalanisation was also reflected in a process of regionalisation of cultural groupings and movements of civic society. As a further significant step, from 1958, the Floral Games of the Vertical Syndicates of the Spanish fascist Falange awarded a prize to the best poem written in Catalan. However, schooling and mass media remained solely in Spanish and these changes, though important, remained symbolic.

Economic change

Throughout the Franco regime, the Catalan economy retained its primacy within Spain. Between 1955 and 1975, the size of the Catalan economic region grew from 17.7 per cent in 1955 to 19.1 per cent by 1975. Over the course of the 1960s, the Catalan economy and society underwent a profound transformation. Major economic reforms had an important Catalan input as the leading architects of the new liberalising economic model came from Barcelona and local elites welcomed the new economic approach.[8] With the enactment of the Stabilisation Plan in July 1959, the regime abandoned the autarkic model in force since 1939. This led to a massive influx of workers from other regions of Spain. Expansion took place without urban planning or democratic control of the economic model. Catalan industry became a supplier of consumer goods to the Spanish market and experienced enormous growth. This was best symbolised by the SEAT 600 car, which began production in Barcelona in 1957 and became representative of private consumption. Road building was broadly welcomed with little concern expressed around environmental degradation or urban planning visions which prioritised the car. Car prices dropped every year between 1959 and 1973 and the regime sought to craft car ownership as a symbol of societal success.

The Spanish state authorities actively promoted a consumer society as it was believed it would produce a de-politicised and de-mobilised population. Yet consumerism had paradoxical effects. It began a process of individual patterns of consumer behaviour, which impacted across the social structure, including with the emergence of a counter-culture. The owning of consumer goods began a rapid process of narrowing of the cultural distinctiveness of the Catalan countryside with urban areas. New social values also appeared with a marked reduction in popular religiosity. The Catalan church began a lengthy crisis marked by a dramatic fall in vocations and declining church attendance. Catalan traditionalists also expressed concern as the young rushed to consume music and fashion that had little to do with Catalan traditions. The advent of television and a modern advertising system produced new social demands, as did the rapid growth of a mass tourist industry aimed at northern Europeans. Cultural practices were now subject to ever greater international impact, with the Beatles performing in a Barcelona bull ring in 1965.

Rapid diffusion of international patterns of consumption impacted on cinema, music, radio, fashion and the cultural impact of cities such as New York and London.[9] For a period from approximately 1960–1965, economic demands were the key element in strike activity but growing regime concern at apparent communist involvement in union activity led to repressive policies which politicised activity that began as economic demands. The emergence of a consumer society meant, however, that even a resurgent labour movement did not seek a revolutionary transformation of society. It is this fact that enabled the broad acceptance of a capitalist economic form.[10] The working class changed in social composition and, whilst highly mobilised for democratic rights, it also sought clear and direct material improvements.

Demographic transformation

The Catalan economy not only continued to grow in importance but it also became a pole of attraction. Over the course of the twentieth century, Catalonia tripled its population, with about three million people arriving between 1915 and 1975.[11] As we have seen, early patterns were marked by internal migration from the Catalan interior and this began to change over the 1920s and 1930s, meaning around 20 per cent of the population in Catalonia in 1939 came from non-Catalan-speaking areas of Spain. Barcelona concentrated by far the largest balance of immigrant inflows, receiving some 75 per cent migration from other parts of Spain to Catalonia. Urban concentration also depopulated areas of the Catalan countryside. It is estimated that in 1975, the year of Franco's death, more than half of Catalan residents were born outside Catalonia. Population growth occurred with little preparation in terms of urban planning and had negative consequences for the environment, particularly amongst rivers and the coast. Towns on the outskirts of Barcelona such as L'Hospitalet, Badalona, Santa Coloma de Gramenet expanded rapidly. The first phase of population arrival was marked by the construction of shanty towns followed by rapid construction of often poorly built urban estate tower block estates, with few amenities. Though a separate phenomenon, the arrival of mass tourism from the late 1960s irreparably damaged the Costa Brava.

This vast migration brought to an end a culturally homogenous Catalonia. All subsequent cultural expressions and voting patterns were testimony to the territory's transformation and social complexity. Migration produced cultures of displacement for both new arrivals and receptor communities. Some Catalan towns on the edge of Barcelona saw populations of around 4,000–5,000 rapidly transformed by the arrival of some 20,000 new arrivals. The personal impact was varied with some arrivals experienced cultural dislocation in a large city, whilst for others, new opportunities were provided for personal liberation from traditional social mores. Contrary to some nationalist myth-making that migration was state policy to dilute Catalan society, the authorities in Franco's Catalonia often turned back new arrivals and demolished their temporary accommodation. Catalan employers were the principal beneficiary as such vast numbers arrived in boom conditions ensured not only economic growth but also the payment of low wages. For the native Catalan population, this vast infusion of new labour partly provided opportunities for social advancement whether as factory foreman or a shift from blue to white collar employment. Some zones of urban Catalonia heavily concentrated overwhelming number of Spanish speakers, meaning many had little everyday encounter with the Catalan language.[12]

As early as 1960, Catalan ceased to be the majority language of those born in Catalonia.[13] Societal transformation had great implications for the future development of the political and cultural movement of Catalanism. The questions of integration and assimilation of half of the population became a constant theme in Catalan nationalist reflection.[14] The arrival of mass migration from the 1950s led to a new labour movement which was principally organised by the forces of communism. The emergence of the Workers Commissions, the CCOO, developed a unitary ideology around the defence of workers, irrespective of national origin. A new sociology of labour in Catalonia was underway. Furthermore, the dominance of Catalan communism prevented the emergence of hostility towards Catalanism, which had certainly existed prior to 1936. Though the new labour movement was hostile to nationalism, it also sought to defend Catalan language and identity as well as offering a broad cross-class programme of democratisation. In spite of outbursts of anxiety and sometimes hostility to this Spanish-speaking migration, the newly emerging nationalist movement was forced to adopt to the postulates crafted by the communists.

Cultural revival

The Catalan cultural revival that became increasingly visible over the course of the 1960s was based on the activities and organisations that bourgeois Catholics had carefully constructed throughout the 1950s. Catalan-language publishing, having its origins in Church-led and Catholic publications, expanded into all areas of cultural life. Prior to 1936, the Catalan church had been deeply unpopular in many sectors of society, and strong anti-clerical traditions culminated in persecution during the Civil War.[15] However, the restoration of the Church after 1939 gave it relative autonomy, allowing it to slowly rebuild and, to some extent, mould a new version of Catalanism. By the mid-1950s, almost all cultural expressions of Catalanism were possible due to Church patronage. Furthermore, from 1965 to 1975, communists and Catholics co-operated, as churches and other religious buildings become sanctuaries for trades union and cultural meetings. For the first time, social issues emerged amongst new Church sectors, in particular through younger urban priests, a generation that had no experience of the pre-war Catholic church or anti-religious persecution. In ideological terms, a proto–liberation theology can be discerned. Symbolic of the breach made with the regime by bourgeois Catholic sectors were the events of the early 1960s. In 1960, Catholics sang publicly a Catalanist song in the presence of regime dignitaries. This resulted in the imprisonment and torture of some individuals including the future president of democratic Catalonia, Jordi Pujol. Catholics also led a boycott of the Barcelona daily, La Vanguardia, when the editor, Luis de Galinsoga, speaking to a parish priest who had given a sermon in Catalan, described all Catalans as 'shits'. The boycott led to his removal as editor. In 1963, the Abbot of Montserrat was forced into exile after describing the regime as 'un-Christian' in Le Monde. Finally, a group a priests demonstrated in Barcelona in 1966 against police torture and were subject themselves to beatings by the police. Whilst the church began to align itself more closely to Catalan society, it was also noticeable that church attendance continued its decline to the point that in Barcelona in 1970, only 6 per cent attended Sunday service. This decline also occurred in rural areas, though at a slower rate.

Permissive tolerance towards Catalan conservative culture culminated in the authorisation of Òmnium Cultural in July 1961, an organisation whose explicit aim was the promotion and support of all areas of Catalan language and culture. Òmnium played a key role as an intermediate organisation, and its directors brought together figures from both sides of the civil war, which allowed it to pivot between regime institutions and sectors of the opposition. In September 1964, Spanish Television announced the creation of a monthly Catalan language programme. Yet a few months earlier, the regime had reversed permission for Òmnium Cultural and closed it down. The prohibition of Òmnium was an indication of the stop–start approach that reigned within the regime, as technocrats and reactionaries jockied for pre-eminence. From 1965, growing social pressure was taking place for the campaign known as 'Català a l'escola': the introduction of the Catalan language into the schooling system. This was partly expressed in the approach towards the incorporation of Catalanism, as the ban on Òmnium was removed in 1967 and the entity remained legal thereafter. The position of the Catalan language remained one of a spoken language with little written presence. In this period, a children's publication Cavall Fort, inspired by the French and Belgian comic book traditions, was launched to encourage familiarity with the language amongst the young. Further opening towards Catalan culture was facilitated by the modest liberalisation associated with the Press Law introduced in April 1966. In the same year, for the first time since 1939, the National Literature prizes of Spain was opened to entries from the Catalan language and other languages of the state.

The second half of the 1960s was marked by enormous international investment in the Catalan economy, drawn by low labour costs. An increasingly affluent society was able to support a variety of new cultural forms. These developments, in terms of social change and evolving class composition, came to explain the re-crafting of Catalanism in the 1960s. By this time, the worst of the persecution of Catalan culture was over and the language increasingly found a presence on the radio, particularly local stations. 1966 remains an important year in the history of popular music through the electrification of folk embodied by Bob Dylan. In Catalonia, this inspired the Nova Cançó, the new song movement. This movement combined cultural expression with an explicit anti-regime message. From this period of the mid-1960s, we see an explosion in cultural production. New publishers emerged such as Edicions 62, which as well as new work written in Catalan, produced numerous translations of European and other works. Though this revival continued unabated until the end of the dictatorship in 1975, even by that year, the number of books published in Catalan remained well behind the pre-war figure of 1936.

Protest and late Francoism

By late Francoism Catalonia had become the centre of cultural revival and also maintained its role as Spain's main industrial city. The city of Barcelona concentrated more urban workers than any other which further explains the intensity of the anti-Francoist struggle in Catalonia. The highly mobilised working class, even if now a majority of Spanish speakers, came into ever-increasing situations of conflict, where it inevitably experienced the brute force of the security forces. The dominant role within the opposition of the PSUC and CCOO ensured that, in the 1960s and 1970s, during the mass mobilisation of protest, both native and Spanish-speaking workers shared a political identity of both opposition to the dictatorship and defence of the rights of Catalonia as a national entity. The PSUC was a Marxist-Leninist party that published in the language of the country: Catalan.[16] Thus, potential division between Catalan- and Spanish-speaking workers was prevented by the unitary strategy of the Catalan communists. The political dominance of the PSUC culminated in the creation of the most important platform of the Catalan opposition, the Assemblea de Catalunya in 1971. Its creation symbolised the transformation in Catalan political culture that took place over the course of the Franco regime. The Assemblea, which brought together almost all sectors of the anti-regime struggle to devise a common programme, was communist-led yet took place under the protection of a monastery, at Montserrat. The absence of an ideological rupture in the Catalan relationship to Spain found expression in the simple demand from the Assemblea for the restoration of a Catalan autonomous government, as had existed in the 1930s. The Catalan national project that emerged into the transition in the mid-1970s had a clear vision: to pick up from where it was abruptly broken in 1939. By the early 1970s, the goals of Catalanism were more widely accepted than at any previous time, a marked contrast with the pre-civil war period. By 1973, the Catalan language was being incorporated into the school system where collaboration was sought with the cultural organisation Òmnium Cultural to facilitate it. Catalan cultural revival shifted over the decades from being excluded to inclusion. The main concern of the Franco regime was of course its self-preservation, but it also sought to maintain the economic boom and to prioritise the repression of the labour challenge. By October 1975, the state referred to all of the languages of Spain as 'national languages . . . whose knowledge and usage will be protected and encouraged'.

The transition to democracy in Catalonia

Organised labour protest and strikes strikingly grew in every year from 1969 to 1976. The working class in Catalonia, now composed predominantly of native

Spanish speakers in the greater Barcelona area, was more radicalised than at any time since the 1930s, though it should not be seen as a revolutionary agent. The sophisticated political culture developed across the opposition had created schools for democracy.[17] Catalan protest, combining Catalanist demands with calls for popular and civic rights, continually mobilised the largest numbers of any protest culture throughout Spain. Popular pressure ultimately forced the transitional government in Spain to go further than projected and restore the full autonomy of 1931–1939. Equally, though democratic local elections were not held until 1979, the organised popular forces extracted meaningful concessions from officials who owed their authority to the regime. The transition in Catalonia built on pre-existing cultural, economic and political trends, concessions and accommodations that had emerged by the late 1960s. Resolution of the Catalan question post-1975 occurred with comparative ease in the transition period, unlike the escalating conflict in the Basque Country. A broad consensus on recognition towards Catalan culture and identity was visible. In September 1977, on Catalan national day, over one million people protested in Barcelona calling for freedom, amnesty for political prisoners and the restoration of a Statute of Autonomy. Only in Catalonia did a political representative of the republican period, Josep Tarradellas, return as the embodiment of pre-Francoist political legitimacy. Catalan autonomy was provisionally restored in 1979 and the first elections to its parliament took place in 1980. Victory went to conservative Catalanism and the left, which had been dominant under Francoism, was defeated. The Catalan question, with varying degrees of intensity, has remained central to the politics of democratic Spain since the end of the Franco dictatorship.

Social change and de-industrialisation

Under the Franco regime, Catalan society underwent the most important and fastest transformation in its history. In just 30 years, Catalonia consolidated itself as a highly industrialised country and doubled its population. The population was concentrated around the city of Barcelona, so that by 1975, two out of three Catalans lived in the metropolitan area. This entailed a culture that was predominantly urban, which experienced patterns of social modernisation comparable to all other urban zones of Southern Europe. An incipient feminist movement became visible during the transition era, with a congress on women's rights organised in May 1976. New social movements also appeared such as locally based environmental campaigns and those against compulsory military service. The end of the Franco regime broadly coincided with a number of structural changes that determined subsequent social and political development. Catalonia ceased to be the economic leader of Spain and embarked on an intense process of de-industrialisation. Structural unemployment intensified in the late 1970s and gradually undermined the historic strength of the Catalan labour movement. Whilst industry never ceased to be an important component in the post-Franco Catalan economy, white collar and services employment played an ever greater role in the labour market. The population, after the vast demographic change of the 1950s and 1960s, entered a period of some 30 years with little in terms of internal migration, a phase we can term stabilisation. By 1986, only 5.8 per cent had arrived to live in the city of Barcelona in the previous eight years. In this period, for the first time since the Spanish Civil War, Barcelona lost population. This was also a population that was increasingly ageing. The relative stability of the population was also determined by there being little population mobility: most were educated and worked close to where they had been born. There was also in this period an increasing homogenisation of sectors of the population in terms of their cultural habits and practices. Following the de-industrialisation of the late 1970s and beyond, the industrial working class declined in Barcelona. The dominant working class culture of the twentieth century, centred on the self-educated working class activist and the workers cultural centre, the ateneu, was eroded as most workers sought to improve their material living standards and embraced consumerism.

Nationalism in power

The Catalan national project, as it emerged in the late nineteenth century and for most of the twentieth century, not only sought autonomy for Catalonia but also to lead Spanish modernisation. Under the new post-Franco political dispensation, the sources of Spanish modernisation came from Madrid and Europe. This determined a historic re-appraisal of the political project of Catalanism. This partly explains why the new Catalan nationalism no longer sought the leadership of Spain. For the movement led by Jordi Pujol, the close imbrication of the Lliga Regionalista with governments in Madrid had been a historical failure and ended in the disaster of collaboration with the Spanish Nationalists during the civil war. Furthermore, the cultural and linguistic destruction of a long-lasting dictatorship determined that political priorities should be centred on Catalonia. Whilst the Catalan regional government could never ignore developments in Madrid, it sought to craft a new political culture from Barcelona. Whilst for most commentators, the transition to democracy in Spain is seen to have ended with the landslide victory of the Spanish socialists in November 1982, for Catalonia, March 1980 marks a new moment in its contemporary development. In an election campaign marked by an employer-led red scare at the prospect of communist influence in a leftist government, the nationalist coalition Convergència i Unió, CiU, obtained victory and held power until 2003. The process that had been developed intellectually since the 1960s in terms of the national re-construction of Catalonia was now implemented. CiU ruled during a successful transition to a western parliamentary democracy and Spain's accession to the EEC. The new Generalitat obtained greater powers in health, education, finance, public works, planning, tourism, language and cultural policy and the media. Compared to the 1932 Statute, however, the Catalan government obtained fewer powers in public order and justice.

Yet in contrast to the views held in much of Spanish political culture that the emergence of the new semi-federal regime marked a dramatic overhaul of the

Spanish political system, for the Catalan national movement, the power obtained was simply seen as a starting point. No opportunity would be missed when Spain was governed by minority governments for Catalonia to obtain and accumulate new powers. It was to be this differential reading of the compromises of the transition to democracy that produced small-intensity conflicts between Madrid and Barcelona post-1980 and after 2010 political crisis. The unexpected victory of the nationalist coalition in 1980, cemented by an overall majority in 1984, meant that Jordi Pujol, who attained symbolic importance due to his imprisonment by the dictatorship, came to embody the new Catalan nationalism of the post-Franco period. Pujol's political movement often combined radical rhetoric with pragmatic practice, a combination necessitated by the transformation of the Catalan population under the Franco regime. Pujol constructed a broad-based dominant political coalition that sought to emulate the dominant position of the Basque nationalist party within its territory. This coalition was built on the Catalan middle classes, from shopkeepers in the small towns to urban professionals in Barcelona but was unable to extend its reach into the upper elites of the richest areas of Barcelona who had developed a transnational capitalist identity. Weak support was also evident amongst most Spanish speakers, particularly those in the industrial and post-industrial zones found between Barcelona and Tarragona. Differential voting behaviour also enabled the repeated victories of CiU. The first refers to the fact that a significant percentage of the Spanish-speaking Catalan population who voted socialist in the general elections tended to abstain in the regional elections, whilst other socialist voters for national elections voted CiU in the regional ones. Thus, whilst CiU averaged figures of over 40 per cent in Catalan elections, its vote fell by an average of 10 per cent in Spanish general elections. Until 2003, CiU was the most important nationalist formation in the Spanish State and the most electorally successful representative of state-less nationalism in Western Europe, winning six consecutive Catalan elections between 1980 and 1999. At various times since the restoration of democracy, CiU played a pivotal role at a Spanish level. CiU's support of minority Madrid governments was instituted in the late 1970s with its external support of Adolfo Suárez and the UCD and was replicated first with the Spanish Socialists (PSOE) from 1993 to 1996, and again from 1996 to 2000, in support of the conservative Popular Party (PP).

Language and cultural policy

On 18 April 1983, the Parliament of Catalonia overwhelmingly approved the Law on Language Normalisation. This was priority legislation whose purpose was not simply to revive the Catalan language but to transform its status within the educational system and thus, throughout society. It established the use of Catalan as the language of instruction in the classroom through a model known as immersion. In 1975, only 14.5 per cent of the population could write Catalan, whilst only around 35 per cent of secondary school teachers had sufficient competence in the language. Thus, extensive teacher training was an important mechanism for the transformation of the school system. Comprehension of Catalan in the populace rose to 95 per cent by 1996, with some 45.8 per cent then having written ability in the language.[18] Radio and television in Catalan became essential components to not only the transformation of the cultural position of the language but also as mechanisms for the crafting of national narratives. These new channels and stations also displayed a high degree of professionalism and sought to be competitive within the audio-visual market.[19] The post-Franco period saw a range of new publications in Catalan, from the historical and cultural monthly L'Avenç to a daily newspaper Avui, all of which in the late 1970s gave an explicit commitment to a Catalanist cultural space. From the 1980s, publications in Catalan expanded and an extensive literary culture was ever more evident.

Urban culture

The Spanish Constitution of 1978 transformed the territorial structure of Spain, leading to increasing regionalisation and the emergence of a tier of sub-national government. The territorial formula adopted was the State of Autonomies, which led to the creation of 17 Comunidades Autónomas (Autonomous Communities). This regionalisation of the Spanish state model was followed by the profound democratisation of the municipal level. Cities and their mayors became part of the vanguard of the civic culture of Spain's new democracy with Barcelona, Madrid and the other urban areas of Spain electing left-wing governments. By 2012, half of Spanish state spending was managed at a regional and municipal level, whilst these two tiers employed 70 per cent of state employees. In European terms, Paris and London are rather unusual in the extent of their overwhelming political, administrative and economic dominance: most European societies have seen competing rivalries between two major cities: Rome/Milan, St Petersburg/Moscow and, in the case of Spain, Madrid/Barcelona. In these cases, it is often only in the latter part of the twentieth century that the political and administrative capitals also became the cultural and economic capitals. In some cases, such as Rome/Milan and Madrid/Barcelona, the second city has often maintained an economic dominance into the contemporary era.

Barcelona is one of the most densely populated cities in the world. By 1975, the greater Barcelona metropolitan area comprised 70 per cent of the total Catalan population. This greater area was comparable in European terms to Milan, Rome and Madrid. There is then a marked demographic and spatial contrast in terms of the size of Barcelona in relation to Catalonia, and the size of Madrid in relation to the rest of Spain. One of the deeply rooted debates that has determined the discourse of political Catalanism has been the dialectic between city and wider territory, the political relations between Barcelona and the rest of Catalonia. With the nationalists of Convergència i Unió dominant in the national terrain and the Catalan socialist party (Partit del Socialistes de Catalunya—PSC) dominant in the main cities and urban areas, it was thus possible to speak of rival parallel power structures rather than alternation. Catalan socialism (urban and municipal) and nationalism (regional and rural) held sole power, respectively, for over 20 years from the late 1970s, and, in the case of the socialists, they continued to hold the most important municipal position, the mayorship and administrative control of the city of Barcelona until 2011. The city council is the second most important in all of Spain and historically Barcelona vied as an alternative capital of Spain. It was to counter socialist strength that in 1987, Jordi Pujol's nationalist government abolished the Área Metropolitana de Barcelona (Metropolitan Area of Barcelona), the body responsible for municipal oversight, believing it to represent a regional counter power. This move deepened hostility between the two largest Catalan political forces, the socialists and the nationalists. The abolition of this authority was rooted in the new narrative of Catalan nationalism, centred on the small towns of the Catalan interior, that the city of Barcelona, metropolitan and multi-cultural, was a challenge to its nationalising project. Thus, a battle for cultural hegemony occurred between these two forces. However, with the comparative decline of industry and its part replacement by services and the knowledge economy, the political culture began to be less threatening to Catalan nationalism by the 2000s, with the city becoming the central location for the pro-sovereignty mobilisations.

1992 and change of model

During the 1980s, CiU's political dominance in Catalonia had grown as regional self-government consolidated, even following the attempted clawing back of powers to Madrid after the failure of the February 1981 coup. PSOE majority governments in Madrid from 1982 to 1993 produced periodic disputes between Barcelona and Madrid. With the loss of the absolute majority of the PSOE in the elections of 1993, CiU was able, until 2000, to obtain direct concessions from Madrid in exchange for ensuring parliamentary stability in Spain. Whilst a push for direct participation in the Spanish cabinet came from some sectors in the nationalist coalition, this was strongly resisted by Jordi Pujol. The coming to power of a renewed Spanish conservatism in 1996, without an overall majority, again gave leverage to Catalan nationalism. However, this period was also marked by a resurgent and confident Spanish nationalism, in part produced by the economic transformation of Spain and in particular of Madrid. This Spanish nationalism increasingly questioned the accumulation of concessions obtained by Basques and Catalans in the 1990s and sought to prevent any further devolution of powers to the regions. It also embarked on challenges to language policies in those regions and sought to harmonise the educational curriculum, partly around areas such as history and geography, where it advocated the teaching of a shared Spanish national story.

The economy

The territory once termed the Manchester of the South, the city of Barcelona, has seen its once enormous industrial strength and comparative weight in Spain eroded. In 1933, Catalan income per capita was 80 per cent higher than the Spanish average and this fell to 19 per cent by 2000. As elsewhere in Europe, the Catalan economy has seen structural transformation since the early 1980s. The industrial sector in Catalonia has seen its importance within the economy fall from 41.1 per cent of Catalan GDP in 1975 to 28.9 per cent in 1996, and just under 20 per cent by 2020. This fall in the industrial sector has brought with it sustained structural unemployment and a weakened trade union movement. The decline in industry has been partly offset by the growth of the service sector. Barcelona has not been completely displaced, remaining important in terms of industry, culture and city of design and tourism. Barcelona obtains 12 per cent of its GDP from tourism. In the post-Franco period, the city, following a crisis associated with de-industrialisation, re-emerged through its hosting of the Olympic Games in 1992. As host city, the urban landscape of the city was re-configured under the terms of what became known as the Barcelona model. This began with the urban revival necessitated by the decline of textiles and other traditional industries in the early 1980s. In this phase, with an ambitious modernising socialist council, with strong communist support, the transformation of the city sought to address the great deficits in terms of infrastructure that the dictatorship had shown little concern with.

The Olympic Game in 1992 initiated the transformation of the city of Barcelona into one of Europe's leading centres for tourism. Within a decade, the city had become one of the most visited in Europe. The city's art and architecture attained ever greater international projection. This cultural rebranding has entailed a cleansing and purification of the social conflicts of the past with the city developing a new urban model as an 'entrepreneurial city' built on the new tourism, with numbers expanding from 2.4 million visitors in 1993 to 9 million by 2019. At the same time, economic change brought about the shift to a new service industry. However, this employment growth occurred in sectors notorious for low wages, little innovation and low productivity and evidence of ever greater social inequality. Since the Olympic Games in 1992, Catalonia attracted substantial foreign investment. Catalonia continues to have the highest share of exports throughout Spain. Catalonia has become one of the most important tourist regions in Europe and its hospitality industry has also made it a prime location on the international conference market.[20] The city as theme park and playground of a tourist industry was not without consequence. The perception of tourism increasingly became viewed as a problem with growing concern that its massification in Barcelona would lead to the city becoming a new Venice in terms of the erosion of its physical environment. Mobilisation against the prioritisation of tourism over the citizenry has regularly produced organised protests in the historic centre of the city.

Comparative economic stagnation

For most of the twentieth century, Catalonia maintained its economic advantage over nearly all other areas of Spain. Calculations have shown that of 173 European regions, in 1900, Catalonia was placed 39th, a placing which had risen to 31st by 1925. However, from the 1970s, the difference between the poorest and richest regions narrowed, a process which has intensified by membership of the European Community, which has ensured a narrowing in economic position amongst the Spanish regions compared to Catalonia. In 1955, Madrid represented just 11 per cent of Spain's GDP. In 1980, Madrid's share had risen to 15.6 per cent but it still remained behind Catalonia at 18.8 per cent. Yet by the early 2020s, Madrid had displaced Catalonia with a figure of 20 per cent. The capital city also surpassed Barcelona as that with the highest per capita income. The ongoing expansion and consolidation of Madrid have major political implications not only for Spain but also for a Catalonia that is having to become accustomed to comparative decline. Madrid enjoys advantages due to its location in the centre of the peninsula and radial Spain, and that it receives privileges derived from public spending and the location of public and private decision-making centres. At the European level, Catalonia's competitiveness has also slipped. By 2020, the Catalan region had fallen to 70th in the overall ranking of European regions. Madrid and Barcelona have transformed their roles since the 1970s, crafting new identities for themselves in the process. Madrid's project to be a great European city has inevitably meant the downgrading of Barcelona's role in the wider Spanish polity.

Societal impact of new economic models

For 120 years Catalonia was the most advanced society in Spain. The Catalonia of industrial and bourgeois textile workers began its decline during the transition to democracy. Whilst Catalonia continues to be an important economic region, it is no longer so in a disproportionate way. Thus, we can begin to trace the emergence of a Catalan existential crisis as its comparative importance in the Spanish political system began to decline. Simply put, Catalonia had lost its leading role in the political and economic development of Spain, which had been a central element to the narrative of political Catalanism since its emergence in the 1880s. Catalan society has converged not only with the broad patterns of much of Spain but also in other areas of Europe, where working patterns combine security and precarious conditions. Poverty is extensive in Catalan society, comprising some 21 per cent by the early 2020s. Child poverty is consistently higher than the European Union average.[21] The older bonds of social solidarity have faded in now post-industrial areas with individual expression increasingly important and dominant. Furthermore, the working class barrio became an ever more heterogenous social area, with new immigration and new middle-class arrivals transforming its make-up. However, class position, in particular middle-class position, were strong indications across the greater Barcelona area that the individual was more likely to speak Catalan in the home and have Catalan ancestry. This was even more strongly evident amongst the business class.[22] As elsewhere in other European societies, immigration has been concentrated in the poorer areas of Barcelona and other Catalan cities. Barcelona received the largest number of immigrants of any Spanish city impacting on society in ever greater demands on transport, schooling and health care. 700,000 new arrivals were added between 2000 and 2005, and by 2020, the overseas population comprised some 16 per cent of the overall Catalan population. This immigration has brought with it ethnic, religious and cultural differentiation and poses a greater cultural change than the extensive Spanish migration of the 1950s and 1960s. The principal way this new international immigration is framed is in terms of its potential impact on the project of what is termed the normalisation of the Catalan language across society.

Language crisis

Though Catalonia experienced vast demographic transformation under Francoism, the learning of Catalan remained a clear aspiration amongst Spanish migrants and ensured broad support for the language policies introduced in the early 1980s. By the mid-1990s, concern was increasingly expressed that the expansion of Catalan had stalled. This was linked to a growing sense amongst international immigrants to Catalonia that the Catalan language had limited utility. This deepened following the economic crisis after 2008, where the prospect of social mobility through knowledge of Catalan halted.[23] Language practice beyond certain social sectors has changed little though the 1983 normalisation law has achieved substantial progress in the status of Catalan. Societal consensus that made the law of 1983 is no longer evident across Catalan society. The impact of the programme of language normalisation has stalled and ever greater evidence emerged of a linguistic situation where the language remained the primary means of communication within the classroom, yet it ceased to be so in a number of social contexts. New social media platforms and an associated internationalisation of cultural production meant that younger cohorts were increasingly attracted by the global reach of the Spanish language. By 2018, only some 36 per cent of Catalans described the Catalan language as their primary source of identification, whilst the figure for Spanish was over 46 per cent. It is in this context of a growing sense of crisis around the prospects for the Catalan language, together with the consolidation of Madrid, the comparative decline of Barcelona and Catalonia and, the disruption produced by the economic crisis after 2008, that we should situate the turn to independence.[24]

Notes

1 Molinero, C. (2001) 'Les actituds polítiques a Catalunya durant el primer Franquisme', *Butlletí de la Societat Catalana d'Estudis Històrics*, no. 12, pp. 97–106.
2 Marín i Corbera, M. (1995) 'Franquisme i poder local. Construcció i consolidació deIs ajuntaments feixistes a Catalunya, 1938–1949', *Recerques, Història, Economia, Cultura*, no. 31, pp. 37–52.
3 Morales Montoya, M. (2009) 'L'Exili a Catalunya al segle XX', *Butlletí de la Societat Catalana d'Estudis Històrics*, no. 20, pp. 169–202.
4 Solé i Sabaté, J. M. and Dueñas i Iturbe, O. (2007) *El franquisme contra Esquerra. Els alcaldes i diputats afusellats d'Esquerra Republicana de Catalunya*, Barcelona: Fundació Josep Irla, pp. 35–36.
5 Nadia Varo, N. (2007) 'Mujeres en huelga. Barcelona metropolitana durante el franquismo', in Babaiano, J. (ed.) *Del hogar a la huelga. Trabajo, género y movimiento obrero durante el franquismo*, Madrid: los Libros de la Catarata, pp. 139–187.

6 Vázquez de Prada, M. (2003) 'La oposición al régimen franquista en Barcelona: algunas muestras entre 1948 y 1951', *Hispania: Revista española de historia*, vol. 63, no. 215, pp. 1057–1078.

7 Dowling, A. (2006) 'The Catholic Church in Catalonia: From Cataclysm in the Civil War to the "Euphoria" of the 1950s', *Catalan Review*, vol. 20, no. 1, pp. 83–100.

8 Balfour, S. (2012) 'La modernització autoritària franquista a Barcelona: arrels intel·lectuals i contradicció', in Balfour, S. (ed.) *Barcelona malgrat el franquisme La SEAT, la ciutat i la represa sense democràcia*, Barcelona: Ajuntament de Barcelona, pp. 13–26.

9 Manel Tresserras, J. M. (2000) 'Els sistemes de comunicació i cultura a Catalunya durant el segle XX. Una proposta d'interpretació', *Cercles: revista d'història cultural*, no. 3, pp. 59–73.

10 Kocka, J. (2016) *Capitalism. A Short History*, Princeton, NJ: Princeton University Press, p. 119.

11 Cabré i Pla, A. and Pujadas i Rúbies, I. (1989) 'La población: inmigració i explosió demogràfica', in V.V.A.A., *Història econòmica de la Catalunya contemporània s. XX Població, agricultura i energia*, Barcelona: Enciclopèdia Catalana, pp. 111–128.

12 Marín i Corbera, M. (2006) 'Franquismo e inmigración interior: el caso de Sabadell (1939–1960)', *Historia Social*, no. 56, pp. 131–152.

13 Vila i Moreno, F. X. (2004) 'Hora de fer balanç? Elements per valorar les polítiques lingüístiques a Catalunya en el periode constitucional', *Revista de Llengua i Dret*, no. 41, pp. 243–286.

14 Domingo i Valls, A. (2014) *Catalunya al mirall de la immigració: demografia i identitat nacional*, Barcelona: L'Avenç, pp. 94–97.

15 Dowling, A. (2013) *Catalonia Since the Spanish Civil War: Reconstructing the Nation*, Portland: Sussex Academic Press, pp. 74–76.

16 Molinero, C. and Ysàs, P. (2010) *Els anys del PSUC. El partit de l'antifranquisme (1956–1981)*, Barcelona: L'Avenç, p. 49.

17 Andreu Acebal, M. (2015) 'Barcelona, els moviments socials i la transició a la democràcia: hegemonia gramsciana, referent espanyol i ruptura catalana', *Segle XX. Revista catalana d'història*, no. 8, pp. 105–134.

18 Milian i Massana, A. (2013) 'La llei de normalització lingüística: el camí cap al redreçament', in *30 anys de política lingüística*, Barcelona: Generalitat de Catalunya, pp. 11–20.

19 Guimerà i Orts, J. A. (2018) 'El papel de la comunicación en la construcción nacional de Cataluña: Jordi Pujol y la instrumentalización política de los medios (1968–1989)', *Historia y política: Ideas, procesos y movimientos sociales*, no. 40, pp. 363–387.

20 Maluquer de Motes, J. (20111) 'El turismo, motor fundamental de la economía de Cataluña (1951–2010)', *Historia Contemporánea*, no. 42, pp. 347–399.

21 Flaquer, L. (2008) 'Diversitat familiar, benestar de la infància i cohesió social a Catalunya', *Nota d'economia*, no. 91, pp. 71–86.

22 Subirats, M., López, P. and Sánchez, C. (2010) 'Classes i grups socials a la Regió Metropolitana de Barcelona', *Papers: Regió Metropolitana de Barcelona: Territori, estratègies, planejament*, no. 52, pp. 8–37.

23 Subirats Martori, M. (2020) 'Catalunya endins:: una comunitat estructuralment esquerdada', *Idees: Revista de temes contemporanis*, no. 50, pp. 1–9.

24 Dowling, A. (2014) 'Accounting for the Turn Towards Secession in Catalonia', *International Journal of Iberian Studies*, vol. 27, nos. 2–3, pp. 219–234.

EPILOGUE

The failed push for Catalan independence

As we have seen throughout this study, social and political revolt is a frequent expression in Catalan society and we witnessed a new phase between 2017 and 2019. We have seen also how so often in the political culture of the country, these rebellions and protests have been defeated. A movement that began an explicit push for the independence of Catalonia from Spain experienced a dramatic political defeat in the autumn of 2017. Whilst a sustained series of protests irrupted in the autumn of 2019 following the sentencing of the political leadership of independence to imprisonment by the Spanish Supreme Court, this protest cycle represented the end of a phase of the movement rather than a new beginning. The full range of memoirs and political analysis that has been published since 2017 has demonstrated that the goal of Catalan independence was certain to fail given the existing correlation of forces. These were a state order in Spain that refused to countenance secession; a parliamentary majority for secession, yet one comprised of less than 48 per cent of the vote and the complete absence of international support for an independent Catalonia. It remains the case that the declaration of independence remains universally unrecognised. Furthermore, pro-independence Catalan political elites had differing interpretations of what the push itself signified. For many it represented an authentic attempt at breaking with Spain, whilst for others, the purpose of the movement was to act as a mechanism of pressure on Madrid to extract meaningful concessions that might include an internationally recognised referendum. There remained throughout the process a marked mismatch between public rhetoric and private belief. Whilst Catalan independence was proclaimed in the Catalan parliament on 27 October 2017, within 24 hours, some of the political leadership had fled the country to avoid imprisonment whilst others who remained submitted to arrest warrants. This was one of the least credible declarations of independence in modern history. Not even the Spanish flag was lowered from the Catalan government building.

DOI: 10.4324/9781003218791-10

Explaining the rise of independence

From the late 1970s, it seemed that Catalonia was embarking on a new direction, with autonomy re-established, wealth maintained and self-confidence restored in a Spain that was seeking to build a new democracy. The Europeanisation of Spanish political culture from the mid-1980s seemed also to provide new potential opportunities within the context of European Community membership. The institutional status of Catalan language and culture was transformed post-1980. The new middle class that emerged in Catalonia over the course of the 1970s and 1980s held both the resources of cultural capital and a degree of political power. They were found across newly emerging economic sectors and professions. They were a social cohort who dominated the culture industries. This social sector had disproportionate influence in Barcelona and its dominance was unchallenged in the small towns and countryside. The new cultural elite that emerged in Catalonia post-1975 had been forged in opposition to the state. Many of the leading cadres of cultural and other activism were rapidly incorporated into the new institutional terrain. Thus, political demobilisation and institutionalisation were marked features of the transition and new period of regional autonomy.

For most of the period from 1980 to 2005, the Catalan question seemed to be resolvable within the contours of Spain's semi-federal autonomous regime. It was political violence in the Basque Country that attracted the greatest national and international attention. As we have noted, sources of discontent had gradually been growing in some sectors of Catalan society but as late as 2005, fewer than 15 per cent of Catalans expressed support for the independence of the country. A left-liberal Catalan coalition government which displaced the Catalan nationalists in 2003 began a process known as the revising of the Catalan statute of autonomy. Due to the unexpected political victory of Spanish socialism in March 20004, in the context of a terrorist attack, an embittered conservative Partido Popular began to use the Catalan question to erode the PSOE government in Madrid. Thus, what in many respects were technical aspects of Catalan autonomy became highly politicised. Popular interest in the autonomy debate were low and barely half of the Catalan electorate approved the measure in a referendum in June 2006. The Partido Popular requested the Supreme Court adjudicate on the constitutionality of the revised autonomy statute in Catalonia. In the midst of this political impasse, the global economic crisis broke out in 2008 and the Spanish economy was one of the hardest hit in Europe. In the context of an increasingly paralysed Catalan political class, nationalist social movements began to take the initiative. Between 2009 and 2011, self-organised micro-referendums were organised throughout the Catalan interior and seemed to demonstrate that support for independence was rapidly growing. In early July 2010, after four years of deliberations, in the context of a major economic crisis profoundly disrupting Catalan society, the Spanish Supreme Court declared a number of elements of the Catalan statute to be unconstitutional. This judgement also touched on important symbolic areas such as the Catalan language and the right of Catalonia to call itself a nation. A broad cross-party and collective societal response interpreted this judgement as an affront and soon after over one million people marched in the centre of Barcelona proclaiming: 'We are a nation. We decide'.

15M and sovereignty

Catalonia has long been one of the richest regions of Spain and the middle classes within the region enjoyed comparative privilege. The province of Girona, deeply imbricated with pro-secessionist sentiment, is the richest region in all of Spain. This social sector, comparatively privileged, was traumatised between 2009 and 2010 by the arrival of the intense economic crisis. With the arrival of the crisis, Spain became a laboratory for new forms of political organisation, culminating in the mobilisation that began in the city of Madrid, becoming known as the 15M movement, due to its foundation on 15 May 2011. The movement rapidly spread throughout Spain, and Barcelona became one of the primary locations in terms of the movement's influence. The 15M emerged in a context of crisis, property bubbles and their subsequent implosions, corruption and conflicts over urban re-zoning and land use. Broadly middle class in terms of their activist and organisational base, these movements also reflected the fact many of new forms of employment, including that of once stable professional sectors, were precarious. Although the 15M movement and Catalan sovereignty did not seem to have much in common, they did share the rejection of the status quo and an ability to mobilise the citizenry. 15M and Catalan independence became in scale some of the most important social and political movements in contemporary Europe. The 15M had a much shorter duration whilst the Catalan sovereignty movement lasted a decade. Finally, between 2012 and 2020, electoral support for Catalan independence movement consistently obtained between 35 per cent and 48 per cent of the vote in a range of elections. In 2021, independence did obtain 52 per cent of the vote, but this was also with the loss of over half a million votes, with a substantially reduced turnout in an election held in the context of the Covid pandemic.

The ritual of independence

The Catalan movement for independence was highly unusual until 2017 in its construction of an optimistic culture of prediction with its claim that the independence of Catalonia was not just a probability but was imminent. Whilst the response and mobilisation of July 2010 can be termed reactive, the development of the Diadas from 2012 can be framed within this optimistic narrative of the future. The street became the stage and the central location of pro-independence protest after 2012. The Diada became the annual ritual of Catalan independence. This was a unique and innovative form of display, visual vocabulary and political communication through the annual Diadas. The Catalan secessionist movement had at its disposal a ready-made toolkit of mechanisms of communication and organisation. The professionalised choreography of patriotic performance was used to express the organisation's power and mobilising capacity. The broader Catalan sovereignty movement until 2017 represented a romantic revolt in politics. It was notably lacking in sophistication or rigorous political assessment, and its intellectual cheerleaders were remarkably naïve in their relentlessly upbeat analysis. Seven successive and vast mass mobilisations, usually totalling one million, each September since 2012 demonstrated their political limitations in the autumn of 2017. The movement had often seemed to interpret its successful annual mobilisations as themselves providing the legitimacy to break with Spain. The Catalan sovereignty movement finally reached a strategic end point in October 2017.

The autumn of 2017

Although it had not formed part of the electoral programme of the pro-independence coalition that won the Catalan regional elections in September 2015, a referendum on independence later became government policy and was promised for 1 October 2017. The Spanish government immediately declared such an action to be illegal and invalid. Prior to this event, a non-binding consultation on independence, held on 9 November 2014, had revealed there was overwhelming pro-independence sentiment in the interior and small towns of Catalonia. However, turnout was around 40 per cent, which was broadly replicated on 1 October 2017. The greater Barcelona area and the city of Tarragona remained the main zones where support for independence is clearly a minority political position. Given the demographic transformation of Catalonia in the 1950s and 1960s, this is not surprising. On both occasions, consultation and referendum, voters against independence simply did not participate. However, the event in 2014 had been tolerated by the Spanish authorities; in 2017, the full weight of the Spanish state was used to prevent a referendum. Yet in a situation where some two million or more Catalans turned out to vote, 1 October 2017 was a political triumph. Spanish police violence not only made the event a global news story but also seemed to give an international moral victory to the Catalan cause. In Catalonia itself, outrage and collective shock at the police violence and the subsequent imprisonment of the civic and political leadership led into a late radicalisation of the movement. The logistics for the referendum on 1 October 2017 was supported by political activists who began to develop a strategy of resistance which occurred with varying degrees of intensity in the next two years. New participatory actions including transport disruption, minor acts of sabotage and a more confrontational political style emerged. Civil disobedience, which had been deemed unnecessary by the pro-independence movement through its repeated affirmation of its peaceful values, became an increasing part of the repertoire of the Catalan sovereignty movement after 2017.

Backlash from Spanish nationalism

The events of 2017 in particular and during the political cycle until 2019 also had a profound societal impact across Spain. One consequence was the explicit re-emergence of an intolerant Spanish nationalism. On the evening of 3 October 2017, King Felipe VI gave a belligerent televised speech against Catalan independence and notably never mentioned the hundreds injured in the Spanish police violence. This speech by the Spanish king seemed to provide the tone for the years to come as much of the Spanish media landscape and the country's political and legal authorities interpreted the Catalan events as an affront to the honour and integrity of Spain. Anger was also expressed at the framing of Spain internationally as a country of harsh police repression. The Spanish government, for the first time in the history of the autonomous system, removed the Catalan government from office and called new elections. By 2019, a newly emergent political force, Vox, had capitalised on the Spanish nationalist backlash and become a new and influential actor in the party system in Spain. The Spanish legal authorities, often acting as a parallel power structure, have been unending in their pursuit against apparent threats to Spanish unity. In this context, the options for political accommodation between Madrid and Barcelona and a meaningful overhaul of the Spanish Constitutional settlement of 1978 have receded. The early 2020s are marked by a period of stasis in terms of reform and wars of position between resurgent Spanish nationalism and a Catalan independence movement on the defensive.

Endgame or pause?

The movement for Catalan independence, that was already able to mobilise hundreds and thousands in 2006 and 2007 in two separate protests, has had a marked impact on Catalan political culture. All political parties must articulate their position on the sovereignty question. The issues that produced the rise of independence: concern at the erosion of the Catalan language, economic deficits, comparative decline, middle-class discontent, remain unresolved. However, the dramatic and rapid growth experienced by the movement reached a ceiling and the independence cause remains unable to craft a sustained and clear social majority. With a Spanish state system unwilling to consider the independence of Catalonia, it remains difficult to envisage the achievement of secession without what is termed in the literature a super-majority. Yet support for secession amongst for the young had stalled by the early 2020s, which closes off the possibility of an inevitable demographic route to independence. Voters under 30, like their counterparts elsewhere, are moving away from traditional fixed identity categories. This may be temporary or may mark a permanent shift in identity construction. It is evident that issues such as climate change are increasingly of much greater concern to this cohort. Over 40 per cent of the Catalan population live along the Catalan coast and rising sea levels have grave potential for upheaval. Loss of flora and fauna has intensified whilst forest and other fires have increased in frequency and intensity. Whether this period of the early 2020s marks a permanent end to the hope for independence of Catalonia or merely a pause before the re-appearance of revitalised political programme for secession will ultimately depend on the character of the political system in Madrid and its willingness to accommodate difference.

Spanish political reality is plural and multi-lingual and the return to political power in Madrid of an intolerant Spanish nationalism can only increase Catalan alienation from Spain. Throughout this book, we have seen how reactions to specific events, grievances and causes can produce dramatic political reactions. We have also seen that Catalan society has internalised a number of social and political values, including a collective sense of justice and the demand for recognition. Should many Catalans feel further political humiliation in the future, historical tradition points to a renewed expression of the deeply rooted Catalan tradition of revolt.

BIBLIOGRAPHY

Abello i Güell, T. (1992) 'El proceso de Montjuïc, la condena internacional al régimen de la Restauración', *Historia Social*, no. 14, pp. 47–60.

Abernethy, D. (2000) *The Dynamics of Global Dominance: European Overseas Empires, 1415–1980*, New Haven: Yale University Press.

Adell Gisbert, J. A. and Menchón i Bes, J. (2004–2005) 'Les fortificacions de la frontera meridional dels comtats catalans, o les fortificacions de la Marca Superior d'al-Àndalus', *Lambard: Estudis d'art medieval*, no. 17, pp. 65–84.

Agustí i Farreny, A. (1994) 'Els bisbes de Lleida i l'espanyolització (segles XVI-XVIII)', *Analecta Sacra Tarraconensia*, vol. 67, no. 2, pp. 233–245.

Ainaud, J. M. (1995) *El Llibre Negre de Catalunya: De Felip V a l'ABC*, Barcelona: Planeta.

Alanyà i Roig, J. (2005) 'Culte i devoció a la Puríssima al bisbat de Tortosa (segles XIII-XXI)', *Analecta Sacra Tarraconensia*, vol. 78, pp. 159–308.

Albareda i Salvadó, J. (1988) 'Els dirigents de la revolta pagesa de 1687–89: de barretines a botiflers', *Recerques*, no. 20, pp. 151–170.

Albareda i Salvadó, J. (1995) 'L'impacte de la guerra dels Nou Anys a Catalunya. L'ocupació francesa de 1697', *Afers: fulls de recerca i pensament*, vol. 10, no. 20, pp. 29–46.

Alcoberro i Pericay, A. (2008) 'Cacera de bruixes, justícia local i Inquisició a Catalunya, 1487–1643: alguns criteris metodològics', *Pedralbes: Revista d'historia moderna*, no. 28(2), pp. 485–504.

Alonso Martinez, N. (2005) 'Agriculture and food from the Roman to the Islamic Period in the North-East of the Iberian peninsula: Archaeobotanical Studies in the City of Lleida (Catalonia, Spain)', *Vegetation History and Archaeobotany*, vol. 14, no. 4, pp. 341–361.

Alter, P. (1989) *Nationalism*, London: Edward Arnold.

Álvarez Junco, J. (2001) *Mater Dolorosa: La Idea de España en el Siglo XIX*, Madrid: Taurus.

Alvarez-Ossorio, I. and Taibo, C. (eds.) (2007) *Nacionalismo Español, Esencias, Memoria e Instituciones*, Madrid: La Catarata.

Amat, J. (2015) *El Llarg Procés: Cultura i Política a la Catalunya Contemporània (1937–2014)*, Barcelona: Tusquets.

Amelang, J. (1992) 'Distribució social i formes de vida', in Sobrequés, J (ed.) *Història de Barcelona. Vol. IV*, Barcelona: Enciclopèdia Catalana, pp. 165–211.

Anderson, P. (1974) *Lineages of the Absolutist State*, London: New Left Books, pp. 75–77.

Anderson, P. (1996) *Passages from Antiquity to Feudalism*, London: Verso, pp. 168–169.

Andreu Acebal, M. (2015) 'Barcelona, els moviments socials i la transició a la democràcia: hegemonia gramsciana, referent espanyol i ruptura catalana', *Segle XX. Revista catalana d'història*, no. 8, pp. 105–134.

Andreu Acebal, M. (2016) *Les Ciutats Invisbles: Viatge a la Catalunya Metropolitan*, Barcelona: L'Avenç.

Anglès, H. (1935) *La música a Catalunya fins al segle XIII*, Barcelona: Institut d'Estudis Catalans, pp. 312–313.

Anguera, P. (1995) *Déu, Rei i Fam. El primer carlisme a Catalunya*, Barcelona: Publicacions de l'Abadia de Montserrat.

Aranegui Gascó, C. and Vives-Ferrándiz Sánchez, J. (2007) 'Encuentros coloniales, respuestas plurales. Los ibéricos antiguos de la fachada mediterránea central', in *De les comunitats locals als estats arcaics. La formació de les societats complexes a la costa del Mediterrani occidental*, Barcelona: Universitat de Barcelona, pp. 89–107.

Arnabat i Mata, R. (1999) 'Notes sobre l'aixecament dels malcontents, 1827', *Butlletí de la Societat Catalana d'Estudis Històrics*, no. 10, pp. 107–128.

Arteaga, O., Padró, J. and Sanmartí, E. (1986) 'La expansión fenicia por las costas de Cataluña y el Languedoc', in Del Olmo, G. and Aubet, M. E. (eds.) *Los fenicios en la Península Ibérica*, Sabadell: Ausa, pp. 303–314.

Ashtor, E. (1988) 'Catalan Cloth on the Late Medieval Mediterranean Markets', *Journal of European Economic History*, vol. 17, no. 2, pp. 227–257.

Aurell Cardona, J. (1998) 'La Imagen del mercader medieval', *Boletín de la Real Academia de Buenas Letras de Barcelona*, no. 46, pp. 23–44.

Aurell i Cardona, J. and Rubiés i Mirabet, J. P. (1993) 'Els mercaders catalans i la cultura de l'Edat Mitjana al Renaixement', *Anuario de Estudios Medievales*, vol. 23, pp. 221–255.

Backman, C. (2003) *The Worlds of Medieval Europe*, Oxford: Oxford University Press, p. 179.

Bada i Elias, J. (1994) 'La religiositat popular al bisbat de Barcelona en la segona meitat del segle XVII: alguns indicadors', *Analecta Sacra Tarraconensia*, vol. 67, no. 2, pp. 259–269.

Bada i Elias, J. (2009) 'L'Expulsió dels jueus, 1492', *Butlletí de la Societat Catalana d'Estudis Històrics*, no. 20, pp. 51–68.

Badia, L, Santanach, L. and Soler, A. (2013) 'Ramon Llull', in Broch, A. (ed.) *Història de la Literatura Catalana. Literatura medieval (I). Dels orígens al segle XIV*, Barcelona: Enciclopèdia Catalana/Editorial Barcino, pp. 377–476.

Badosa Coll, E. (1990) '*Endeutament col·lectiu i desaparició de béns comunals a Catalunya a la segona meitat del segle XVIII*', *Pedralbes: revista d'història moderna*, no. 10, pp. 51–66.

Baer, Y. (1961) *A History of the Jews in Christian Spain: From the Age of Reconquest to the Fourteenth Century*, Philadelphia: Jewish Publication Society, p. 140.

Bainton, R. H. (2000) *Christianity*, Boston: Houghton Mifflin, pp. 141–143.

Balcells, A. (1983) *Historia Contemporanea de Cataluña*, Barcelona: Edhasa.

Balcells, A. (1991) *El Nacionalismo Catalan*, Madrid: Historia 16.

Balcells, A. (2015) 'La inmigració i la política catalana durant la Segona República', *Cercles: revista d'història cultural*, no. 18, pp. 21–41.

Balcells, A., Pujol, E. and Sabater, J. (1996) *La Mancomunitat de Catalunya i l'Autonomia*, Barcelona: Institut d'Estudis Catalans, pp. 441–449.

Baldor Abril, E., Cáceres, I. and Farràs Royo, N. (1995) 'Els recursos econòmics de la pagesia altafullenca: Segona meitat del segle XVIII', *Estudis altafullencs*, no. 19, pp. 19–38.

Balfour, S. (1989) *Workers, Dictatorship and the City: Labour in Greater Barcelona Since 1939*, Oxford: Clarendon Press.

Balfour, S. (2012) 'La modernització autoritària franquista a Barcelona: arrels intel·lectuals i contradicció', in Balfour, S. (ed.) *Barcelona malgrat el franquisme La SEAT, la ciutat i la represa sense democràcia*, Barcelona: Ajuntament de *Barcelona*, pp. 13–26.

Ballbé i Sans, N. (2018) 'La "Real Cédula de Aranjuez" del 23 de juny de 1768: propòsits d' uniformització lingüística en un context de Despotisme "il·lustrat"', *Revista de Catalunya*, no. 303, pp. 43–56.

Baraut, C. (1996) 'Els inicis de la inquisició a Catalunya i les seves actuacions al bisbat d'Urgell (segles XII-XIII)', *Urgellia: Anuari d'estudis històrics dels antics comtats de Cerdanya, Urgell i Pallars, d'Andorra i la Vall d'Aran*, no. 13, pp. 407–438.

Barberá i Farras, J. (2001) 'La ceràmica griega arcaica a la laietània', in Cabrera Bonet, P. and Santos Retolaza, M. (eds.) *Ceràmiques jònies d'època arcaica: centres de producció i comercialització al Mediterrani occidental*, Barcelona: Museu d'Arqueologia de Catalunya, pp. 277–284.

Barceló Perelló, M. (2005) 'Enganya-l'ull: el guerrer, el comerciant i la noble causa en la història medieval de Catalunya', *L' Espill*, no. 21, pp. 6–26.

Barnosell, G. (2012) 'Guerra i religió a Catalunya: 1792–1840', in Barnosell, G. and Galofré, J. (eds.) *La Guerra del Francès al Pla de l'Estany*, Banyoles: Centre d'Estudis Comarcals de Banyoles, pp. 15–24.

Barrio, J. A. (2013) 'El concepto de frontera en la Edad Media. La frontera meridional del reino de Valencia. Siglos XIII-XV', *Sharq al-Andalus*, no. 20, pp. 41–65.

Barton, T. (2019) *Victory's Shadow. Conquest and Governance in Medieval Catalonia*, Cornell: Cornell University Press, p. 30.

Basso, P. (2003) *Modern Times, Ancient Hours: Working Lives in the Twenty-First Century*, London: Verso.

Bastardas, J. (1992) 'El llatí de la Catalunya romana i l'origen i formació de la llengua catalana', *Fonaments: prehistòria i món antic als Països Catalans*, no. 8, pp. 99–116.

Baulenas, L. (2004) *El Català No Morirà: Un Moment Decisiu per al Futur de la Llengua*, Barcelona: Edicions 62.

Baydal Sala, V. (2015) 'Los orígenes historiográficos del concepto de "pactismo"', *Historia y Política*, no. 34, pp. 269–295.

Bel, G. (2011) *Espanya, Capital París: Tots els Camins Porten a Madrid*, Barcelona: La Campana.

Bel, G. (2013) *Anatomía de un Desencuentro: La Cataluña que es y la España que no Pudo Ser*, Barcelona: Destino.

Belenguer Cebria, E. (1993) 'La monarquia hispànica i la Corona d' Aragó. El progressiu qüestionament del pactism a Catalunya', *Pedralbes: Revista d'historia moderna*, no. 13(1), pp. 207–216.

Bell, N. (2011) 'The Iberian peninsula', in Everist, M. (ed.) *The Cambridge Companion to Medieval Music*, Cambridge: Cambridge University Press, pp. 161–170.

Bellavista i Ramon, J. (1998) 'El culte al màrtir sant Cugat a través dels textos de les misses de manuscrits litúrgics de Catalunya', *Analecta sacra tarraconensia: Revista de ciències histori-coeclesiàstiques*, no. 71, pp. 115–130.

Beltrán de Heredia Bercero, J. (2013) 'Barcino, de colònia romana a sede regia visigoda, medina Islàmica i ciutat comtal: una urbs en transformació', *Quarhis: Quaderns d'Arqueologia i Història de la Ciutat de Barcelona*, no. 9, pp. 16–118.

Belzunces, M. (2008) *Suport Social a la Independència de Catalunya (1991–2008)*, Barcelona: Centre d'Estudis Sobiranistes.

Bengoechea, S. (1998) *El Locaut de Barcelona (1919–1920): Els Precedents de la Dictadura de Primo de Rivera*, Barcelona: Curial.

Bensch, S. (2002) *Barcelona and Its Rulers, 1096–1291*, Cambridge: Cambridge University Press, pp. 60–61.

Benton, L. (1990) *Invisible Factories: The Informal Economy and Industrial Development in Spain*, New York: SUNY Press.

Berger, S. (ed.) (2007) *Writing the Nation: A Global Perspective*, Basingstoke: Palgrave.

Berger, S. and Smith, A. (eds.) (1998) *Nationalism, Labour and Ethnicity 1870–1939*, Manchester: Manchester University Press.

Billig, M. (1995) *Banal Nationalism*, London: Sage Publications.

Bisson, T. (1986) *The Medieval Crown of Aragon. A Short History*, Oxford: Oxford University Press, p. 31.

Boadas i Raset, J. (1986) *Girona després de la guerra de succesió: riquesta urbana i estructura social al primer quart del segle XVIII*, Girona: Ajuntament, pp. 84–85.

Bolòs i Masclans, J. (1998) 'Els masos al'edat mitjana. Historia i arqueologia in El mas medieval a Catalunya', *Quaderns*, no. 19, pp. 95–111.

Bolòs i Masclans, J. (2004), *Els orígens medievals del paisatge català. l'arqueologia del paisatge com a font per a conèixer la història de Catalunya*, Barcelona: Institut d'Estudis Catalans, p. 48.

Bolòs i Masclans, J. (2014) 'L'arqueologia del Paisatge de la Catalunya Medieval', *Butlletí de la Societat Catalana d'Estudis Històrics*, no. 25, pp. 101–170.

Boltanski, L. and Chiapello, E. (2007) *The New Spirit of Capitalism*, London: Verso.

Bou, J. (2004) 'La Jamància: el naixement de l'última bullanga popular (juny-agost de 1843)', *Barcelona, Quaderns d'Història*, no. 10, pp. 171–186.

Boyd, C. (1997) *Historia Patria: Politics, History, and National Identity in Spain, 1875–1975*, Princeton: Princeton University Press.

Bramon, D. (2013) *Moros, jueus i cristians en terra catalana: Memòria del nostre passat*, Lleida: Pagès, p. 63.

Bran García, F. (2021) 'Sobre la epidemia en la Antigüedad: la peste antonina y la plaga de Justiniano', in Pageaux, D. (ed.) *Pandemia y cultura*, Madrid: Instituto Juan Andrés de Comparatística y Globalización, pp. 37–46.

Breuilly, J. (1982) *Nationalism and the State*, Manchester: Manchester University Press.

Brines i García, L. (2006) 'La Filosofía Social y Política de Francesc Eiximenis (1ª part)', *Estudios franciscanos: publicación periódica de Ciencias Eclesiásticas de las Provincias Capuchinas Ibéricas*, vol. 107, no. 440, pp. 41–232.

Brotons, R. and Albertí, E. (2014) *300 Anys de Lluita*, Barcelona: Albertí.

Brufal i Sucarrat, J. (2013) 'La medina andalusina de Lleida en el segle XI: Identitat i societat', *Rivista dell'Istituto di Storia dell'Europa Mediterranea*, no. 10, pp. 219–244.

Brufal i Sucarrat, J. (2018) 'La arquitectura del poder en los distritos islámicos de Lleida, Tortosa y Huesca', in Sabaté i Curull, F. (ed.) *El poder entre la ciutat i la regió*, Lleida: Pagès editors, pp. 17–42.

Buechler, S. (2016) *Understanding Social Movements: Theories from the Classical Era to the Present*, London: Routledge.

Burch, J., Castanyer i Masoliver, P., Nolla Brufau, J. M. and Tremoleda i Trilla, J. (2010) 'Temps de canvis. La romanització del nord-est de Catalunya', in *Època de canvis: als inicis de la romanització = Time of changes: in the beginning of the romanization*, Girona: Laboratori d'Arqueologia, Universitat de Girona, pp. 89–108.

Burns, F. (2013) 'The Many Crusades of Valencia's Conquest (1225–80): An Historiographical Labyrinth', in Perry, M. (ed.) *Warrior Neighbours. Crusader Valencia in its International Context, Collected Essays of Father Robert I. Burns, SJ*, Turnhout: Brepols, pp. 103–113.

Buxó, J. and Coll Riera, J. (2010) 'El jaciment de la Plaça Major de Castellar del Vallès: de l'Assentament del Neolitic al viatge de l'antiguitat tardana. 5000 anys d'evolució històrica', *Recerca: Revista d'història i ciències socials i humanes de Castellar del Vallés*, no. 7, pp. 77–108.

Buxó, R. (2005) 'L'agricultura d'època romana: estudis arqueobotànics i evolució dels cultius a Catalunya', *Cota Zero*, no. 20, pp. 108–120.

Cabana, F. (2000) *37 Anys de Franquisme a Catalunya: Una Visió Econòmica*, Barcelona: Pòrtic.

Cabana, F. (2009) *Madrid i el centralisme. Un fre a l'economia catalana*, Barcelona: Pòrtic.

Cabanilles, J. (et al.) (2017) 'New Approaches to the Neolithic Transition: The Last Hunters and First Farmers of the Western Mediterranean', in García Puchol, O. and Salazar García, C. (eds.) *Times of Neolithic Transition Along the Western Mediterranean*, Dordrecht: Springer International Publishing, 2017, pp. 33–65.

Cabré i Pla, A. and Pujadas i Rúbies, I. (1989) 'La población: inmigració i explosió demogràfica', in V.V.A.A., *Història económica de la Catalunya contemporània s. XX Població, agricultura i energia*, Barcelona: Enciclopèdia Catalana, pp. 111–128.

Cabrelles, I. (2013) 'Elits urbanes i propietat rural durant l'Alt Imperi. El cas dels Clodii de Tarraco', *Pyrenae: revista de prehistòria i antiguitat de la Mediterrània Occidental*, vol. 44, no. 2, pp. 7–32.

Cabruja i Vallès, E. (2008) 'Inestabilitat i conflictes socials. La baronia de la Conca d'Òdena en el transcurs dels segles moderns', *Pedralbes, Revista d'historia moderna*, no. 28, pp. 505–520.

Cacho Viu, V. (1998) *El Nacionalismo Catalán como Factor de Modernización*, Barcelona: Quaderns Crema.

Campabadal i Bertran, M. (2006), 'La Reial Acadèmia de Bones Lletres de Barcelona al segle XVIIIl'interès per la història, la llengua i la literatura catalanes', *Butlletí de la Societat Catalana d'Estudis Històrics*, no. 17, pp. 215–227.

Campmany, J. (2008) 'El Garraf entre dos imperis. Conquesta franca i reculada sarraïna (900–970)', in *V Trobada d'Estudiosos del Garraf*, Barcelona: Diputació de Barcelona, pp. 147–155.

Camprubí i Pla, X. (2015) 'L'impacte dels allotjaments a Tona: de la Revolta dels Barretines (1687) al pas de l'exèrcit austriacista durant la Guerra de Successió (1711)', *Ausa*, no. 175, pp. 61–87.

Canal i Roquet Jalmar, J. (1985) 'De la "Marca Hispànica" a la constitució de l'estat: Especial significació de la petició d'ajuda de Girona als francs', *Quadern de treball*, no. 6, pp. 45–49.

Canela Gràcia, J. (2012) 'De la cabana a la ciutat. El poblament a la cessetània occidental entre el bronze final i l'ibèric final (XII-VIII ane-II/I ane)', *Cypsela*, no. 19, pp. 141–157.

Capdevila Muntadas, M. A. (2004a) 'La inmigració francesa un factor decisiu de la recuperació demogràfica de la comarca del Maresme a l'època moderna?' *Estudis d'història agrària*, no. 17, pp. 231–242.

Capdevila Muntadas, M. A. (2004b) 'Pagesos, mariners i comerciants a la Catalunya litoral. El Maresme *a l'època* moderna', *Butlletí de la Societat Catalana d'Estudis Històrics*, no. 25, pp. 193–203.

Capra, R. (2015) 'Chariot Racing in Hispania Tarraconensis: Urban Romanization and Provincial Identity', in Kemezis, A. (ed.) *Urban Dreams and Realities in Antiquity: Remains and Representations of the Ancient City*, Leiden: Brill, pp. 370–92.

Caprile, M. and Sanz de Miguel, P. (2016) 'La Precarització del Treball Abans i Durant la Crisi', in Giner, S. and Homs, O. (eds.) *Raó de Catalunya: La Societat Catalana al Segle XXI*, Barcelona: Institut d'Estudis Catalans, pp. 225–248.

Carles, V. (2006) 'Abdalà és un nom català? La presència sarraïna a Catalunya a l'Edat Mitjana', *Mot so razo*, vol. 5, pp. 52–62.

Carr, K. (2002) *Vandals to Visigoths. Rural Settlement Patterns in Early Medieval Spain*, Ann Arbor: University of Michigan Press, pp. 189–190.

Carrió Arumí, J. (2014) 'La política militar hispànica i la persecució de bandolers a Catalunya en els segles XVI-XVII', *Recerques: història, economia, cultura*, no. 69, pp. 99–130.

Casals, X. (2010) *El Oasis Catalán (1975–2010)¿Espejo o Realidad?*, Barcelona: Edhasa.

Casals, X. (2013) *El Pueblo Contra el Parlamento: El Nuevo Populismo en España. 2009–2013*, Barcelona: Pasado y Presente.

Casassas i Ymbert, J. (1990) 'La Catalunya d'Entreguerres, 1917–1936', in V.V.A.A., *Lluís Companys, Trajectòria d'un President*, Barcelona: L'Avenç, p. 79.

Casey, J. (1999) *Early Modern Spain. A Social History*, London: Routledge, pp. 120 and 172.

Castanyer i Masoliver, P., Tremoleda i Trilla, J., Colominas Barberà, L. and Antolín i Tutusaus, F. (2015) 'Després de les villæ. La transformació del camp al nord-est català en els segles VI i VII a partir de l'exemple de Vilauba/Villa Alba (Pla de l'Estany)', *Estudis d'història agrària*, no. 27, pp. 43–65.

Castanyer i Masoliver, P., Tremoleda i Trilla, J., Dehesa, R. and De Vilauba a Villa, A. (2010) 'L'hàbitat dels segles VI-VII dC de la vil·la romana de Vilauba (Camós, Pla de l'Estany)', *Tribuna d'arqueologia*, no. 2010–2011, pp. 9–21.

Castell Granados, P. (2012) 'La persecución de la brujería en el Pirineo leridano (ss. XV-XVI)', in Villanueva, C. (ed.) *Estudios Recientes de Jóvenes Medievalistas*. Lorca: Universidad de Murcia-Sociedad Española de Estudios Medievales, pp. 25–38.

Cata Tur, J. (2016) 'La repressió després de 1714: execucions, empresonaments i exili', in Puig i Oliver, J. (ed.) *1714*, Barcelona: Institut d'Estudis Catalans, pp. 101–107.

Catalunya 1714: la Guerra de Successió: Ruta pels escenaris, Barcelona: Ohdigital, 2014, p. 116.

Catlos, B. (2004) *The Victors and the Vanquished: Christians and Muslims of Catalonia and Aragon, 1050–1300*, Cambridge: Cambridge University Press, pp. 72–73.

Chandler, C. (2013) 'Carolingian Catalonia: The Spanish March and the Franks, c.750—c.1050', *History Compass*, vol. 11, no. 9, pp. 739–750.

Chandler, C. (2019) *Carolingian Cataloni. Politics, Culture, and Identity in an Imperial Province, 778–987*, Cambridge: Cambridge University Press, pp. 52–54.

Claude, D. (1998) *Remarks About Relations Between Visigoths and Hispano-Romans in the Seventh Century*, Leiden: Brill, pp. 118–120.

Climent, V. (2004) *Estructura Social de España y Cataluña*, Barcelona: Universitat de Barcelona.

Colectivo Ioe. (2008) *Trabajo Sumergido, Precariedad e Inmigración en Catalunya: Una Primera Aproximación*, Barcelona: Fundació Jaume Bofill.

Collins, R. (1989) *The Arab Conquest of Spain 710–797*, Oxford: Blackwell, pp. 96–97.

Collins, R. (2008) *Visigothic Spain 409–711*, Oxford: Blackwell, pp. 211–212.

Colominas, L., Fernandez Rodriguez, C. and Iborra Eres, M. (2017) 'Animal Husbandry and Hunting Practices in Hispania Tarraconensis: An Overview', *European Journal of Archaeology*, vol. 20, no. 3, pp. 510–534.

Congost i Colomer, C. (2008) 'Una societat rural dinàmica i canviant. El segle XVIII', in Salrach Marés, J. M. and Giralt i Raventós, E. (ed.) *Història agrària dels Països Catalans*, vol. 3, pp. 559–583.

Congost i Colomer, R. (2015) 'Els canvis en l'Empordà del segle XVIII: la tesi d'una revolució industriosa', *Annals de l'Institut d'Estudis Empordanesos*, vol. 46, pp. 371–388.

Congrés de Cultura Catalana. (2000) 'Resolucions i Propostes del III Congrés de Cultura Catalana', in *Països Catalans Segle XXI: Identitat, Societat i Cultura*, Lleida: El Jonc, pp. 41–46.

Cortada i Colomer, L. (1998) *Estructures territorials, urbanisme i arquitectura poliorcètics a la Catalunya preindustrial: De l'antiguitat al segle XVII*, Barcelona: Institut d'Estudis Catalans, pp. 96–97.

Corteguera, L. (2018) *For the Common Good Popular Politics in Barcelona, 1580–1640*, Ithaca, NY: Cornell University Press, p. 105.

Coulon, D. (2005) 'Barcelona i el gran comerç amb Orientun segle de relacions comercials de Barcelona amb Egipte i Síria (c. 1330—c. 1430)', *Butlletí de la Societat Catalana d'Estudis Històric*, no. 16, pp. 165–170.

Crameri, K. (2008) *Catalonia. National Identity and Cultural Policy, 1980–2003*, Cardiff: University of Wales Press.

Crexell, Joan. (1998) *Català a l'Escola, les Campanyes Populars sota el Franquisme*, Barcelona: La Magrana.

Cuadrada, C. (1997) 'Senyors i ciutadans, les senyories catalanes a la Baixa Edat Mitjana', *Revista d'Historia Medieval*, no. 8, pp. 57–77.

Cuadrada, C. (2012) *El llibre de la pesta*, Barcelona: Rafael Dalmau Editor, p. 303.

Cuadrada, C. (2017) 'Dones i terres catalanes medievals (segles X-XIII)', *Studis d'Història Agrària*, no. 29, pp. 35–63.

Cucurella, S. (2000) *Catalunya 2000: Situació Política. Quins Escenaris Dibuixen els Resultats Electorals de la Dècada dels 90*, Barcelona: Pòrtic.

Culla i Clarà, J. (ed.) (2001) *El Pal de Paller: Convergència Democràtica de Catalunya (1974–2000)*, Barcelona: Editorial Pòrtic.

Culla i Clarà, J. (2013) *Esquerra Republicana de Catalunya 1931–2012: Una Història Política*, Barcelona: La Campana.

Cuscó i Clarasó, J. (2005) *Els beguins, l'heretgia a la Catalunya medieval*, Barcelona: Publicacions de l'Abadia de Montserrat, pp. 78–79.

Damià del Clot i Trias. (2007) *L'Espai Nacionalista a Catalunya (1999–2006): Crònica d'un Enfrontament*, Barcelona: La Busca Edicions.

Dannecker, A. and Barriendos i Vallvé, M. (1999) 'La sequía de 1812–1824 en la costa central catalana consideraciones climáticas e impacto social del evento', in *La climatología española en los albores del siglo XXI*, Barcelona: Publicaciones de la Asociación Española de Climatología, pp. 53–61.

Dantí i Riu, J. (1986) 'El Vallès Oriental a l'època moderna: el creixement demogràfic i econòmic als segles XVI i XVII', *Pedralbes: Revista d'historia moderna*, no. 6, pp. 197–207.

Dantí i Riu, J. (2012) 'Catalunya entre el redreç i la revolta: afebliment institucional i diferenciació social', *Manuscrits. Revista d'Història Moderna*, no. 30, pp. 55–76.

Degen, M. (2004) 'Barcelona's Games: The Olympics, Urban Design and Global Tourism', in Sheller, M. and Urry, J. (eds.) *Tourism Mobilities*, London: Routledge, pp. 131–142.

Delgado, L. (2014) *La Nación Singular: Fantasías de la Normalidad Democrática Española (1996–2011)*, Madrid: Siglo XXI de España Editores.

Díaz Gijón, J., Fernández Navarrete, D., González, M., Martínez Lillo, P. and Soto Carmona, Á. (1998) *Historia de la España Actual 1939–1996: Autoritarismo y Democracia*, Madrid: Marcial Pons.

Díez Medrano, J. (1995) *Divided Nations: Class, Politics and Nationalism in the Basque Country and Catalonia*, Ithaca: Cornell University Press, p. 94.

Doll-Petit, R. (2004) 'Repressió, salvament i fugida a la reraguarda catalana, 1936–1939', *Ebre 38: revista internacional de la Guerra Civil, 1936–1939*, no. 2, pp. 49–60.

Domenech, X. (2011) *Lucha de Clases, Dictadura y Democracia (1939–1977)*, Barcelona: Icaria.

Domènech, X. (2014) *Hegemonías: Crisis, Movimientos de Resistencia y Procesos Politicos (2010–2013)*, Madrid: Akal.

Domingo, A. (2014) *Catalunya al Mirall de la Immigració: Demografia i Identitat Nacional*, Barcelona: L'Avenç.

Dowling, A. (2006) 'The Catholic Church in Catalonia: From Cataclysm in the Civil War to the "Euphoria" of the 1950s', *Catalan Review*, vol. 20, no. 1, pp. 83–100.

Dowling, A. (2013a) 'The Leading Role of the Party: Catalan Communism and the Franco Regime, 1939–1975', *European History Quarterly*, vol. 43, no. 3, pp. 489–507.

Dowling, A. (2013b) *Catalonia Since the Spanish Civil War: Reconstructing the Nation*, Portland: Sussex Academic Press.

Dowling, A. (2013c) *La Reconstrucció Nacional de Catalunya 1939–2012*, Barcelona: Pasado y Presente.

Dowling, A. (2014) 'Accounting for the Turn Towards Secession in Catalonia', *International Journal of Iberian Studies*, vol. 27, nos. 2–3, pp. 219–234.

Dowling, A. (2019) 'When National Symbols Divide: The Case of Pan-Catalanism and the *Països Catalans*', *Journal of Iberian and Latin American Studies*, vol. 25, no. 1, pp. 143–157.

Duch Plana, M. (2020) 'Els feminismes del segle XX a Catalunya', *Butlletí de la Societat Catalana d'Estudis Històrics*, no. 31, pp. 233–290.

Dunbabin, K. (1999) *Mosaics of the Greek and Roman World*, Cambridge: Cambridge University Press, p. 145.

Edwards, G. (2014) *Social Movements and Protest*, Cambridge: Cambridge University Press.

Ehrlich, C. (2004) *Lliga Regionalista: Lliga Catalana 1900–1936*, Barcelona: Alpha.

Elliott, J. H. (1984) *The Revolt of the Catalans: A Study in the Decline of Spain (1598–1640)*, Cambridge: Cambridge University Press.

Elliott, J. H. (1997) 'Revolution and Continuity in Early Modern Europe', in Parker, G. and Smith, L. (eds.) *The General Crisis of the Seventeenth Century*, London: Routledge, pp. 109–127.

Enrich, J. and Pedraza, L. (1995) 'Vilaclara de Castellfollit de Boix (Bages): un assentament rural de l'antiguitat tardana', *Tribuna d'arqueologia*, no. 1993–1994, pp. 95–106.

Escribano, D. (2015) 'Política lingüística a la Catalunya autònoma de la Segona República (1933–1938)', *Recerques: Història, economia i cultura*, no. 71, pp. 159–187.

Esmonde Cleary, S. (2013) *The Roman West, AD 200–500. An Archaeological Study*, Cambridge: Cambridge University Press, p. 364.

Espadaler, A. M. (2007) 'Els Almogàvers, les cares d'un mite', *Butlletí de la Societat Catalana d'Estudis Històrics*, no. 18, pp. 35–51.

Espinet, F. and Tresserras i Gaju, J. (1999) *La Gènesi de la Societat de Masses a Catalunya, 1888–1939*, Barcelona: University Autònoma de Barcelona.

Espino López, A. (2003) 'El coste de la guerra para la población civil: la experiencia catalana, 1653–1714', *Millars: Espai i historia*, no. 26, pp. 155–184.

Evans, R. J. and Marchal, G. (2011) *The Uses of the Middle Ages in Modern European States History, Nationhood and the Search for Origins*, Basingstoke: Palgrave Macmillan.

Feliu i Montfort, G. (1996) 'El règim senyorial català als segles XVI i XVII', *Pedralbes: Revista d'historia moderna*, no. 16, pp. 31–46.

Feliu i Montfort, G. (1999) 'La demografia baixmedieval catalana estat de la qüestió i propostes de futur', *Revista d'historia medieval*, no. 10, pp. 13–44.

Feliu i Montfort, G. (2010) *La llarga nit feudal. Mil anys de pugna entre senyors i pagesos*, Valencia: Publicacions de l'Universitat de Valencia, p. 80.

Femández Trabal, J. (1999) 'De Prohoms a ciudadanos honrados. Aproximación al estudio de las elites urbanas de la sociedad catalana bajomedieval (s. XIV-XV)', *Revista d'Historia Medieval*, no. 10, pp. 331–372.

Fernández i Trabal, J. (2002) 'El conflicte remença a la Catalunya del segle xv (1388–1486)', *Afers*, nos. 42–43, pp. 582–624.

Fernández i Trabal, J. (2004) 'Les indústries rurals', in Salrach Marés, J. M. and Giralt i Raventós, E. (eds.) *Història agrària dels Països Catalans*, Barcelona: Universitat de Barcelona, vol. 2, pp. 361–394.

Fernández-Cuadrench, J. (2014) 'L'Estat que no va ser catalans i occitans entre els segles VIII i XIII: a propòsit del vuitè centenari de la Batalla de Muret', *Butlletí de la Societat Catalana d'Estudis Històrics*, no. 25, pp. 47–85.

Ferrando i Francés, A. and Amorós, M. (2011) *Història de la Llengua Catalana*, Barcelona: Editorial UOC.

Ferrer i Mallol, M. T. (1987) 'Causes i antecedents de la guerra dels dos Peres', *Boletín de la Sociedad Castellonense de Cultura*, nos. 63–4, pp. 445–508.

Ferrer i Mallol, M. T. and Coulon, D. (1999) *L'expansió catalana a la Mediterrània a la Baixa Edat Mitjana*, Barcelona: CSIC, Institució Milà i Fontanals, pp. 341–359.

Ferrer i Mallol, M. (1999) 'El Consolat de Mar i els consolats d'Ultramar, instrument i manifestació de l'expansió del comerç català', in Ferrer i Mallol, M. and Coulon, D. (eds.) *L'Expansió Catalana a la Mediterrània a la Baixa Edat Mitjana*, Madrid: Consejo Superior de Investigaciones Científicas, pp. 53–80.

Ferrer, A. (2019) 'Captives at the Conquest of Mallorca. September 1229-July 1232', *Imago Temporis. Medium Aevum*, no. 13, pp. 151–176.

Ferrer, L. (2007) 'Una revisió del creixement demogràfic de Catalunya en el segle XVIII a partir dels registres parroquials', *Estudis d'història agrària*, no. 20, pp. 17–68.

Flaquer, L. (2008) 'Diversitat familiar, benestar de la infància i cohesió social a Catalunya', *Nota d'economia*, no. 91, pp. 71–86.

Flocel, F. (2007) *La feudalización de la sociedad catalana*, Granada: Editorial Universidad de Granada, Granada and Barceló, M., Feliu, G., Furió, A., Miquel, M. and Sobrequés, J. (2003). *El feudalisme comptat i debatut. Formació i expansió del feudalisme català*, València: Universitat de València.

Folch Iglesias, C. (2003) 'Estratègies de conquesta i ocupació islàmica del nord-est de Catalunya', *Quaderns de la Selva*, no. 15, pp. 139–154.

Font Rius, J. M. (1985) *Estudis sobre els drets i institucions locals en la Catalunya medieval*, Barcelona: Universitat de Barcelona, p. 345.

Fontana, J. (2014) *La formació d'una identitat. Una història de Catalunya*, Vic: Eumo Editorial, pp. 224–225.

Fradera, J. M. (1986) 'El comerç americà durant el segle XIX', in *El comerç entre Catalunya i Amèrica, segles xviii i xix*, Barcelona: L'Avenç, pp. 109–121.

Fradera, J. M. (2009) *La Pàtria dels Catalans: Història, Política, Cultura*, Barcelona: La Magrana.

France, J. (2020) 'Armies and Bands in Medieval Europe', in Gordon, M., Kaeuper, R. and Zurndorfer, H. (eds.) *The Cambridge World History of Violence*, vol. II 500–1500, Cambridge: Cambridge University Press, pp. 79–99.

Fraser, R. (2008) *Napoleon's Cursed War: Spanish Popular Resistance in the Peninsular War*, London: Verso, pp. 114–115.

Freedman, P. (1991) *The Origins of Peasant Servitude in Medieval Catalonia*, Cambridge: Cambridge University Press, 1991, pp. 38–40.

Freedman, P. (1999) *Images of the Medieval Peasant*, Stanford: Stanford University Press, pp. 117–118.

Fundacio Jaume, Bofill. (2005) *Estructura Social i Desigualitats a Catalunya. Volum I. Classes socials, educación, treball i usos del temps*, Barcelona: Editorial Mediterrània.

Fundación BBV. (1998) *Capitalització i Creixement de l'Economia Catalana 1955–1995*, Bilbao: Fundación BBV.

Furió, A. (2001) *Història del País Valencià*, Valencia: Tres i Cuatre, pp. 110–112.

Fuster, J. (1978) *El Congrés de Cultura Catalana: Què És i Què Ha Estat?* Barcelona: Editorial Laia.

Gabriel Sirvent, P. (1988) 'Sous i cost de la vida a Catalunya a l'entorn dels anys de la Primera Guerra Mundial', *Recerques: Història, economia i cultura*, no. 20, pp. 61–91.

Galera Monegal, M. (2015) 'Estudi raonat de les fonts documentals de l'Atles català de 1375. Des del seu inici fins a l'actualitat', *Treballs de la Societat Catalana de Geografia*, no. 80, pp. 9–66.

Garcia Espuche, A. (2014), 'Lliçons del setge de Barcelona (1713–1714)', *Gimbernat. Revista d'Història de la Medicina i de les Ciències de la Salut*, vol. 61, pp. 11–22.

García-Varela, J. (1997) 'Moviments de protesta i resistència a la fi de l'Antic Règim (1714–1808): cap a una integració de les actituds i les trajectòries socials', in Arnabat i Mata, R. (ed.) *Moviments de protesta i resistència a la fi de l'Antic Règim*, Barcelona: Abadia de Montserrat, pp. 7–36.

Gifre i Ribas, P. (2003) 'La consolidació d'un grup pagès: els senyors útils i propietaris de masos (1486–1730)', *Revista Pedralbes*, no. 23, pp. 513–536.

Gillespie, R. and Gray, C. (eds.) (2015) *Contesting Spain? The Dynamics of Nationalist Movements in Catalonia and the Basque Country*, London: Routledge.

Giner, S., Flaquer, L., Busquet, J. and Bultà, N. (1996) *La Cultura Catalana: El Sagrat i el Profà*, Barcelona: Edicions 62.

Glick, T. (2005) *Islamic and Christian Spain in the Early Middle Ages*, Lleiden: Brill, pp. 157–158.

Goldstein, R. (1983) *Political Repression in 19th Century Europe*, Oxford: Routledge.

González Calleja, E. (1999) *El Máuser y el Sufragio: Orden Público, Subversión y Violencia Política en la Crisis de la Restauración (1917–1931)*, Madrid: CSIC.

González Casanova, J. (1974) *Federalisme i Autonomia a Catalunya 1868–1938*, Barcelona: Curial.

González Casanova, J. (1979) *La Lucha por la Democracia en Catalunya*, Barcelona: Dopesa.

Gonzalvo i Bou, G. (1996) 'Els Jueus i Els Usatges de Barcelona', *Barcelona Quaderns d'Història*, nos. 2–3, pp. 117–124.

Gonzalvo i Bou, G. (2010) 'Les Assemblees de Pau i Treva', *Revista de Dret Històric Català*, vol. 10, pp. 95–103.

Gost, P. (2001) 'La primera articulación del estado feudal en Cataluña a través de un impuesto: el bovaje (SS. XII-XIII)', *Hispania*, vol. 61, no. 209, pp. 967–997.

Grafe, R. (2012) *Distant Tyranny: Markets, Power, and Backwardness in Spain, 1650–1800*, Princeton: Princeton University Press.

Graham, E. (2016) 'Heresy, Doubt and Identity: Late Medieval Friars in the Kingdom of Aragon', *Studies in Church History*, vol. 52, pp. 135–149.

Grau i Fernández, R. (2011) 'Un patriota d'altres temps: Antoni de Capmany i la historiografia racionalista', *Butlletí de la Societat Catalana d'Estudis Històrics*, no. 22, pp. 93–112.

Green, D. H. (2000) *Language and History in the Early Germanic World*, Cambridge: Cambridge University Press, 2000, p. 323.

Gual, V. (2008) 'El punt de partida de l'agricultura moderna. De la Sentència arbitral de Guadalupe i les Germanies a la crisi de finals del cinc-cents', in Giralt, A. (ed.) *Història agrària dels Països Catalans. Vol. 3. Edat moderna*, Barcelona: Universitat de Barcelon, pp. 13–30.

Guibernau, M. (1996) *Nationalisms: The Nation State and Nationalism in the Twentieth Century*, Cambridge: Polity Press.

Guibernau, M. (1999) *Nations without a State: Political Communities in a Global Age*, Cambridge: Polity Press.

Guimerà i Orts, J. A. (2018) 'El papel de la comunicación en la construcción nacional de Cataluña: Jordi Pujol y la instrumentalización política de los medios (1968–1989)', *Historia y política: Ideas, procesos y movimientos sociales*, no. 40, pp. 363–387.

Halperin, S. (2004) *War and Social Change in Modern Europe: The Great Transformation Revisted*, Cambridge: Cambridge University Press.

Halsall, G. (2007) *Barbarian Migrations and the Roman West, 376–568*, Cambridge: Cambridge University Press, pp. 45–47.

Halsall, G. (2008) *Warfare and Society in the Barbarian West 450–900*, London: Routledge, pp. 90–91.

Hourigan, N. (2004) *Escaping the Global Village: Media, Language, and Protest*, Lanham: Lexington Books.

Huertas Claveria, J. (1994) *Obrers a Catalunya: Manual d'Història del Moviment Obrer (1840–1975)*, Barcelona: L'Avenç.

Ibars, T. (1994) *La delinqüència a la Lleida del Barroc*, Lleida: Pagès editors, pp. 133–136.

Ichijo, A. and Uzelac, G. (eds.) (2005) *When Is the Nation? Towards an Understanding of Theories of Nationalism*, London: Routledge.

Illa, M. (1983) *El Segon Congrés Catalanista. Un congrés inacabat (1883–1983)*, Barcelona: Generalitat de Catalunya, p. 25.

Illa, O. (2010) *Independentisme Català: Entre el Símbol i la Institució*, Barcelona: Angle Editorial.

Isla Frez, A. (2011) 'Del món tardoantic a la Tarragona visigoda, Història de Tarragona', in Bonet Donato, M. and Isla Frez, A. (eds.) *Tarragona medieval, capital eclesiàstica i del camp*, Tarragona: Universitat Rovira i Virgili, pp. 21–56.

Jacoby, D. (2015) 'The Catalan Company in the East: The Evolution of an Itinerant Army (1303–1311)', in Halfond, G. (ed.) *The Medieval Way of War Studies in Medieval Military History in Honor of Bernard S. Bachrach*, Farnham: Ashgate, pp. 153–182.

Jarne, A. and Porta, J. (2012) *Un Horitzó Nacional: Història del Pensament Politic Catalanista Contemporani*, Lleida: Pagès Editors.

Jimenez Garnica, A. M. (2003) 'Settlement of the Visigoths in the Fifth Century', in Heather, P. (ed.) *The Visigoths from the Migration Period to the Seventh Century. An Ethnographic Perspective*, Rochester: Boydell Press, pp. 93–128.

Junyent Sánchez, E., Garcés i Estallo, I., López Melción, J. and Lafuente Revuelto, A. (1993) 'Els Vilars (Arbeca, Les Garrigues): primera edat del ferro i època ibèrica a la plana occidental catalana', *Laietania: Estudis d'historia i d'arqueología de Mataró i del Maresme*, no. 8, pp. 41–60.

Kagay, D. and Andrew Villalon, A. (2021) *Conflict in Fourteenth-Century Iberia. Aragon Vs. Castile and the War of the Two Pedros*, Leiden: Brill, pp. 409–412.

Kamen, H. (1993) *The Phoenix and the Flame. Catalonia and the Counter Reformation*, New Haven and London: Yale University Press, p. 436.

Keating, M. (1996) *Nations Against the State: The New Politics of Nationalism in Quebec, Catalonia and Scotland*, London: Macmillan.

Kennedy, H. (1996) *Muslim Spain and Portugal. A Political History of al-Andalus*, London: Routledge, 1996.

King, P. D. (1972) *Law and Society in the Visigothic Kingdom*, Cambridge: Cambridge University Press, pp. 60 and 64.

Kirchner, H., Virgili Colet, A. and Antolín i Tutusaus, F. (2014) 'Un espacio de cultivo urbano en al-Andalus: Madîna Turtûsa (Tortosa) antes de 1148', *Historia agraria: Revista de agricultura e historia rural*, no. 62, pp. 11–45.

Kleinschmidt, H. (2000) *Understanding the Middle Ages. The Transformation of Ideas and Attitudes in the Medieval World*, Woodbridge: Boydell Press, p. 156.

Knutsen, G. W. (2009) *Servants of Satan and Masters of Demons: The Spanish Inquisition's Trials of Superstition, Valencia and Barcelona, 1478–1700*, Valencia and Barcelona, 1478–1700, Turnhout: Brepols Publishers, pp. 85–86.

Kocka, J. (2016) *Capitalism. A Short History*, Princeton, NJ: Princeton University Press, p. 119.

Kulikowski, M. (2011) *Late Roman Spain and Its Cities*, Baltimore: Johns Hopkins University Press, p. 272.

Ladero Quesada, M. (1994) 'El ejercicio de poder real en la Corona de Aragón: Instituciones e instrumentos de gobierno (siglos xiv yxv)', *En la España Medieval*, no. 17, pp. 31–93.

Lara Peinado, F. (1978) 'Materiales para el estudio de la esclavitud romana en las tierras de Lérida', *Ilerda*, no. 39, pp. 79–84.

Latowsky, A. (2013) *Emperor of the World. Charlemagne and the Construction of Imperial Authority, 800–1229*, Ithaca and London: Cornell University Press, p. 215.

Lillios, K. (2019) *The Archaeology of the Iberian Peninsula. From the Paleolithic to the Bronze Age*, Cambridge: Cambridge University Press, pp. 150–152.

Lladonosa Latorre, M. (2013) *La Construcció de la Catalanitat: Evolució de la Concepció d'Identitat Nacional a Catalunya 1860–1990*, Lleida: Espais.

Llobera, J. (1994) *The God of Modernity: The Development of Nationalism in Western Europe*, Oxford: Macmillan.

Llobera, J. (2004) *Foundations of National Identity: From Catalonia to Europe*, Oxford: Bergahn.

Lluch i Bramon, R. (2008) 'Les Viles medieval franqueses i mals usos', *Butlletí de la Societat Catalana d'Estudis Històrics*, no. 19, pp. 9–28.

Lluch i Bramon, R. (2013) 'Tot pensant en el conflicte remença: reflexions i propostes', *Estudis d'història agrària*, no. 25, pp. 29–46.

Lluch i Bramon, R. (2018) 'El Conflicte de Mir Geribert en el marc de la feudalització del Penedès (1041–1058)', *Anuario de Estudios Medievales*, vol. 48, no. 2, pp. 793–820.

Lluch i Bramon, R. (2000) 'Els pagesos medievals: els remences', *Revista de Girona*, no. 202, pp. 63–66.

Lluch, E. (1996) *La Catalunya vençuda del segle XVIII: foscors i clarors de la Il.lustració*, Barcelona: Edicions 62, pp. 109–111.

Lo Cascio, P. (2008) *Nacionalisme i Autogovern: Catalunya 1980–2003*, Barcelona: Editorial Afers.

López Esteve, M. (2013) 'Els Fets d'octubre de 1934 a Catalunya: entre l'acció de govern i la mobilització social', *Butlletí de la Societat Catalana d'Estudis Històrics*, no. 24, pp. 631–649.

Mallorquí i Garcia, E. (1998) 'El mas com a unitat d'explotació agrària. Repàs dels seus orígens, El mas medieval a Catalunya', *Quaderns*, no. 19, pp. 45–64.

Mallorquí i Garcia, E. (2011) *Parròquia i societat rural al bisbat de Girona, segles XIII-XIV*, Barcelona: Fundació Noguera, p. 251.

Mallorquí i Garcia, E. (2011) 'Masos medievals i cognoms endèmics a les terres de Girona', *Quaderns de la Selva*, no. 23, pp. 11–55.

Maluquer de Motes, J. (1992) 'Los pioneros de la segunda revolución industrial en España: La Sociedad Española de Electricidad (1881–1894)', *Revista de Historia Industrial*, no. 2, pp. 121–142.

Maluquer de Motes, J. (2011) 'El turismo, motor fundamental de la economía de Cataluña (1951–2010)', *Historia Contemporánea*, no. 42, pp. 347–399.

Manel Tresserras, J. M. (2000) 'Els sistemes de comunicació i cultura a Catalunya durant el segle XX. Una proposta d'interpretació', *Cercles: revista d'història cultural*, no. 3, pp. 59–73.

Marc Álvaro, F. (2003) *Ara Sí Que Toca! Jordi Pujol, el Pujolisme i els Successors*, Barcelona: Edicions 62.

Marco Palau, F. (2014) *Plataforma per la Llengua: 20 Anys Defensant el Català*, Barcelona: Editorial Base.

Marfany, J. L. (2001) *La llengua maltractada*, Barcelona: Empúries, p. 237.

Marfany, J. L. (2012) *Land, Proto-Industry and Population in Catalonia, c. 1680–1829, an Alternative Transition to Capitalism?* Farnham: Ashgate, pp. 96–97.

Marín i Corbera, M. (1995) 'Franquisme i poder local. Construcció i consolidació deIs ajuntaments feixistes a Catalunya, 1938–1949', *Recerques, Història, Economia, Cultura*, no. 31, pp. 37–52.

Marín i Corbera, M. (2006) 'Franquismo e inmigración interior: el caso de Sabadell (1939–1960)', *Historia Social*, no. 56, pp. 131–152.

Marta Prevosti i Monclús, M. (1995) 'Prospecciones sistemáticas en el Maresme y los orígenes de la romanización del territorio', *Studia historica. Historia antigua*, nos. 13–14, pp. 125–141.

Martí Castelló, R. and Viladrich, M. (2018) 'Les torres de planta circular de la frontera extrema d'al-Andalus a Catalunya (segles VIII-X)', *Treballs d'Arqueologia*, no. 22, pp. 51–81.

Martí i Escayol, M. A. (2002) 'Indústria, medicina i química a la Barcelona de finals del segle XVIII: el tintatge i la introducció del carbó mineral des d'una perspectiva ambiental', *Recerques: Història, economia i cultura*, no. 44, pp. 5–20.

Martin, B. (1990) *The Agony of Modernization: Labor and Industrialization in Spain*, Ithaca: Cornell University Press.

Martín Alvira Cabrer, M. (2014) 'El rey de Aragón Pedro el Católico y sus batallas. Del triunfo de Las Navas de Tolosa al desastre de Muret', in Cressier, P. and Salvatierra, V. (eds.) *Las Navas de Tolosa 1212–2012, miradas cruzadas*, Jaén: Universidad de Jaén, Servicio de Publicaciones, pp. 229–242.

Martínez Shaw, C. (1981) *Cataluña en la carrera de Indias: 1680–1756*, Barcelona: Crítica, pp. 54–56.

Marvin, L. (2008) *The Occitan War. A Military and Political History of the Albigensian Crusade, 1209–1218*, Cambridge: Cambridge University Press, p. 195.

Mas Ferrer, J. (2020) 'Pautes de consum i condicions de vida dels treballadors de la terra a partir dels inventaris post mortem a Catalunya: el cas de la Selva (1750–1805)', *Estudis d'Història Agrària*, no. 32, pp. 69–96.

Masferrer i Domingo, A. (1999) 'La Influència dels Usatges de Barcelona en l'ordenament jurídicopenal dels municipis de la Catalunya Nova: notes per a un estudi', in Serrano Daura, J. (ed.) *El Territori i les seves institucions històriques*, Lleida: Pagès Editors, pp. 809–838.

Massot i Muntaner, J. (1979) *Els Creadors del Montserrat Modern*, Montserrat: Biblioteca Serra d'Or, p. 35.

Mayayo i Artal, A. (2002) *La Ruptura Catalana*, Barcelona: Editorial Afers.

McKitterick, R. (1983) *The Frankish Kingdoms Under the Carolingians, 751–987*, London: Routledge, p. 88.

McRoberts, K. (2001) *Catalonia: Nation Building Without a State*, Oxford: Oxford University Press.

Medrano, J. (1995) *Divided Nations: Class, Politics, and Nationalism in the Basque Country and Catalonia*, Ithaca: Cornell University Press.

Menchón i Bes, J. (2010) 'De l'ager Tarraconensts a la marca extrema d'Al-Andalus. Algunes reflexions entorn al (des)poblament del Camp de Tarragona, la Conca de Barberá i el Priorat entre l'antiguitat tardana i la conquesta feudal', in Prevosti i Monclús, M. and Guitart i Duran, J. (eds.) *Ager Tarraconensis, Paisatge, poblament, cultura material i història*, Barcelona: Institut Català d'Arqueologia Clàssica, pp. 57–73.

Mestre i Godes, J. (1994) *Els càtars problema religiós, pretext polític*, Barcelona: Edicions 62.

Mierse, W. (1999) *Temples and Towns in Roman Iberia. The Social and Architectural Dynamics of Sanctuary Designs, from the Third Century B.C. to the Third Century A.D.*, Berkeley: University of California Press, p. 132.

Milian i Massana, A. (2013) 'La llei de normalització lingüística: el camí cap al redreçament', in *30 anys de política lingüística*, Barcelona: Generalitat de Catalunya, pp. 11–20.

Milian, L. (2019) 'La estructura del primer banco público de Europa: la Taula de Canvi de Barcelona (siglo XV)', *Medievalismo*, no. 29, pp. 297–321.

Millàs i Castellví, C. (2005) *Els altres catalans dels segles XVI i XVII. La immigració francesa al Baix Llobregat*, Barcelona: Publicacions de l'Abadia de Montserrat, p. 85.

Milton, G. (2012) *Market Power: Lordship, Society, and Economy in Medieval Catalonia (1276–1313)*, Basingstoke: Palgrave Macmillan, pp. 112–113.

Miró i Tuset, C. (2016) 'L'adopcionisme, una excusa de Domini Polític i Cultural dels Carolingis sobre Septimània i la Marca Hispànica. El Cas D'Urgell (788–798)', *Institut d'Estudis Comarcals de l'Alt Urgell*, pp. 67–82.

Molincro, C. (2001) 'Les actituds polítiques a Catalunya durant el primer Franquisme', *Butlletí de la Societat Catalana d'Estudis Històrics*, no. 12, pp. 97–106.

Molinero, C. and Ysàs, P. (eds.) (2010a) *Construint la ciutat democràtica. El movement veïnal durant el tardofranquisme i la transició*, Barcelona: Icaria.

Molinero, C. and Ysàs, P. (2010b) *Els anys del PSUC. El partit de l'antifranquisme (1956–1981)*, Barcelona: L'Avenç.

Molinero, C. and Ysàs, P. (2014) *La Cuestión Catalana: Cataluña en la Transición Española*, Barcelona: Crítica.

Moncunill Martí, N. (2011) 'La llengua dels ibers: preguntes i respostes', *Quaderns de Vilaniu*, no. 59, pp. 5–20.

Monés, J. (2005) *Formació professional i desenvolupament econòmic i social català (1714–1939)*, Barcelona: Societat d'Història de l'Educació dels Països de Llengua *Catalana*, p. 341.

Montalbán Martínez, C., Llinàs i Pol, J. and Ramírez, A. (1996–1997) 'L'hort d'en Bach (Maçanet): una vil·la romana a la selva interior', *Annals de l'Institut d'Estudis Gironins*, no. 37, pp. 841–852.

Morales Montoya, M. (2009) 'L'Exili a Catalunya al segle XX', *Butlletí de la Societat Catalana d'Estudis Històrics*, no. 20, pp. 169–202.

Morán i Ocerinjauregui, J. (1984) 'Notes sobre la formació de la llengua catalana', *Anuario de filología*, no. 10, pp. 335–346.

Mora-Sitjà, N. (2011) 'El primer proletariat català. Mà d'obra i relacions laborals a les fàbriques d'indianes de Barcelona', *Barcelona: quaderns d'història*, no. 17, pp. 237–252.

Moreno Claverías, B. (2004) 'Les condicions materials de vida dels rabassers penedesencs al segle XVIII: treball, mercat i consum', *Estudis d'història agrària*, no. 17, pp. 615–630.

Morley, N. (2010) *The Roman Empire: Roots of Imperialism*, London: Pluto Press, pp. 52–54.

Muniesa, B. (1985) *La Burgesia Catalana Ante la Segunda República Española*, Barcelona: Anthropos, two vols.

Munilla Cabrillana, G., Garcia i Rubert, D. and Gracia Alonso, F. (1998) 'San Jaume- Mas d'en Serra (Alcanar, Tarragona) Un asentamiento de transición entre los S. VII y VI a. C en el área de la desembocadura del Ebro: primeros resultados', *Revista de estudios ibéricos*, no. 3, pp. 23–44.

Muñoz Peña, P., Díez de Revenga Torres, P. and Puche Lorenzo, M. (2010) *Discurso sobre el origen y progreso de la lengua castellana*, Murcia: Universidad de Murcia Editum, pp. 42–43.

Muñoz Pradas, F. (1997) 'Fluctuaciones de precios y dinámica demográfica en Cataluña (1600–1850)', *Revista de Historia Económica = Journal of Iberian and Latin American Economic History*, year 15, no. 3, pp. 507–543.

Nadia Varo, N. (2007) 'Mujeres en huelga. Barcelona metropolitana durante el franquismo', in Babaiano, J. (ed.) *Del hogar a la huelga. Trabajo, género y movimiento obrero durante el franquismo*, Madrid: los Libros de la Catarata, pp. 139–187.

Narváez Cases, C. (2005) 'El patronatge de les noves oligarquies urbanes a l'art català dels segles XVI i XVII', *Recerques: Història, economia i cultura*, no. 51, pp. 5–25.

Navarro, N. (2009) 'La inserció de les dones a la vida pública i política durant la Segona República (1931–1939)', *Eines per a l'esquerra nacional*, no. 9, pp. 151–163.

Negre, J. and Suñé, J. (2019) 'Territorio, Fiscalidad y Actividad Militar de un Espacio Fronterizo. La Consolidación de Tortosa como límite extremo del Al-Andalus Omeya', *Anuario de Estudios Medievales*, vol. 49, no. 2, pp. 705–740.

Noguera Guillén, J., Asensio Vilaró, D., Ble, E. and Jornet, R. (2014) 'The Beginnings of Rome's Conquest of Hispania. Archaeological Evidence for the Assault on and Destruction of the Iberian Town Castellet de Banyoles', *Journal of Roman Archaeology*, no. 26, pp. 60–81.

Nolla i Brufau, J. M. (2001) 'Aspectes de la romanització. De la llengua dels indigets al llatí. Algunes dades', *Estudi General*, no. 21, pp. 415–428.

Nolla i Brufau, J. M. (2019) 'El món romà i la Hispània Tarraconense precatalana', *Butlletí de la Societat Catalana d'Estudis Històrics*, no. 30, pp. 21–78.

O'Callaghan, J. (2003) *Reconquest and Crusade in Medieval Spain*, Philadelphia, PA: University of Pennsylvania Press, p. 209.

O'Callaghan, J. (2018) *A History of Medieval Spain*, Ithaca, NY: Cornell University Press, pp. 71–72.

Ogilvie, S. (2011) *Institutions and European Trade. Merchant Guilds, 1000–1800*, Cambridge: Cambridge University Press, p. 54.

Olivares Periu, J. (1995) 'Plets i endeutament comunal en la immediata postguerra dels Segadors', *Recerques: Història, economia i cultura*, no. 33, pp. 33–52.

Ollich, I. (1999) 'Roda: l'Esquerda. La ciudad carolingia', in Camps, J. (ed.) *Cataluña en la época carolingia: arte y cultura antes del románic (siglos IX y X)*, Barcelona: Museu nacional d'art de *Catalunya*, pp. 84–88.

Oltra, B., Mercadè, F. and Hernandéz, F. (1981) *La Ideologia Nacional Catalana*, Barcelona: Anagrama, pp. 45–47.

O'Reilly, W. (2009) 'Lost Chances of the House of Habsburg', *Austrian History Yearbook*, vol. 40, pp. 53–70.

Orlandis, J. (2003) *Historia del Reino Visigodo español*, Madrid: Ediciones Rialp, pp. 119–121.

Pages i Branch, P. (ed.) (2004a) *Franquisme i Repressió: La Repressió Franquista als Països Catalans (1939–1975)*, Valencia: Universitat de València.

Pagès i Blanch, P. (2004b) 'La justicia revolucionaria i popular a Catalunya (1936–1939)', *Ebre 38. Revista Internacional de la Guerra Civil (1936–1939)*, no. 2, pp. 1–14.

Pagès i Blanch, P. (ed.) (2005) *La Transició Democràtica als Països Catalans: Història i Memòria*, Valencia: Universitat de València.

Palau Elcacho, L. (2020) 'L'evolució demogràfica de la Catalunya interior al llarg dels segles XVIII i XIX: El cas del Pla d'Urgell', *Estudis d'història agrària*, no. 32, pp. 139–172.

Panosa, M. A. (2012) *Els ibers del Vallès Oriental*, Barcelona: Publicacions de l'Abadia de Montserrat, pp. 176–177.

Parareda, A. and Sala, P. J. (2003) *Via fora, lladres! la revolta dels remences contra la servitud feudal*, Barcelona: Barcanova, pp. 33–34.

Pèlachs, A., Nadal, J., Soriano, J. M., Molina, D. and Cunill, R. (2009) 'Changes in Pyrenean Woodlands as a Result of the Intensity of Human Exploitation: 2,000 Years of Metallurgy in Vallferrera, Northeast Iberian Peninsula', *Vegetation History and Archaeobotany*, no. 18, pp. 403–416.

Pérez Centeno, M. (1998) 'Análisis evolutivo de "Gerunda, Baetulo e Iluro" en el siglo III DC', *Annals de l'Institut d'Estudis Gironins*, no. 39, pp. 31–38.

Pérez i Conill, J. (2010) 'La Segarra entre els lacetans i els ilergetes. Una aproximació a la cultura ibèrica en aquesta comarca', *Miscel·lània cerverina*, no. 20, pp. 11–22.

Pérez Moreda, V. (2017) 'Spain', in Alfani, G. and Ó Gráda, C. (eds.) *Famine in European History*, Cambridge: Cambridge University Press, pp. 48–72.

Phillips, C. (2007) 'Family and Community in the Spanish World', in Parker, C. and Bentley, J. (eds.) *From the Middle Ages to Modernity: Individual and Community in the Early Modern World*, Lanham, MD: Rowman & Littlefield, pp. 71–90.

Pinhasi, R., Fort, J. and Ammerman, A. J. (2005) 'Tracing the Origin and Spread of Agriculture in Europe', *PLoS Biology*, vol. 3, no. 12, p. e410.

Pladevall i Font, A. (2013) 'Les iniciatives de l'Esglesia catalana durant el regnat de Jaume I', in Ferrer i Mallol, M. (ed.) *Jaume I: commemoració del VIII centenari del naixement de Jaume I*, vol. 2, pp. 212–225.

Plaza, C. and Fuguet, J. (2020) *Història de la Conca de Barberà. Cultura tradicional i cultural*, Tarragona: Publicacions URV, p. 270.

Posner, R. (1966) *The Romance Languages*, Cambridge: Cambridge University Press, pp. 122 and 197.

Pounds, N. (1973) *An Historical Geography of Europe 450 BC to AD 1330*, Cambridge: Cambridge University Press, pp. 228–229.

Prevosti i Monclús, M. (2010) 'Els grans canvis del poblament a Catalunya: de la protohistòria a l'antiguitat', *Butlletí de la Societat Catalana d'Estudis Històrics*, no. 21, pp. 45–76.

Puig i Oliver, J. (2016) *1714*, Barcelona: Institut d'Estudis Catalans.

Puig Vallverdú, G. (2020) 'La terra en comú. La col·lectivització agrària a Catalunya durant la Guerra Civil, 1936–1939', *Segle XX: revista catalana d'història*, no. 13, pp. 51–72.

Puigvert i Sola, J. (1997) 'Església i territori en els orígens de la Catalunya contemporània', *Treballs de la Societat Catalana de Geografia*, no. 44, pp. 85–111.

Pujol Puigvehí, A. (1979) 'Los cráneos de Ullastret y su posible significado', *Pyrenae: revista de prehistòria i antiguitat de la Mediterrània Occidental*, nos. 15–16, pp. 267–276.

Ramon, J. (2008) 'El comercio púnico en occidente en época tardorepublicana (siglos II-I aC). Una perspectiva actual según el tráfico envasado en ánforas. Los Fenicios y el Atlántico', in González, R., López, F. and Peña, V. (eds.) *Iberia e Italia: modelos romanos de integración territorial*, Madrid: Universidad Complutense, pp. 67–100.

Recasens i Comes, J. M. (1972) *A propòsit de l'ocupació àrab de Tarragona i l'emigració de Sant Pròsper a Itàlia*, Tarragona: Real Sociedad Arqueológica Tarraconense, pp. 209–213.

Recolons, L. (1974) *La Població de Catalunya: Distribució Territorial i Evolució Demogràfica 1900–1970*, Barcelona: Institut d'Estudis Catalans.

Reddy, W. (1987) *Money and Liberty in Modern Europe. A Critique of Historical Understanding*, Cambridge: Cambridge University Press, pp. 114–115.

Reglà i Campistol, J. (1952) 'El comercio entre Francia y la Corona de Aragón en los siglos XIII y XIV y sus relaciones con el desenvolvimiento de la industria textil catalana', in *Actas del Primer Congreso Internacional de Estudios Pirenáicos*, San Sebastián: Instituto de Estudios Pirenaicos, vol. 6, pp. 47–65.

Reglà i Campistol, J. (1965) *El bandolerisme català del barroc*, Barcelona: Edicions 62, pp. 187–188.

Ribas, P. G. (2011) *Delmes, censos i Lluïsmes. El feudalisme tardà a la Catalunya vella (Vegueria de Girona, S. XVI-XVIII)*, Girona: Documenta Universitària.

Riera i Fortiana, E. (1982) 'El estamento eclesiástico catalán en la guerra de la Independencia', *Pedralbes: Revista d'historia moderna*, no. 2, pp. 211–236.

Riera, R. (2017) 'The Beginnings of Urban Manufacturing and Long Distance Trade', in Sabaté, F. (ed.) *The Crown of Aragon. A Singular Mediterranean Empire*, Leiden: Brill, pp. 201–236.

Riera, S. (2013) *Onze de Setembre: Història de la Commemoració de la Diada a Barcelona*, Barcelona: Editorial Efadós.

Riquer, B. de and Culla, J. (1993) *El Franquisme i la Transició Democràtica 1939–1988*, Barcelona: Edicions 62.

Riquer, I. de (1996) 'Presencia trovadoresca en la Corona de Aragón', *Anuario de Esludios Medievales*, no. 26, pp. 933–966.

Riutort, J. (2018) 'Estudio macroscópico de las cerámicas de cocina tardoantiguas de Plaça Major de Castellar del Valles (Barcelona)', in Martín Viso, I., Fuentes Melgar, P., Sastre Blanco, J. and Catalán Ramos, R. (eds.) *Cerámicas altomedievales en Hispania y su entorno: (siglos V- VIII d. C.)*, Valladolid: Arbotante Patrimonio e Innovación, pp. 563–572.

Rodà de Llanza, I. (2016) 'Tarraco y Barcino en el Alto Imperio', *Revista de historiografía*, no. 25, pp. 245–272.

Rodrigo y Alharilla, M. (2015) 'From Periphery to Centre: Transatlantic Capital Flows, 1830–1890', in Leonard, A. B. and Pretel, D. (eds.) *The Caribbean and the Atlantic World Economy Circuits of Trade, Money and Knowledge, 1650–1914*, Basingstoke: Palgrave Macmillan, pp. 217–237.

Roig, J. (1988) *Llibre de les dones*, Barcelona: Laertes, p. 132.

Roma i Casanovas, F. (2014) 'Canvi social i conflictivitat als segles XVIII i XIX. El cas d'Osona', *AUSA*, no. 26, pp. 925–944.

Roma i Casanovas, F. (2017) 'El magne diluvi de 1617 en les seves fonts', *AUSA*, no. 179, pp. 213–231.

Romero Baeza, M. (1996) 'Julio-septiembre de 1936: las guerras civiles de Euskadi y Catalunya', *Historia y comunicación Social*, no. 1, pp. 109–130.

Romero-Salvadó, F. (2008) *The Foundations of Civil War: Revolution, Social Conflict and Reaction in Liberal Spain, 1916–1923*, London: Routledge, p. 94.

Rosselló Bordoy, G. (1989) 'Notes sobre la conquesta de Mallorca (1229–1232): El testimoni dels vençuts', *Mayurqa: revista del Departament de Ciències Històriques i Teoria de les Arts*, no. 22(2), pp. 541–550.

Roth, N. and Roth, A. M. (1999) *Jews, Visigoths, and Muslims in Medieval Spain. Cooperation and Conflict*, Leiden: E. J. Brill, pp. 11 and 141.

Roura i Aulinas, L. (2010) 'Guerra, frontera i absolutisme (Guerra Gran, Guerra del Francès i -de reüll- Guerra de Successió)', *Annals de l'Institut d'Estudis Gironins*, no. 51, pp. 89–108.

Roura i Aulinas, L. (2013) 'Il·lustració i projectes per al país', in Albareda, J. (ed.) *Catalunya, nació d'Europa, 1714–2014*, Barcelona: Enciclopèdia Catalana, pp. 178–223.

Rubiera Mata, M. (1993) 'Els arabismes del català. Història d'un rebuig', in Ferrando Francés, A., Lluís Meseguer, L. and Alemany Ferrer, R. (eds.) *Actes del novè Col·loqui Internacional de Llengua i Literatura Catalanes*, Barcelona: Abadia de Montserrat, vol. 2, pp. 301–317.

Ryder, A. (1976) *The Kingdom of Naples Under Alfonso the Magnanimous: The Making of a Modern State*, Oxford: Clarendon Press, pp. 303–305.

Ryder, A. (2007) *The Wreck of Catalonia. Civil War in the Fifteenth Century*, Oxford: Oxford University Press, pp. 262–265.

Sabaté, F. (2010) 'The Catalonia of the 10th to 12th centuries and the historiographic definition of feudalism', *Catalan Historical Review*, vol. 3, pp. 31–53.

Sacasasi Lluís, J. (2007) *Geografia de Catalunya*, Barcelona: Publicacions de l'Abadia de Montserrat.

Safran, J. (2013) *Defining Boundaries in Al-Andalus. Muslims, Christians, and Jews in Islamic Iberia*, Ithaca and London: Cornell University Press, 2013, pp. 99–100.

Salrach Marés, J. M. (1997) 'Orígens i transformacions de la senyoria a Catalunya (segles IX-XIII)', *Revista d'historia medieval*, vol. 8, pp. 25–55.

Salrach Marés, J. M. (2000) *Catalunya a la fi del primer mil·lenni*, Vic-Lleida: Eumo, p. 80–86.

Salrach Marés, J. M. (2014) 'La Història de Catalunya, avui: La llarga edat mitjana', *Butlletí de la Societat Catalana d'Estudis Històrics*, no. 25, pp. 261–297.

Salvadó i Montoriol, J. (2003) *Història medieval d'un territori, Sant Fruitós de Bages segles X-XVI*, Barcelona: Publicacions de l'Abadia de Montserrat, pp. 375–376.

Sam, S. and Wood, J. (2009) 'Unity from Disunity: Law, Rhetoric and Power in the Visigothic Kingdom', *European Review of History=Revue européene d'histoire*, vol. 16, no. 6, pp. 793–808.

Sanllehy i Sabi, M. À. and Bringué i Portella, J. M. (2005) 'Les muntanyes i els homes: una aproximació a la societat, l'economia i la història', *Estudis d'història agrària*, no. 18, pp. 15–46.

Sanmartí Grego, J. (2014) 'L'Estat del coneixement sobre la cultura ibèrica a Catalunya', *Butlletí de la Societat Catalana d'Estudis Històrics*, no. 25, pp. 227–260.

Sanmartí Grego, J., Asensio i Vilaró, D., Belarte Franco, M. C. and Noguera Guillén, J. (2009) 'Comerc colonial, comensalitat i canvi social a la protohistòria de Catalunya', *Citerior: arqueologia i ciències de l'Antiguitat*, no. 5, pp. 219–238.

Santirso Rodríguez, M. (1994) 'Revolució liberal i guerra civil a Catalunya, 1833–1840', *Butlletí de la Societat Catalana d'Estudis Històrics*, no. 6, pp. 205–212.

Sanz Martínez, M. (1979) 'Población ibérica del valle del Ebro (III). Aportación al estudio del oppidum ibérico de San Miguel, Vinebre', *Butlletí arqueològic de la Reial Societat Arqueològica Tarraconense*, no. 1, pp. 11–42.

Scheidel, W. (2019) *The Science of Roman History Biology, Climate, and the Future of the Past*, Princeton: Princeton University Press, pp. 33–34.

Sentañes, E. M. (2006) *Lleida a les corts. Els síndics municipals a l'època d'Alfonso el Magnànim*, Lleida: Edicions de la Universitat de Lleida, pp. 91–92.

Serra i Puig, E. (1980) 'El règim feudal català abans i després de la sentència arbitral de Guadalupe', *Recerques: història, economia, cultura*, no. 10, p. 17–32.

Serra i Puig, E. (2003) 'Poder polític: municipi, Generalitat i virrei', *Barcelona: quaderns d'història*, no. 9, pp. 25–50.

Serra i Puig, E. (2013) 'La crisi del segle XVII i Catalunya', *Butlletí de la Societat Catalana d'Estudis Històrics*, no. 24, pp. 297–315.

Serra i Puig, E. (2016) 'Naixement de la concepció de la ciutadania: el marc històric', in *Dret, conflictes i justícia. Barcelona 1700*, Barcelona: Ajuntament de Barcelona, pp. 51–93.

Serrano Daura, J. (2019) 'Una aproximación a la Corona de Aragón de Fernando el Católico', *Revista de Dret Històric Català*, no. 18, pp. 35–97.

Sesma Muñoz, J. A. (2014) 'Parlamentarismo y sucesión al trono en la Corona de Aragón: el compromiso de Caspe', *Hidalguía: la revista de genealogía, nobleza y armas*, no. 362, pp. 55–84.

Simon i Tarrés, A. (1992) 'La població catalana a l'època moderna. Síntesi i actualització', *Manuscrits. Revista d'història moderna*, no. 10, pp. 217–258.

Simon i Tarrés, A. (1999) 'Ideologia i identitat nacional a la Revolució Catalana de 1640', *Cercles: revista d'història cultural*, no. 2, pp. 10–23.

Smith, A. (1999) *Myths and Memories of the Nation*, Oxford: Oxford University Press.

Smith, A. (2003) *Chosen Peoples*, Oxford: Oxford University Press.

Smith, A. (2007) *Anarchism, Revolution and Reaction: Catalan Labour and the Crisis of the Spanish State, 1898–1923*, Oxford: Bergahn.

Smith A. (2010) 'The Lliga Regionalista, the Catalan Right and the Making of the Primo de Rivera Dictatorship', in Romero-Salvadó, F. and Smith, A. (eds.) *The Agony of Spanish Liberalism: From Revolution to Dictatorship, 1914–1923*, Basingstoke: Palgrave Macmillan, pp. 145–174.

Smith, A. (2014) *The Origins of Catalan Nationalism, 1770–1898*, Basingstoke: Palgrave Macmillan, pp. 204–205.

Sobrequés, S. (1973) 'La política remença de la monarquia en temps d'Alfons el Magnànim', in Sobrequés i Vidal, S. and Sobrequés i Callicó, J. (eds.) *La guerra civil catalana del segle xv. Estudis sobre la crisi social i econòmica de la Baixa Edat Mitjana, vol. 1: Causes i desenvolupament de la crisi*, Barcelona: Edicions 62, pp. 11–39.

Solà i Colomer, X. (2016) 'Petits hospitals rurals: caritat, misèria i supervivència en els segles XVI i XVII. Alguns exemples de pobles de la Garrotxa i la Selva', *Annals del Patronat d'Estudis Històrics d'Olot i Comarca*, no. 27, pp. 99–134.

Solà i Colomer, X. (2017) 'Notes sobre la indústria drapera a la Vall d'Hostoles en el segle XVIII', *Annals del Patronat d'Estudis Històrics d'Olot i Comarca*, no. 28, pp. 141–166.

Solé i Sabaté, J. M. and Dueñas i Iturbe, O. (2007) *El franquisme contra Esquerra. Els alcaldes i diputats afusellats d'Esquerra Republicana de Catalunya*, Barcelona: Fundació Josep Irla, pp. 35–36.

Solé i Sabaté, J. M. and Villarroya, J. (1989) *La Repressió a la Reraguardia de Catalunya 1936–1939*, Barcelona: Ediciones Península, p. 179.

Soler, A. (2018) 'El català i altres llengües en concurrència a la cort i a la cancelleria napolitanes d'Alfons el Magnànim', *Caplettra*, no. 65, pp. 43–67.

Soler i Simon, S. (2017) 'Tortellà al segle XVIII una època de creixement i transformacions', *Annals del Patronat d'Estudis Històrics d'Olot i Comarca*, no. 28, pp. 113–140.

Soler Sala, del M. (2015) 'Forum Granate a la fira de Vilafranca. Origen, creació i articulació d'una xarxa de mercats al Penedès feudal (segles ix–xii)', *SVMMA*, no. 6, pp. 67–86.

Stocking, R. (2008) 'Early Medieval Christian Identity and Anti-Judaism: The Case of the Visigothic Kingdom', *Religion Compass*, vol. 2, no. 4, pp. 642–658.

Streeck, W. (2014) *Buying Time: The Delayed Crisis of Democratic Capitalism*, London: Verso.

Streeck, W. and Schäfer, A. (2013) *Politics in the Age of Austerity*, London: Polity Press.

Subías Pascual, E., Puig Griessenberger, E., Codina i Reina, D. and Fiz Fernández, J. (2016) 'El castrum visigòtic de Puig Rom revisitat', *Annals de l'Institut d'Estudis Empordanesos*, no. 47, pp. 75–96.

Subirats Martori, M. (2020) 'Catalunya endins:: una comunitat estructuralment esquerdada', *Idees: Revista de temes contemporanis*, no. 50, pp. 1–9.

Subirats Martori, M., López, P. and Sánchez, C. (2010) 'Classes i grups socials a la Regió Metropolitana de Barcelona', *Papers: Regió Metropolitana de Barcelona: Territori, estratègies, planejament*, no. 52, pp. 8–37.

Subirats, Marina (ed.) (2010) *Societat Catalana 2010*, Barcelona: Institut d'Estudis Catalans.

Taibo, C. (2014) *Sobre el Nacionalismo Español*, Madrid: Catarata.

Tarradell, M. (1979) 'La ciutat antiga: Dels orígens urbans als visigots', *Cuadernos de historia económica de Cataluña*, no. 20, pp. 17–22.

Tarrow, S. (1995) *Power in Movement: Social Movements, Collective Action and Politics*, Cambridge: Cambridge University Press.

Tello, E. (1997) 'La conflictividad social en el mundo rural catalán, del Antiguo Régimen a la Revolución liberal, 1720–1833', *Noticiario de historia agraria. Boletín informativo del seminario de historia agraria*, year 7, no. 13, pp. 89–104.

Teschke, B. (1998) 'Geopolitical Relations in the European Middle Ages: History and Theory', *International Organization*, vol. 52, no. 2, pp. 325–358.

Thomson, J. K. J. (1992) *A Distinctive Industrialization: Cotton in Barcelona 1728–1832*, Cambridge: Cambridge University Press, p. 71.

Thomson, J. K. J. (2005) 'Explaining the "Take-Off" of the Catalan Cotton Industry', *Economic History Review*, vol. 58, no. 4, pp. 701–735.

Tilly, C. (1992) *Coercion, Capital, and European States, AD 990–1992*, Oxford: Blackwell, p. 188.

To Figueras, L. (1993) 'Señorío y Familia: Los Orígenes del "Hereu" Catalán (Siglos X–XII)', *Studia Historica-Historia Medieval*, vol. 11, pp. 57–79.

Torra Fernández, L. (2001) 'Botigues de teixits, crèdit comercial i crèdit al consum: Xarxes comercials a la Catalunya del segle XVIII', *Recerques: Història, economia i cultura*, no. 41, pp. 5–30.

Torra Fernández, L. (2014) 'Origen i Desenvolupament de les Fires a Catalunya', *La Resclosa*, no. 18, pp. 75–88.

Torras Elias, J. (1970) 'Societat rural i moviments absolutistes. Nota sobre la guerra dels malcontents (1827)', *Recerques: Història, economia i cultura*, no. 1, pp. 123–130.

Torras i Bages, J. (1984) *Obres Completes*, Montserrat: Publicacions de l'Abadia de Montserrat, 1984, vol. 1, p. 242.

Torras i Ribé, J. M. (1984) 'Aproximació a l'estudi del domini baronial del monestir de Ripoll (1266–1711)', *Primer Congrés d'Història Moderna de Catalunya, Actes*, vol. 1, p. 204.

Torres i Sans, X. (1985) 'Les bandositats de Nyerros i Cadells a la Reial Audiència de Catalunya (1590–1630) Policia o Alto gobierno?' *Pedralbes: Revista d'historia moderna*, no. 5, pp. 147–174.

Torres i Sans, X. (1995) 'Pactisme i patriotisme a la Catalunya de la Guerra dels Segadors', *Recerques: Història, economia i cultura*, no. 32, pp. 45–62.

Torres i Sans, X. (1998) 'Les bandositats de "nyerros" i "cadells": bandolerisme català o "feudalisme bastard"?' *Pedralbes: Revista d'historia moderna*, no. 18(1), pp. 227–242.

Torró Abad, J. (2006) *El naixement d'una colònia: dominació i resistència a la frontera valenciana (1238–1276)*, València: Publicacions de la Universitat de València, p. 99.

Torró Abad, J. (2010) 'Els camperols musulmans del regne de València. De la conquesta a la conversió', *La Rella: anuari de L'Institut d'Estudis Comarcals del Baix Vinalopó*, no. 23, pp. 201–212.

Tortella Casares, G. (2000) *The Development of Modern Spain: An Economic History of the Nineteenth and Twentieth Century*, Harvard: Harvard University Press.

Tov Assis, Y. (2012) 'The Jews of Barcelona in Maritime Trade with the East', in Ray, J. (ed.) *The Jew in Medieval Iberia, 1100–1500*, Brighton, MA: Academic Studies Press, pp. 180–226.

Tünde Mikes, T. (2017) 'Leglislació Històrica de la Família Catalana Medieval i Moderna', *Butlletí de la Societat Catalana d'Estudis Històrics*, no. 26, pp. 163–196.

Tussell, T. and Queipo de Llano, G. (1990) *Los Intelectuales y la República*, Madrid: Nerea, p. 93.

Valls Junyent, F. (2010) *La Cataluña atlántica: Aguardiente y tejidos en el arranque industrial catalán*, Zaragoza: Prensas de la Universidad de Zaragoza, Universidad de Zaragoza, pp. 286–288.

Vallverdú i Martí, R. (1995) 'La defensa de Montblanc durant la tercera carlinada. Aproximació sociològica als guerrillers carlins', *Aplec de treballs*, no. 13, pp. 143–170.

Vallverdú i Martí, R. (2019) 'La Guerra dels Matiners en Cataluña. Crisis económica y revuelta social, Aportes', *Revista de historia contemporánea*, no. 100, pp. 99–121.

Vallverdú Poch, J., Gómez de Soler, B., Vaquero Rodríguez, M. and Bischoff, J. (2012) 'The abric romaní site and the Capellades region, High Resolution Archaeology and Neanderthal Behavior: Time and Space in Level J of Abric Romaní (Capellades, Spain)', in Carbonell i Roura, E. (ed.) *High Resolution Archaeology and Neanderthal Behavior*, Dordrecht: Springer, pp. 19–46.

Vázquez de Prada, M. (2003) 'La oposición al régimen franquista en Barcelona: algunas muestras entre 1948 y 1951', *Hispania: Revista española de historia*, vol. 63, no. 215, pp. 1057–1078.

Vázquez Osuna, F. (21017) 'L'anihilació de la República del general Franco i l'administració de justícia de Catalunya (1936–1939)', *Revista de Dret Històric Català*, no. 16, pp. 297–319.

Vega, E. (2004) 'La CNT a Catalunya entre revolució i reforma, 1930–1936', *Butlletí de la Societat Catalana d'Estudis Històrics*, no. 15, pp. 157–168.

Vicens Vives, J. (1936) *Ferran II i la ciutat de Barcelona*, Barcelona: Universitat de Catalunya, vol. 1, p. 374.

Vila i Bover, M. (1993) 'La pesta negra del segle XIV a Vic', *Gimbernat: Revista d'Història de la Medicina i de les Ciències de la Salut*, vol. 20, pp. 165–72.

Vila i Moreno, F. X. (2004) 'Hora de fer balanç? Elements per valorar les polítiques lingüístiques a Catalunya en el periode constitucional', *Revista de Llengua i Dret*, no. 41, pp. 243–286.

Vilaginés, J. (1988) 'El fenòmen parroquial en la societat del Vallès Oriental a l'Alta Edat Mitjana', *Acta historica et archaeologica mediaevalia*, no. 9, pp. 125–42.

Vilar, P. (1962) *Catalunya dins l'Espanya Moderna, Vol. III, Les transformacions agràries del segle XVIII català: de l'impuls de les forces productives a la formació d'una burgesia nova*, Barcelona: Edicions 62, pp. 121–141.

Vilar, P. (1992) 'Les transformacions del segle XVIII', in Nadal i Farreras, J. and Wolff, P. (eds.) *Història de Catalunya*, Barcelona: Oikos-Tau, pp. 385–420.

Villegas-Aristizábal, L. (2017) 'Spiritual and Material Rewards on the Christian-Muslim Frontier: Norman Crusaders in the Valley of the Ebro in the First Half of the Twelfth Century', *Medievalismo*, no. 27, pp. 353–376.

Vinyoles, T. and Varela-Rodríguez, M. (1998) 'Vocacions femenines del segle XV', *Analecta Sacra Tarraconensia*, vol. 71, pp. 889–906.

Virgili Colet, A. (1995) 'Conquesta i feudalització de la regió de Tortosa 1148–1200', *Recerca*, no. 1, pp. 33–50.

Virgili Colet, A. (2001) *Ad detrimentum Yspanie la conquesta de Turtusa i la formació de la societat feudal (1148–1200)*, Barcelona: Universitat Autònoma de Barcelona, Servei de Publicacions, pp. 73–75.

Westin, A., Crumley, C. and Lennartsson, T. (2018) *Issues and Concepts in Historical Ecology. The Past and Future of Landscapes and Regions*, Cambridge: Cambridge University Press, p. 47.

Whittle, A. W. R. (1996) *Europe in the Neolithic. The Creation of New Worlds*, Cambridge: Cambridge University Press, p. 309.

Wickham, C. (2009) *The Inheritance of Rome. A History of Europe from 400 to 1000*, London: Penguin, pp. 530–532.

Wilson, S. (1998) *The Means of Naming. A Social and Cultural History of Personal Naming in Western Europe*, London: UCL Press, p. 133.

Woolard, K. (2016) *Singular and Plural: Ideologies of Linguistic Authority in 21st Century Catalonia*, Oxford: Oxford University Press.

Wunder, A. (2019) 'Spanish Fashion and Sumptuary Legislation from the Thirteenth to the Eighteenth Century', in Riello, G. and Rublack, U. (eds.) *The Right to Dress: Sumptuary Laws in a Global Perspective, c.1200–1800*, Cambridge: Cambridge University Press, pp. 243–272.

Xavier Payà i Mercè. (2003) 'Les termes públiques de la ciutat romana d'Ilerda (Lleida, Segrià)', *Tribuna d'arqueologia*, nos. 1999–2000, pp. 147–164.

Yeste, E. (2015) *Un Conflicte de Llengües: De la Nova Planta a la Llei Wert*, Barcelona: Angle Editorial.

Ysàs i Solanes, P. (ed.) (1997) *La Transició a Catalunya i Espanya*, Barcelona: Fundació Doctor Lluís Vila d'Abadal.

Ysàs i Solanes, P. (2004) *Disidencia y Subversion: La Lucha del Régimen Franquista por su Supervivencia, 1960–1975*, Barcelona: Crítica.

INDEX

Milton Keynes UK
Ingram Content Group UK Ltd.
UKHW020946081223
433929UK00005B/47